Revolution in Central America

Revolution in Central America

D. Fogel

ism
∞
press

San Francisco

We will not endulge here in such childish absurdities as to insist that "no part of this book may be reproduced or transmitted in any form or by any means, electronic or mechanical, including photocopying, recording, or by any information storage and retrieval system, without written permission from the publisher." Having to get written permission from the publisher before you photocopy a few pages from a book, e.g., would be rather like having to get written permission from the architect every time you let a friend into your house. Indeed the colossal growth and diffusion of social technology has far outstripped the legal superstructure standing above society and stifling its development—which superstructure, in turn, reflects the relationships of ownership dominating society. The fruits of intellectual labor, as well as the material means of production, must therefore cease to be private property, and become the common property of society as a whole.

Library of Congress Cataloging in Publication Data

Fogel, D. (Daniel), 1953-
    Revolution in Central America.

    Bibliography: p.
    Includes index.
    1. Central America—Politics and government—1979-
2. Revolutions—Central America—History—20th century.
3. Mosquito Indians—Government relations.   4. Indians
of Central America—Nicaragua—Government relations.
5. Church and social problems—Central America.
6. Church and social problems—Catholic Church.
7. Women—Central America—Social conditions. I. Title.
F1439.5.F64   1985   972.8'05   84-27805
ISBN 0-910383-08-1

Ism Press, Inc.
P.O. Box 12447
San Francisco, CA 94112

Correspondence and criticism welcome.

Manufactured in the United States of North America

Acknowledgments

Thanks to the following publishing companies for permission to reprint excerpts from the works indicated:

Bobbs-Merrill Co., Inc. 4300 West 62nd Street, P.O. Box 7083, Indianapolis, Indiana 46206:
CARIBBEAN EDGE, copyright © 1979, by Bernard Nietschmann, used with permission of the publisher, The Bobbs-Merrill Company.

Monthly Review Press. 62 West 14th Street, New York, NY 10011:
Guatemala: Occupied Country, by Eduardo Galeano. Translated by Cedric Belfrage. Copyright © 1969 English Language edition, by Monthly Review Press. Reprinted by permission of Monthly Review Press.

Pathfinder Press. 410 West Street, New York, NY 10014:
Rosa Luxemburg Speaks. Copyright © 1970, Pathfinder Press, Inc. Reprinted by permission of Pathfinder Press.

Random House. 201 East 50th Street, New York, NY 10022:
ONE DAY OF LIFE, by Manlio Argueta. Translated by Bill Brow. Copyright © 1983.

Cover Photo: *Mass demonstration on the streets of San Salvador. This was during the 1979-80 wave of mass mobilization and ferment, before the ferocious military repression drove all the radical people's organizations underground.* (from *The Guardian*)

Table of Contents

Preface *8i*

**Glossary of Revolutionary and
Mass Organizations** *15i*

1. El Salvador: Which Class Will Win the Civil War? . . . 1

The Agrarian Crisis (3) — Agrarian Reform, Agrarian Repression:
Phase 1 (3) — Phase 2: The Phase That Never Was (8) — Phase 3:
'Land to the Tiller' (9) — Archbishop Romero Sides with the
Poor...(11) — ...and Is Murdered by the Dictatorship...(13) —
...and Is Buried Amidst a Massacre of the Poor (13) — Church
Hierarchy Retrenches to the Right (14) — Class Structure of
El Salvador (16) — The FMLN (26) — The Death of Anaya
Montes and Cayetano Carpio (35) — Which Class is to Lead the
Revolution? (36) — Revolutionary Rift in the FMLN (38) —
Revolutionary Combatants Under the Political Lead of Liberal
Noncombatants (40) — The Contadora Process of Sabotaging
the Revolution (41) — The 'Political Solution' and the Political
Solution (43) — Revolutionary vs. Bourgeois Negotiations (44) —
The 'Zimbabwe Solution' or the 'Nicaragua Solution'? (47)

2. Nicaragua: The Workers and Peasants Triumph . . . 51

February 1978: Insurrection in Monimbó (52) — The Masses
Prepare for Revolution...(53) — ...and the FSLN Reunites (53)
The September 1978 Revolution (54) — From Revolutionary
Defeat to Revolutionary Victory (55) — Workers' State, Petty-
Bourgeois Government (57) — Class Struggle Sharpens (59) —
The Coalition Government Is Wrenched (60) — Revolutionary
Democracy vs. Counterrevolutionary Liberalism (65) —
Agrarian Revolution, FSLN Reform (67) — The Women's
Struggle (70) —Bureaucratically Deformed Workers' State (73)
FSLN Leaders Abandon the Salvadoran Revolution (74) —
Bureaucracy or Revolutionary Democracy? (76) —
Revolutionary Youth, Senile Leaders (77)

3. The Miskitu Question in Nicaragua 79

Historical Background to the Conflict (81) — U.S. Monopolies Invade, Proletariat Emerges (84) — The Miskitu and Sandino (85) Decline of the Atlantic Coast (85) — Men and Women in Miskitu Society (86) — The Moravian Church and Capitalism (87) The Trauma of Dependent Capitalism (88) — The Miskitu and the Revolution (90) — The Situation After Somoza's Overthrow (91) — In the Name of Sandino...(92) — ...a Chauvinist Policy is Imposed (93) — Contradictions of the Literacy Campaign...(94) ...and State Industrial Policy...(94) — ...and Heavyhanded Bureaucracy...(95) — ...and Land Rights Policy (95) — The Case of Steadman Fagoth (96) — The Turning Point (97) — A General Strike against the FSLN (98) — Fagoth Bolts to Honduras (99) — Chauvinism Assumes Legal Form (100) — Lenin vs. the FSLN (101) Positive Aspects of FSLN Policy (102) — The 'Red Christmas' Plot (103) — Mass Relocation of the Miskitu from their Ancestral Home (104) — A Heavy Hand against the Miskitu, a Light Hand against the Somocistas (107) — Miskitu Leaders Choose Up Sides (108) — FSLN's Amnesty and Self-Criticism (109) — The Miskitu Question as Viewed by North American Indians (110) Repression of Miskitu by Honduran Army (112) — Brooklyn Rivera's Return (112) — A New Miskitu Organization (113)

4. Guatemala and the Fate of the Americas 115

The Partial Revolution of 1944 (117) — Arbenz is Elected (118) — Arbenz' Agrarian Reform (118) — Arbenz is Overthrown (119) — Guatemala 1954 vs. Nicaragua Today (120) — Guevara's Contra-dictory Legacy (121) — Lessons of the Cuban Revolution (121) — The False Foco Theory (122) — The FAR and *Foquismo* in Guatemala (123) — A Ghost from the Arbenz Regime Fronts for Military Dictatorship (124) — The Revolutionary Movement is Crushed (126) — Economic Boom, Growth of Dependent Capitalism (126) — Capitalism Recruits its Gravediggers (127) — Onslaught of the Military/Bureaucratic Bourgeoisie (128) — Transformation of the Revolutionary Movement (129) — The ORPA (129) — The EGP (130) — A New Mass Movement Raises its Head (130) — The Coca-Cola Workers' Struggle (131) — The Earthquake and the People's Movement (132) — 'We Don't Want Elections, We Want Revolution' (134) — Rise of the Committee for Farmworkers' Unity (134) — The Semi-

Insurrection of September 1978 (136) — Carter's 'Break' with
the Lucas Garcia Regime (137) — Massacre at the Spanish
Embassy (138) — Farmworkers' Mass Strike (139) — Lucas
Garcia's Armored Car Race to Hell...(140) — ...and Rios Montt's
'Born Again' Dictatorship (145) — A Counterinsurgency Verging
on Genocide (147) — The Army's Model Villages and Civil
Defense Patrols (148) — Economic Devastation...(149) — ...and
Another Turn in the Military's Fortune Wheel (150) — The Best
Men of the Counterrevolution Step to the Fore (151) —
The U.S. Stake (151) — Latin America's Future (152)

5. *The Church Torn by Class Struggle* 153

The Vatican Moves with the Times (154) — The New Christian
Movement (155) — Origins of Christianity (156) — Internal
Contradiction of Jesus' Teachings (157) — Christianity Spreads
to the Dispossessed of Rome (159) — Social Contradictions
Emerge within the Christian Movement (161) — The Pontius
Pilates of the Vatican against the Christs of the Peoples'
Movements (162) — The Inquisition and 'Witch' Perse-
cutions (163) — From Protestant Revolution...(163) — ...to
Protestant Reaction (165) — The People's Revenge (166) —
The Church Moves into the Capitalist Epoch...(166) — ...and
Competes against the Marxist Workers' Movements (167) —
The Second Vatican Council (170) — The Medellin Confer-
ence, 1968: The Bishops Espouse Liberation Theology (170) —
El Salvador (172) — Archbishop Romero and the People's
Movement (175) — The Reactionary Church Hierarchy (178) —
Democratic Bishops vs. Fascist Bishops (180) — The Puebla
Bishops' Conference, 1979 (185) — Romero and the 'Radical
Civilian/Military Regime' (186) — Romero vs. the Pope (187) —
As Rivera y Damas Moves to the Right...(188) — ...The People's
Church Struggles for its Life (188) — The People's Church vs.
the Oligarchy's Church (189) — Rivera's Balancing Act (190) —
Is the People's Church Struggling to Win? (191) — The Pope's
Visit (192) — Guatemala (194) — Nicaragua (196) — Christian
Charity Serves the Counterrevolution (198) — The Bishops Go
Over to Counterrevolution (199) — The People Defend their
Priests (200) — The Pope's Letter to Obando (201) — The
Struggle in Santa Rosa Parish (202) — Against the Counter-
revolutionary Sects (203) — Naked Came the Priest...(204) —
...and Up in Arms Went the Reactionaries (205) — The Pope

Meets the Revolution (206) — The Dispute over Military
Policy (212) — Rightist Clerics Join the Contras (212) —
Christians to the Left of Christ, Marxist-Leninists to the
Right of Marx and Lenin (213) — Which Class Does the
Bible Really Serve? (214)

6. Women's Liberation 217

The Trans-Atlantic Inquisition (218) — Conquest of America,
Conquest of Women (219) — Capitalist Greed Undermines the
Patriarchal Family (221) — El Salvador (222) — Guatemala (224)
— Nicaragua (226) — The Demilitarization of Women (231) —
Progressive and Reactionary Women's Legislation (232) — How
Did Henry Hyde Get to Stand on Both Sides of the Barricade in
Nicaragua? (235) — The Gay Question (239) — Women in
Catholicism, Women against Catholicism (240) — The
Hemisphere Stood on its Head (241)

Reference Notes 243

Index 259

Preface

My first piece on Central America appeared as an article by the same title as this book, published in *Proletariat* no. 2 (fall 1981). I have endeavored here to correct the factual errors and faulty lines of analysis contained in that article, while updating, expanding and deepening my treatment of the Central American revolutions in all their key aspects.

The most burning task, it seems to me, is to connect the victory of the Nicaraguan revolution with the future victories of the workers' and peasants' revolutions in El Salvador, Guatemala, and ultimately throughout the Americas, from south to north. This connection is by no means automatic, and it presents serious tasks for theory as well as practice.

After the triumph of a social revolution, the overthrown oppressor class, the victorious revolutionary class, and all the intermediary political forces in class society strive to sum up the lessons of that revolution from their own class standpoint—as a guide to their future political action and as a lever of influence among the masses of people they hope to win to their political banner. Naturally, in this summing up process, the bourgeoisie, which has dominated the world for some 200 years, is far more experienced, sure of itself, and firm of will than is the proletariat, which has scarcely grappled with the problems of wielding political power in a few isolated countries, and as yet does not exist as a cohesive and politically conscious international force.

The spontaneous tendency among bourgeois ideologists and their "junior partners" among the petty bourgeoisie after the victory of a proletarian revolution is to trivialize and caricature the revolution as a "freak" historical occurrence, the product of external conditions (fantastic "interference" by revolutionary outsiders) and of strictly chance events (the "exceptional" corruption of this dictator, the "exceptional" softness of that U.S. president or congress). Such a superficial viewpoint mentally sweeps the laboring masses and their revolutionary achievements off the stage of history: The peasant revolts, the active awakening of the workers to the burning problems of the whole country, the urban mass insurrections, the massive participation of women, the self-sacrificing spirit of an entire generation of youths, the passionate radicalization at the base of traditionally conservative mass institutions like the catholic church—all this is glibly dissolved into the "takeover" of the country by a supposedly small and elite group of revolutionaries. Thus the people's victory in Nicaragua in 1979, the culmination of the most profound civil war in the western hemisphere to date, is transmogrified, by the bourgeois analysts and pundits, into the *"sandinista takeover"* of Nicaragua.

This intellectual sleight of hand is convenient, indeed necessary, for the bourgeoisie. For the bourgeoisie to perpetuate its rule, it must successfully continue to represent bourgeois interests as the general interests of the people. The profit drive of Wall Street and the transnational banks and corporations must be made synonymous with freedom and democracy, and the war aims of the Pentagon must be made synonymous with security for the hemisphere. Whenever and wherever the laboring masses become politically conscious, rise up and overthrow the tyranny of U.S. imperialism and its allied local ruling class, this must not be represented as a people's war of national and social liberation, the natural and inevitable outcome of the contradictions imposed upon society by imperialism itself: It must be represented as a devious, communist "plot," whose success was the lamentable result of a lack of vigilance and will (according to the conservative view) or a lack of tactical finesse (according to the liberal view) by the Washington watchdogs of imperialism.

The bourgeois distortion of the reality of proletarian revolution *abstracts* the revolutionary leaders from the deepgoing historical process which produced them, and transforms them into superhuman agents of evil. Bourgeois ideologists within the working-class and radical movement, for their part, strive to transform the victorious revolutionary leaders into superhuman agents of good. Once again, the working masses are mentally shoved aside, and the motive forces of history seem to be tiny groups of "well placed" people and "charismatic" individuals. If the bourgeois ideologists can banish the truth of proletarian revolution from the minds of the masses, then the bourgeoisie has a fighting chance of isolating and crushing the revolutionary uprisings in the future, and of overthrowing the workers' states which exist as the more or less calcified products of the proletarian revolutions of the past.

It is characteristic of bourgeois political thought to overestimate the strength of the propertied ruling class, and underestimate the strength of the laboring masses. And opportunism is the politics of the bourgeoisie in the workingclass movement. After the victory of the Nicaraguan revolution, the watchword of the U.S. ruling class and its Latin American allies was, "Never again—We must not permit another Nicaragua!" After the Salvadoran and Guatemalan ruling classes launched a desperate struggle to annihilate the increasingly combative people's movements and it became clear that the victory of the Salvadoran and Guatemalan revolutionary forces was not around the corner, opportunists of various stripes began moaning that "another Nicaragua," another insurrectionary victory of the armed people, was *"impossible."*

Reinforcing the intimidating effect of military/death-squad repression with the intellectually corrosive effect of political capitulation, the opportunists (trailing in the wake of the bourgeois Contadora group) have argued that the "only way out" of the civil war in El Salvador is a "negotiated political solution" that would involve a "power sharing" arrangement between the FMLN/FDR and the existing parties of the ruling class (excepting the fascist ARENA), and some kind of "integration" of the revolutionary FMLN army with the counterrevolutionary government army. If the North American civil war had ended in such a way (with a coalition government between the abolitionists and the slaveowners' parties and an "integration" of the union army with the slaveowners' army), the black people would have remained enslaved. If the Nicaraguan civil war had ended in such a way, the capitalist class would still be in power, the bourgeoisie would still be armed, the people would be disarmed, and the revolution might well be crushed. But ironically, the *sandinista* leaders have become some of the leading exponents of the anti-revolutionary "political solution" in El Salvador.

How are the sharp contradictions of the *sandinista* regime in Nicaragua to be theoretically summed up? I have had this argument many times with "marxist" blockheads of various stripes, who have rejected my characterization of the social/political regime created upon the revolutionary destruction of the Somoza regime as a *workers' state*, headed by a *petty-bourgeois government*. Most people seem baffled by the notion that there could be a contradiction between the state and the government of a given country. Aren't the state and the government basically one and the same?

Not necessarily. A state is the dictatorship of one class over another, centering on the armed power reinforcing the leading property relations that serve the interests of the ruling class. A government is the political leadership and administration of the class dictatorship. In today's world, only two basic types of *states* are possible: bourgeois states and workers' states. As for the *governments* sitting atop these two antagonistic types of states, *several* types are possible in each case.

The bourgeois dictatorship is capable of being served by an absolute monarchy (Saudi Arabia), a parliamentary monarchy (Britain), a fascist regime (Iran), a military regime (Chile), a presidential/parliamentary system (France, U.S.), or a "pure" parliamentary system (West Germany, Italy). The bourgeoisie, strong and stable in the imperialist countries but weak and insecure in the underdeveloped countries, tends to choose consciously the type of government that best serves its interests in a given country and in a given historical period. When a government emerges that stands in contradiction to the bourgeois dictatorship (above all, the imperialist dictatorship), the bourgeoisie knows from its long and varied historical experience how to rid itself of such a government. Thus in Argentina, the vacillating, bonapartist regime of Isabel Perón proved inadequate to crush the combative workingclass and revolutionary movements; it was replaced in 1976 by a military/fascist dictatorship which re-secured bourgeois rule. Seven years later, after the military regime's debacle in the Malvinas/Falklands war against England, it was too discredited and openly riddled with corruption to suppress the mass movement any longer; it was replaced by a bourgeois democratic regime with far greater flexibility and moral authority to deceive and pacify the masses, for the time being. Governments come and go, but the bourgeois state remains...until the proletarian revolution destroys it.

In the case of a workers' state, two main types of government are possible: a *revolutionary democratic government*, in which the aroused workers directly wield their own state (the Paris commune, the early Soviet republic, and the Shanghai commune in January 1967)—and a *bureaucratic regime*, in which the workers are politically demobilized and smothered by a parasitic bureaucracy, which usurps and distorts the gains of the proletarian revolution (the Soviet bloc countries and China today, Vietnam, Angola, Cuba, etc.). The proletariat, totally inexperienced in ruling society and lacking concentrated financial means outside of its state power, has incomparably greater difficulty than does the bourgeoisie in ridding itself of a government that does not serve the interests of its class dictatorship. If the bourgeoisie confronts a government atop a bourgeois state that stands in contradiction to its class interests, it can generally get rid of that government within a few years at the most. But historical experience has shown that, when the proletariat confronts a bureaucratic, anti-revolutionary regime sitting atop a workers' state, it may have to endure the regime for several decades, while it grapples for the strategic and tactical means to make a new revolution to reconquer its own state.

The Nicaraguan revolution has presented a new example of the contradictions that can emerge between a workers' state and the government resting atop it. The overthrow of the Somoza regime by the armed workers and peasants surely brought a new class to power (the scribblings of vulgar marxist and anarchist pedants notwithstanding). The working masses were armed, the bourgeoisie unarmed. But the new workers' state did not give rise to a revolutionary democratic workers' government. Instead the vanguard organization of the workers and peasants, the FSLN, formed a coalition government with the liberal ("anti-Somoza") bourgeoisie, and committed itself to respect all "patriotic" bourgeois property. The bourgeoisie was in the government, but the state was not its state. The workers and peasants, in their continuing struggle against bourgeois exploitation and reaction, were no longer repressed by the standing army; the *sandinista* army, when it has taken sides in the class struggle, has generally sided with the laboring masses. But the masses have been restrained and stifled by a bourgeois style bureaucratic/judicial apparatus, which strives to maintain bourgeois property and social relations in contradiction to the revolutionary foundations of the new, proletarian state.

This explosive situation has played itself out in a series of sharp class struggles. The laboring masses dragged their FSLN leaders to the left, and the liberal bourgeoisie, frustrated by their lack of command over the new state, staged a series of rebellions and resignations from the coalition government. By 1984, the bulk of the bourgeoisie who had remained in Nicaragua following Somoza's overthrow had gone over actively to the counterrevolution, joining forces with the armed *somocista* units invading Nicaragua from Honduras (and Costa Rica).

In November 1984, the government held nationwide elections, and the FSLN won 63% of the votes in a field of seven competing parties. The major bourgeois opposition parties boycotted the elections, only because they knew that free and fair elections would result in their defeat. The remnants of the unelected coalition government (the junta of national reconstruction) were replaced by a presidential/parliamentary democratic system, with the FSLN holding the presidency and an absolute majority in the national assembly.

The new FSLN government, however, has by no means resolved the sharp contradiction between the government and the revolutionary workers' state. For the FSLN leaders continue pursuing a policy of economic and political collaboration with what remains of the "patriotic" bourgeoisie, and of support to the "Contadora process" of sabotaging the Salvadoran revolution. In this sense, the formulation "petty-bourgeois government" still applies. Moreover, the Nicaraguan workers' state is still *bureaucratically deformed: The sandinista* defense committees, which are *potential* organs of workers' political rule, have no direct input into the government, far less command over it. The resolution of the contradiction between the revolutionary workers' state and the anti-revolutionary FSLN government remains a problem for the future.

The monstrous U.S. military buildup in Honduras is an ominous prelude to the all-out struggle by imperialism to drown the Central American revolution in blood. Many have compared the situation to Vietnam in the early 1960's, when the failure of the U.S. advised counterinsurgency war to crush the revolutionary people's movement in the south gave way to fullscale invasion by U.S. troops (half a million by 1967) and the most massive campaign of aerial bombardment ever seen in history, directed first against Vietnam and Laos, and then—after the Paris "peace" treaty in 1973—against Kampuchea. The comparison between Central America and Indochina is apt, and the peoples of Central America have the advantage of a far greater cultural unity and potential for mutual solidarity than the peoples of Indochina have had.

Sofía Montenegro, a soldier in the *sandinista* army and formerly a reporter and editor for the FSLN's daily paper *Barricada*, has sharply summed up the lessons of Vietnam for North Americans: "You are the only nation that has ever dropped an atomic bomb. You are the nation that has destroyed other cultures without a sense of disgust or revolt. Other countries like Vietnam. And you did not stop that war. It was the struggle of the people under the bombs who stopped it. You protested, you went into the streets, only when the war was beginning to affect you..."*

But the human impact of the U.S. sponsored wars against the peoples of El Salvador, Guatemala and Nicaragua is being driven home to broad sections of the North American people at an earlier stage than was the case during the Vietnam war—thanks to the massive influx of desperate refugees from the military/death-squad terror in El Salvador and Guatemala. History, geography, and U.S. imperialism itself are more and more intermingling the Central American and Mexican peoples with the North American peoples, binding their historical destinies together. This truth has been recognized and acted upon by many people who are by no means partisans of the proletarian revolution—notably, liberal churchpeople of various denominations, who are defying the U.S. government and its repressive apparatus by providing asylum to Central American refugees, sheltering them from deportation into the hands of the death squads.

Most U.S. leftists, meanwhile, are lagging far behind this burning historical development, and have much catching up to do. Any North American leftist who has not learned Spanish, or is not struggling to become competent in the language, is not an internationalist. And any North American leftist who is not grappling with the rich lessons of the Central American revolution, with an eye towards applying them to the future civil war in this country, is not a revolutionary.

—D. Fogel

December 1984

---

*Interview with Carol Swann, *Rolling Stone* magazine, 5 July 1984. (Reference notes documenting the text of this book are numbered, and appear at the back of the book).

Glossary of Revolutionary and Mass Organizations

El Salvador

The following five political/military organizations make up the **FMLN,** *Frente Farabundo Martí de Liberación Nacional,* Farabundo Martí National Liberation Front:

ERP—*Ejército Revolucionario del Pueblo,* Revolutionary Army of the People. Its political vanguard is the PRS, Partido de la Revolución Salvadoreña. Its mass organization is **LP-28,** *Ligas Populares 28 de Febrero (1977).* Its top leader is Joaquín Villalobos.

FPL—*Fuerzas Populares de Liberación/Farabundo Martí,* People's Liberation Forces. Its mass organization is the **BPR,** *Bloque Popular Revolucionario.* Leader: Leonel González.

PCS—*Partido Comunista Salvadoreño,* Salvadoran Communist Party. Its mass organization is the **UDN,** *Unión Democrática Nacional.* Leader: Schafik Jorge Handal.

PRTC—*Partido Revolucionario de Trabajadores Centroamericanos,* Central American Revolutionary Workers Party. Its mass organization is the **MLP,** *Movimiento de Liberación Popular.* Leader: Roberto Roca.

RN—*Resistencia Nacional,* National Resistance. Its mass organization is **FAPU,** *Frente de Acción Popular Unificada.* Leader: Fermán Cienfuegos.

In addition, the **FCER,** *Frente Metropolitano Clara Elizabeth Ramírez,* Clara Elizabeth Ramírez Metropolitan Front, emerged in 1983 from an internal struggle in the FPL. Around the same time, the **MOR,** *Movimiento Obrero Revolucionario,* emerged from a struggle within the BPR.

The **FDR,** *Frente Democrático Revolucionario,* Revolutionary Democratic Front, is a cross-class coalition including: the mass organizations affiliated to the FMLN vanguard groups, an array of other mass organizations (labor unions, teachers', students' and women's associations, etc.), professional associations (of lawyers, doctors, engineers, professors, etc.), and bourgeois liberal politicians and grouplets (social democrats and left christian democrats).

Following are three of the most important mass organizations in the FDR:

AMES—*Asociación de Mujeres de El Salvador*, Women's Association of El Salvador.

ANDES—*Asociación Nacional de Educadores Salvadoreños*, National Association of Salvadoran Teachers. Affiliated with the BPR.

FTC—*Federación de Trabajadores del Campo*, Rural Workers' Federation. Affiliated with the BPR.

The following three mass organizations are not part of the FDR:

MUSYGES—*Movimiento Unido Sindical y Gremial de El Salvador*, United Labor Union and Guild Movement of El Salvador. Formed in the 1970's, it was driven underground along with the FDR mass organizations by the heavy repression beginning in 1980. After the election of Duarte in 1984, which brought a partial easing of military repression against the urban labor movement, MUSYGES re-emerged on the wave of a series of workers' strikes, putting forward economic and political demands similar to those of the FDR.

UCS—*Unión Comunal Salvadoreña*, Salvadoran Communal Union. Affiliated to the Christian Democratic Party (PDC), it claims the largest membership of any rural organization. It is the only major peasant or farmworkers' organization not driven underground since 1980. Supported by the American Institute for Free Labor Development (AIFLD).

UPD—*Unión Popular Democrática*, Democratic People's Union. Labor union and guild confederation affiliated to the Christian Democratic Party. Duarte's "political opening" following his 1984 election was geared primarily for its benefit.

Guatemala

The following four political/military organizations make up the **URNG**, *Unidad Revolucionaria Nacional Guatemalteca*, Guatemalan National Revolutionary Unity:

EGP—*Ejército Guerrillero de los Pobres*, Guerrilla Army of the Poor. Leader: Rolando Morán.

FAR—*Fuerzas Armadas Rebeldes*, Rebel Armed Forces. Leader: Pablo Monsanto.

ORPA—*Organización del Pueblo en Armas*, Organization of the People in Arms. Leader: Gaspar Ilom.

PGT/Nucleo de Dirección Nacional, radical faction of the *Partido Guatemalteco del Trabajo*, Guatemalan Labor Party.

In 1982, a new political/military organization emerged: The **MRP-Ixim**, *Movimiento Revolucionario del Pueblo*, Revolutionary Movement of the People, was formed by dissidents of the ORPA later joined by militants expelled from the other political/military organizations. It rejects membership in the URNG.

Following are the two most important mass organizations in Guatemala:

CNUS—*Comité Nacional de Unidad Sindical*, National Committee of Labor Union Unity. Labor union confederation.

CUC—*Comité de Unidad Campesina*, Committee for Farmworkers' Unity. Works closely with the EGP.

Nicaragua

The **FSLN**, *Frente Sandinista de Liberación Nacional*, Sandinista National Liberation Front, is the political/military organization that led the revolution. Following are the most important mass organizations in Nicaragua:

AMNLAE—*Asociación de Mujeres Nicaragüenses 'Luisa Amanda Espinoza,'* Luisa Amanda Espinoza Nicaraguan Women's Association.

ATC—*Asociación de Trabajadores del Campo*, Rural Workers' Association.

CDC—*Comités de Defensa Civil*, Civil Defense Committees. Grassroots organizations of mass political agitation, education, mobilization, and military training and combat, formed in the heat of the insurrections of 1978-9.

CDS—*Comités de Defensa Sandinista*, Sandinista Defense Committees. The renamed CDC following the victory of the revolution.

UNAG—*Unión Nacional de Arrendatarios y Ganaderos*, National Union of Farmers and Ranchers.

List of Maps   (page)

El Salvador *18i*
Contadora countries **42**
Nicaragua **50**
Guatemala **116**

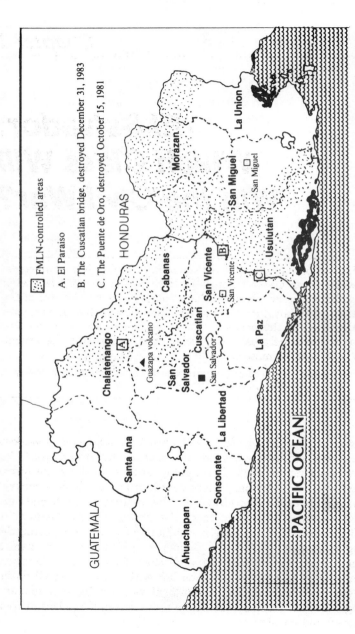

EL SALVADOR

FMLN-controlled areas

A. El Paraiso
B. The Cuscatlan bridge, destroyed December 31, 1983
C. The Puente de Oro, destroyed October 15, 1981

GUATEMALA

HONDURAS

Santa Ana

Ahuachapan

Sonsonate

Chalatenango

Guazapa volcano

San Salvador

San Salvador

La Libertad

Cuscatlan

La Paz

Cabanas

San Vicente

San Vicente

Morazan

San Miguel

San Miguel

Usulutan

La Union

PACIFIC OCEAN

(from *NACLA Report on the Americas*)

18i

El Salvador: Which Class Will Win the Civil War?

"Liberation movements must learn that the cost of their struggle will be even greater than ours. If there had been a less costly path to victory, we would have taken it. I can conceive of no triumph in any part of Latin America without this massive participation of the people... Our guerrilla columns were not the axis, but merely part of a larger axis, which was the armed struggle of the masses."

—**Humberto Ortega,** *sandinista* revolutionary leader, today Nicaragua's minister of defense.[1]

San Salvador, 22 January 1980. Over 150,000 people — workers, peasants, students—take to the streets of the capital city.[2] They are opposing military dictatorship and celebrating the formation of a "revolutionary mass coordinator" of all the country's mass democratic organizations. The military junta, formed in a U.S. sponsored coup against the hated general Romero on 15 October 1979, has quickly shed its "reformist" image, murdering a thousand leftists and democrats in the last two months of the decade and driving away all the reformist politicians who had joined it, until it has been left with only a thin Christian Democratic figleaf. The demonstrators carry banners demanding an end to military rule and a reduction in the prices of cooking oil and gasoline.

As the front lines of demonstrators reach the national palace at the city center, national guard sharpshooters posted within the palace and on the roofs of surrounding buildings open fire upon them. The unarmed masses seek refuge in the metropolitan cathedral across the street from the national palace. Members of the revolutionary organizations, armed with handguns to defend the march, fire back against the assailants. Wearing bandanas to hide their faces, the young revolutionaries continue struggling against the national guardsmen for over an hour.

The people's organizations have anticipated such a bloody attack by the regime, and prepared for it; yesterday, they occupied all the churches in San Salvador, to provide sanctuary for the demonstrators. As word of the national guard attack spreads through the demonstration, the people scatter into refuge in nearby churches and the national university. But the regime has prepared too. Its helicopters spray the fleeing marchers with Malathion, an insecticide used by cotton growers which causes nausea, convulsions and diarrhea among exposed humans.[3] At day's end, 30 people lie dead, over 200 wounded.

It is 75 years, to the day, since the "bloody Sunday" march of 200,000 workers to the tsar's palace in St. Petersburg, Russia in 1905. The Russian workers, many of them carrying religious icons behind the leadership of the christian priest Gapon, attempted to present a petition to the tsar demanding the right to strike, the eight-hour working day and the convening of a constituent assembly. Instead of receiving their petition, the tsar ordered his soldiers to open fire on the unarmed workers, killing hundreds. The "bloody Sunday" massacre triggered a mass political strike wave that began the 1905 revolution, bringing the tsarist monarchy to its knees until the defeat of the insurgent people of Moscow. And the defeated 1905 revolution was, as Lenin put it, the "dress rehearsal" for the victorious revolution of 1917. It marked the dawn of a new epoch in human history: the epoch of proletarian revolution.

The San Salvador massacre triggered a political strike by teachers against the repression. As the revolutionary movement conected its several years' experience of guerrilla struggle with a dynamic mass movement of people aroused from every oppressed layer of society, the country was soon plunged into civil war.

The Agrarian Crisis

El Salvador's most burning social problem was the agrarian problem. The lion's share of the country's fertile land was long monopolized by a tiny clique (oligarchy) of large capitalist land-owners. They stubbornly resisted increasing the productivity of their coffee, cotton and sugarcane plantations through mechanization; their systematic expropriation of peasants' lands had assured them a ready supply of supercheap, seasonal farm labor. Keeping large tracts of their fertile land out of cultivation, they forced the peasant masses into desperate struggle for survival on tiny plots of poor land *(minifundios)*. As the poor peasants plunged into economic ruin, the proportion of the landless among the rural population grew from 12% in 1960 to 40% in 1975; by 1980, landless people made up an estimated 60% of the rural population.[4] Today, El Salvador has the highest rate of labor underutilization in Latin America. Over half of the rural labor force is unemployed for two-thirds of the year.[5]

The growing army of agricultural proletarians and poor peasants, making up the majority of El Salvador's population of 5.5 million, took passionately to mass organization and struggle under the influence of the revolutionary Left and the radicalizing rural cadres of the catholic church. Towards the end of 1979, farmworkers and peasants occupied 72 large plantations. And the rural mass movement was providing the base of support for the protracted guerrilla resistance against the junta's regular forces and death squads.

Agrarian Reform, Agrarian Repression: Phase 1

On 6 March 1980, the "civilian"/military junta, headed by the rightwing christian democrat José Napoleón Duarte, suddenly announced an agrarian reform which would expropriate the largest plantations with compensation. As the army along with some 500 agricultural technicians occupied some 30 plantations, they encountered little resistance from the landowners; most of these were absentee owners who had already moved millions of their dollars out of the country in fear of land reform. A state of siege was declared throughout the country—supposedly for 30 days, but extended indefinitely.

Three hundred cadres of the *Unión Comunal Salvadoreña* (UCS), a peasant and farmworker organization linked to the Christian Democratic party, accompanied the government troops with the mission of forming peasant "cooperatives" on the expropriated plantations. The UCS was set up in 1968 in collaboration with the American Institute for Free Labor Development (AIFLD), an arm of the AFL-CIO and U.S. state department.* To qualify for official land redistribution, the cooperatives had to submit their finances to review by government officials and turn over a list of all their members.

A cadre for the Salvadoran Institute for Agrarian Transformation (ISTA) described the true workings of the "reform" campaign: "...The troops came and told the workers the land was theirs now. They could elect their own leaders and run it themselves. The peasants couldn't believe their ears, but they held elections that very night. The next morning the troops came back, and...they shot every one of the elected leaders." Hundreds of similar examples of counterrevolutionary army terror were reported across the country. When asked what the agrarian reform had meant to the peasants, an old peasant woman replied that it meant others took their land and tried to kill them. [7]

From the standpoint of military and political stratregy, the agrarian reform served as a public relations cover for a counterinsurgent campaign of "forced draft urbanization": driving the rural masses into the cities through military terror, to "dry up" the guerrillas' mass base of support in the countryside, paving the way for saturation aerial bombing to exterminate the guerrillas. This tactical plan was first formulated for the U.S. war against Vietnam by Samuel Huntington, a Harvard professor and later adviser to the Jimmy Carter administration.

From the standpoint of the caste interest of the Salvadoran army officers who led the campaign, the agrarian reform provided cover for them to enrich themselves. Their reign of terror victimized many Christian Democratic mayors and leaders of the

*AIFLD, sponsored by the AFL-CIO, was created in 1962 with financial assistance from the U.S. state department, Agency for International Development (AID), ITT, Exxon, Shell, W.R. Grace, Kennecott, Anaconda, American Smelting and Refining, IBM, Koppers, Gillette, and 85 other transnational conglomerates and corporations. Launched as part of Kennedy's "alliance for progress" campaign, AIFLD has built company unions for United Brands and Standard Fruit in Central America. It has also helped support military dictatorships in Chile, Brazil, and Uruguay. [6]

new cooperatives, as well as farmworkers and peasants. Their economic motive was to intimidate the new coops into paying them "protection" money. Many army officers, in the whirlwind of the agrarian reform and their agrarian repression, were themselves becoming medium landowners.[8] "...In the past, landowners paid local members of the national guard or treasury police to maintain 'order' among the workers. Now the military extorts money from the coops in exchange for not repressing them. The protection racket has the same victim but a different cashier."[9]

At the beginning of May 1980, ISTA technicians working on the newly formed coops went on mass strike. They were protesting the escalation of army violence against the farmworkers, and grave shortcomings in the administration and provision of credit to the coops. Yet when their strike subsided, these technicians, along with the local bureaucrats and the more pliant coop leaders, became the heavyhanded elite of the "cooperatives"—totally excluding the farmworkers from decision making. Skilled and permanent plantation workers—mechanics, tractor drivers, and bookkeepers—benefitted from the formation of the coops. But the seasonal farm laborers, never mobilized by the agrarian reform cadres, received nothing from the reform, and everything from the repression.[10]*

Phase 1 of the agrarian reform formally expropriated only those plantations of 500 hectares** and over. This was supposed to involve some 15% of El Salvador's arable land: rich lands used for cotton, sugarcane, coffee growing and cattle raising. Over 60% of these rich lands were either used for grazing or were lying fallow.[12] The expropriated plantation owners were to be compensated for the first 500 hectares by 25% in cash and 75% in bonds—and for their holdings beyond 500 hectares, by 100% in bonds. The bonds were declared redeemable for investment "in industrial, agro-industrial and agro-chemical activities, and

*In terms of organizational affiliation, UCS members "were the principal—almost the sole—beneficiaries, and became the nucleus of peasant support for the ruling Christian Democratic Party."[11] Other peasant beneficiaries of the reform were members of ORDEN, the fascist paramilitary organization sponsored by the oligarchy as a bludgeon against farmworker and peasant militancy. By the early 1970's, ORDEN was estimated to have 10,000 members and 60,000 collaborators. Its ranks were recruited largely from peasants bribed with permanent jobs, farm credits, etc.

**One *hectare* equals 10,000 square meters, or around 2.5 acres.

rural housing activities in the social interest..."[13] The government, under pressure from U.S. imperialism, thus hoped to modernize the stagnant capital of the big landed oligarchs and stimulate them to reinvest in industrialization.

But such a bureaucratic scheme to "dynamize" the big landowners' capital without *breaking their political power* which is rooted in the *army*, is doomed to fail. Dozens of reformist agrarian reform projects in underdeveloped countries have become shipwrecked on just this contradiction. Notable examples are the agrarian reform campaigns launched by the radical bourgeois military regimes of Nasser in Egypt, Mengistu in Ethiopia, and Velasco in Perú—where radical (junior) officers have endeavored to bite the landowners' hands which fed them, in an effort to stave off a genuine social revolution. The goal of deflecting and crushing the rural revolutionary movement, to be sure, may well be served by such a bourgeois/bonapartist agrarian reform. But the landowning capitalists, interested above all in getting a rapid return on their capital, will always prefer to invest in speculative rackets (commodity futures, urban housing, etc.), rather than make risky, longterm investments in industrial development of "their own" countries.

In El Salvador, many big landowners moved to dump part of their holdings off on relatives to get them below the 500-hectare limit and avoid expropriation.* Many big ranch owners, hell bent on cashing in their assets before parting with some of their land, ordered the wholesale slaughter of their livestock; by 5 May 1980, just two months after the agrarian reform was launched, an estimated 30% of the country's livestock had thus been slaughtered.[14]** Other landowners packed their bags for Guatemala or

*In December 1979, Enrique Alvarez Córdova, minister of agriculture in the reformist "civilian"/military junta, froze property transfers, retroactive to 15 October 1979. Alvarez's intention was to prevent the big landowners from subdividing their holdings among relatives in anticipation of land reform, and to combat their decapitalization campaign. But this reformist bureaucratic maneuver proved impotent. Alvarez soon resigned from the junta and became a leader of the *Frente Democrático Revolucionario* (FDR—Revolutionary Democratic Front). A liberal politician who came from a large landowning family, Alvarez, along with five other FDR leaders, was kidnapped and murdered by a rightist paramilitary squad in November 1980.

**An amendment to the "Evaluation and Payment" chapter of the Basic Law of Agrarian Reform (decree 153) inserted "the cattle" and "the fixed and movable property referred to in article 3 of this law" among the forms of legitimate compensation for expropriated estates.[15] This gave *de jure* approval to the landowners' decapitalization drive to sabotage the agrarian reform.

Miami, taking their farm machinery and livestock with them. Those who remained in the country scrambled to bribe military officers to get their estates back. Through a government "plan of devolution," over 45 big landowners received their estates right back.[16] As of May 1982, only seven titles had been issued to coops created under the reform.[17]

Moreover, the phase 1 agrarian reform decrees themselves allowed all big landowners to claim up to 150 hectares from their estates, and add up to 20% more if they carried out improvements. This enabled them quite legally to slice the richest heart out of the phase 1 reform.[18] And the compensation many landowners received for expropriated land was grossly inflated, since they had overvalued their estates in previous years, to get easy access to bank credit.[19] On the other hand, other landowners who had *under*valued their estates to minimize their tax payments, now felt shortchanged by the compensation they received.

The whole compensation process, in fact, was fraught with bureaucratic haggling and delays that infuriated the big landowners. By the end of 1981, only 20% of the expropriated landowners had received compensation.[20] By mid-1982, the total compensation received by landowners worked out to 9% in cash, and 91% in bonds.[21] In 1983, some landowners tried to use these bonds to pay their taxes; but the government rejected the bonds as "worthless paper."[22]

On the other hand, the establishment of a rightwing civilian regime through the rigged elections of March 1982, allowed the fascist ARENA party to seize control of the agrarian reform ministry (ISTA). The ARENA bureaucrats accommodated the desires of a number of expropriated landowners by allowing them to cash in their bonds (which were originally supposed to be redeemable only after a minimum of 20 years). One might well wonder where the ARENA bureaucrats got the cash to shell out for these bonds—given that the whole Salvadoran government, reeling under the impact of a deep agroexport slump and an increasingly parasitic war economy, has been desperately short of cash in recent years. One astute answer might be corruption: The ARENA agrarian bureaucrats used their posts to embezzle powdered milk, which they sold on the illegal market for around $9 a can.[23]*

---

*This was exposed in the course of the mud-slinging electoral campaign between ARENA head Roberto d'Aubuissón and Christian Democratic Party

Back in 1980, José Rodolfo Viera, director of ISTA, publicly exposed the massive corruption and murder that accompanied the agrarian reform campaign which his institute was supposedly leading. On 2 January 1981, Viera was meeting with two North American AFL-CIO functionaries in a San Salvador hotel, when all three were assassinated by rightist thugs under military command. And despite the anti-revolutionary intentions of their agrarian reform campaign, dozens of ISTA and UCS cadres were murdered by the repressive forces in the pay of the oligarchy.

Many muleheaded oligarchs, equating *any* social reform campaign with "communism," refused to see that the agrarian reform was designed precisely to *save* capitalist rule in the long run, by clipping their manes a bit in the short run. As the jesuit analyst Italo López Vallecillos observed: "Given the prevailing ideological confusion and meager political development, the agro/industrial/financial bourgeoisie did not understand, and still have not understood, that the so-called spoliation of the agrarian reform and the other nationalizations [of banking and foreign trade] were more a restructuring of the system than the establishment of a new one. A modernization, and not a socialization dangerous to their interests."[24]

Phase 2: The Phase That Never Was

"Phase 2" of the agrarian reform was supposed to expropriate the medium sized plantations. This would have struck at the heart of the fertile coffee and cotton plantations owned by the oligarchy as well as the newly rich military officers and state bureaucrats. To ask the military junta, traditionally the mailed fist of the oligarchy, to carry through this phase of the reform would be like asking the mafia to shut down the drug and gambling rackets. So it was no surprise when, on 14 May 1980, phase 2 was "indefinitely postponed." It has since been formally scrapped altogether.

---

head José Napoleón Duarte in 1984. Duarte's apparent contribution to government corruption has been as follows: Following Duarte's nationalization of banking in March 1980, his wife and son, working for the national bank, embezzled money orders sent by Salvadoran exiles to their relatives back home. Rumor has it that some half a million dollars have been stolen by corrupt postal functionaries, from exiles trying to send money back to their relatives.

Phase 3: 'Land to the Tiller'

On 28 April 1980, at the height of the military repression unleashed by the phase 1 rural campaign, the junta announced phase 3 of the agrarian reform, dubbed "land to the tiller." It was supposed to transfer land titles to the masses of poor tenant farmers producing the bulk of El Salvador's food crops on tiny rented plots of mostly hilly, erosion prone land.

Phase 3 was imposed on an unwilling Salvadoran state bureaucracy by U.S. imperialism, through its international "development" and labor agencies, AID and AIFLD.[25] It was conceived by "Imperialist Ploy" Roy Prosterman, a University of Washington law professor and AIFLD consultant. Prosterman and the AIFLD had launched a similar agrarian reform scheme in south Vietnam in 1969-70, in a last ditch effort to drive a wedge between the Vietnamese peasants and the National Liberation Front.

The Vietnamese people's war against the Saigon military clique and the U.S. armed forces was powered mainly by the revolutionary agrarian program of the National Liberation Front; the peasant masses gladly participated in a war which was liberating them from the tyranny of the absentee landlords and providing them with land. The counterinsurgent agrarian reform designed by Prosterman turned land over to peasants corralled into "strategic hamlets," and to those whose loyalty to the Saigon regime could be bought. Other peasants were terrorized and killed. In fact, Prosterman's Vietnamese campaign served as a social reformist cover for the CIA's "operation phoenix" drive to exterminate the revolutionary political infrastructure in the south Vietnamese countryside. The result was over 40,000 peasants and revolutionary cadres dead. "If the reforms are carried out successfully here," said Prosterman of El Salvador, "the armed movement of the Left will be effectively eliminated by the end of 1980."[26]

The social strategy of phase 3 was to groom a layer of middle peasants to serve as a prop for the dictatorship in the countryside. The poor peasants/tenant farmers were to be steered *away from* collectivization, and instead granted titles to the tiny plots they were working and renting.

But poor tenant farmers, whose numbers grew dramatically in the 1960's and 1970's with the ruination of the independent peasantry, have eked out a measure of subsistence by working the plot they were renting for a short period (usually less than two years), and then moving to a new rented plot and tilling it, to allow the original plot to regenerate its fertility. The peasant beneficiaries of phase 3 were now locked into their tiny plots for 30 years—the mortgage period specified by their "ownership" titles. "This effectively plunged the peasant into a more precarious situation than he had been in before the agrarian reform."[27] Lacking technical assistance or credit from the government, the poor beneficiaries are bound to work "their" soil to exhaustion and erosion, destroying what was left of their livelihoods. And the average size of plots distributed to the beneficiaries was 1.64 hectares.[28] The minimum size of a plot necessary to maintain a family of six in El Salvador is 9 hectares.[29]

As with phase 1, the main purpose of phase 3 was *political.* A U.S. AID official noted: "There is no one more conservative than a small farmer. We're going to be breeding capitalists like rabbits."

Things have not turned out that way. Some tenant farmers were reluctant to take over the plots offered them, because they had been renting these plots from their own poor relatives, whom they did not want to hurt. As for the larger owners of the land fractured into rented *minifundios,* they reacted furiously against the tenant farmers slated to become phase 3 beneficiaries. Many owners of between 20 and 100 hectares returned rent money to their tenants, and threw them off the land. Some middlesized landowners hired lawyers to write up documents stating that the tenants renounce all landownership rights—and coerced the tenants to sign.[30] With the army getting into the act, over 33,000 tenant farming families were illegally evicted from the land.[31] Far from "breeding capitalists like rabbits," the so-called agrarian reform has had the effect of "breeding" a growing army of revolutionary fighters recruited from the ruined peasant masses. Phase 3 was formally suspended by the constituent assembly in May 1982, and again in June 1984.

As for the cooperatives which phase 1 managed to establish, they have utterly failed to resolve El Salvador's agrarian crisis. A sample of western region cooperatives taken by ISTA showed that, during the 1981-2 harvest, only 43.5% of their cultivable land was actually worked; the remaining 56.5% of their land was left idle or abandoned. "The situation was virtually the same with the old landowners."[32]

Archbishop Romero Sides with the Poor...

On 22 March 1980, catholic archbishop Oscar Romero denounced the agrarian reform campaign: "...In reality, repression against the people has increased tremendously... People are fleeing the countryside, coming here to San Salvador, or going into the mountains to sleep because if they are found at night by the security forces they will be killed." He concluded: "The popular organizations are voicing the needs of the people...and I have tremendous hope in the popular organizations."[33]

Romero, originally a highly conservative bishop, began firmly to defend his radical priests against the military dictatorship right after his elevation to the archbishop's position by the Vatican in 1977. The revived christian doctrine of liberation theology, preached by the Vatican in the early 1960's, was put into practice in the 1960's and 1970's by the boldest and most passionate priests, nuns, and church layworkers. Going out to live among the rural masses, the practicing preachers of liberation theology plunged into the work of building selfgoverning peasant cooperatives, which tended to grow into combative mass organizations of farm laborers. Radically interpreting the bible in the spirit of the early christian communes, they preached to the peasants that their crushing poverty and suffering were *not* god's will: God's will was for them to inherit the earth. When the oligarchy's forces cracked down against the aroused peasants and farm laborers, the radical priests and nuns would help shelter them and their guerrilla partisans from the white terror. The priests, nuns and layworkers became a prime target of the death squad/military assaults as well.

Archbishop Romero, while maintaining the church's traditional, anitiwoman positions against divorce, contraception and abortion rights, began to give bold expression and support to the sharply radicalizing mass base of his church. His sincere defense of his radical priests against the white terror led him logically into an active alliance with the mass revolutionary movement. His passionate denunciations of the military dictatorship, broadcast nationwide from the church's radio station, became rallying cries for the movement of the oppressed masses across the country.

He politically wavered after the overthrow of general Romero by a reformist "civilian"/military junta, counselling the revolutionary movement to adopt a "wait and see" attitude towards the new regime, to give it an opportunity to implement its promised reforms. But by the beginning of 1980, when the junta had shed its reformist façade and revealed its ruthless campaign of military repression, Romero turned sharply against the junta. And he did not hesitate to denounce the top Christian Democratic politicians for continuing to provide the military dictatorship with a civilian figleaf: "...If the junta members do not wish to be accomplices in these abuses of power and outright criminal behavior, they should publicly announce the names of those responsible and apply the necessary sanctions, for their hands are red with blood."[34]

In a pastoral letter, Romero declared: "When a dictatorship seriously violates human rights and attacks the common good of the nation, when it becomes unbearable and closes all channels of dialog, of understanding, of rationality—when this happens, the church speaks of the legitimate right of insurrectional violence."[35]

The Vatican, the world's largest corporate landowner, now rued the day it appointed Romero archbishop. Pope John Paul 2 held a private meeting with Romero. Although the relationship between the pope and archbishop Romero has not been made public, it was certainly a conflictive one. The pope evidently hammered Romero with the same reactionary message he gave to the bishops of Latin America at the Puebla bishops' conference in Mexico in February 1979: No more preaching and practice of liberation theology, no more worldly opposition to worldly oligarchies and dictatorships; tell your priests and nuns to stick to purely churchy, purely spiritual endeavors, get them back to preaching redemption *in the afterlife* but not here on earth. After his private meeting with the pope, Romero is said to have remarked: "I never felt so alone in all my life."[36]

On 23 March 1980, Romero broadcast his most combative sermon of all to the Salvadoran people, championing rebellion within the armed forces themselves: "No soldier is obliged to obey an order contrary to the law of God. It is time that you come to your senses and obey your conscience rather than follow out a sinful command."[37] "...I wish to make a special appeal to the men of the army and in particular to the rank and file of the national guard, of the police and the garrisons... Brothers, you are from among the people themselves... You kill your very brothers. In the name of God...I beseech you, I beg you, I order you to stop the repression."

...and Is Murdered by the Dictatorship...

On 24 March, Romero was murdered by a rightist gunman while he was saying mass. On 25 March, the U.S. government, headed by Jimmy Carter and Walter Mondale, announced a $55 million economic and military aid package to the Salvadoran government. This was Carter/Mondale's response to Romero's plea, in a letter to Carter one month earlier, for a halt to U.S. military aid to the repressive regime.

...and Is Buried Amidst a Massacre of the Poor

On Palm Sunday morning, 30 March 1980, over 100,000 people assembled in San Salvador for Romero's funeral and a protest demonstration called by the revolutionary mass coordinator. The junta set up military roadblocks to prevent thousands of more peasants from getting into the capital. The protest demonstration, sponsored jointly by the popular organizations BPR, FAPU, LP-28, and UDN, got under way around 9:30. The march route was directed to the metropolitan cathedral, where preparations for the funeral were under way.

As they approached within a block of the cathedral, the demonstrators raised their left fists high into the air while maintaining complete silence, expressing their combative homage to archbishop Romero.[38] When they arrived at the Plaza Barrios facing the cathedral, the funeral mass was already under way. They laid a crown of flowers before the bier of Romero. The people already attending the funeral welcomed the demonstrators with spirited cheers.[39] The protest march soon blended into the massive throng at the cathedral. "The cheers and applauding were mixed with prayers and religious songs."[40]

At the national palace across the street, many windows opened, and the barrels of automatic rifles appeared through them. Military and paramilitary troops appeared in the neighboring building, wielding their heavy arms. The president of El Salvador's human rights commission—himself later assassinated by a death squad—noted that North Americans were spotted in the cathedral's courtyard, with others spotted outside speaking English over walkie talkies.

In the middle of the funeral homily delivered by the pope's special envoy, several bombs exploded around the crowd. The deafening roar of the bombs froze the crowd in terror for a few seconds. Then the troops from the national palace opened fire upon the unarmed multitude. The masses, surrounded by a ring of flying bullets, were seized by panic. At least 5,000 jammed into the cathedral, together with church officials, in search of shelter. Thousands more tried to squeeze in, but the cathedral was too small to hold them. Dozens fainted, and others died of asphyxiation inside the cathedral. Amidst this terrible scene, the coffin of archbishop Romero was hustled inside the cathedral and buried.

Outside, people were falling beneath the hail of bullets, and some were being horribly trampled in the desperate rush to escape. Shoes, shawls, prayer books, blood, and corpses lay strewn across the plaza. Young revolutionaries, charged with the task of defending the mass demonstration, fought back with light arms against the military for half an hour. When it was over, more than 35 people lay dead, most of them older women.[41] The junta, headed by the christian democrat Duarte, cynically blamed the Left, the revolutionary mass coordinator, for the army's massacre that ended archbishop Romero's funeral that Palm Sunday.

Church Hierarchy Retrenches to the Right

Romero's successor and close collaborator, Arturo Rivera y Damas, retreated from Romero's, and his own bold commitment to the liberation struggle of the poor. In contrast to Romero's daring partisanship for the mass struggle against the dictatorship, Rivera began "evenhandedly" condemning *both* the state's repression and the violence of the revolutionary movement—placing the murder of tens of thousands on roughly the same level as the burning of buses and the destruction of electrical power installations. Rivera has failed to offer his beleaguered radical priests, nuns and layworkers more than contemplative moral support, and has chided them for becoming "a little too ideological."

Even so, Rivera has continued to support the church's legal aid commission, which meticulously compiles and exposes every known case of political murder and human rights violation in El Salvador. Since it is overwhelmingly the rightist death

*Once more they are out to stain
my land in the blood of the workers.
They talk about liberty,
yet their hands are smeared foul with crime.
They're scheming to separate
the mother from her own children...*

—from "Winds of the People," a song by Chilean communist poet, composer and singer Víctor Jara, who resisted the Pinochet/U.S. military coup in September 1973 but was captured and executed by the junta. (translated by DF)

"...Not everyone in the army was like me. A man who entered the same time I did was promoted to sergeant in only one month's time. This was because he had no reluctance whatsoever to kill.

The officers knew this man had brothers in the guerrilla army. But they told him he was going to be loyal to his country. Family wasn't important. What was important, they said, was money. And they offered him good money if he would go out and kill.

That man eventually killed his own family—his father, his mother, his brothers and sisters. He even killed a woman who was eight months pregnant. And he killed with such brutality!

People became aware of that, and he was promoted very quickly..."

—testimony from a former soldier in the Salvadoran government army, 1981. (*Counterspy* magazine, May/June 1982)

squads and the military which commit political murder, the church under Rivera has continued to be a thorn in the side of the dictatorship—even if a much duller thorn than it was under Romero.

Within the church hierarchy, Rivera has been besieged by reactionary and fascist bishops tied to the oligarchy and the military—notably, bishop/colonel José Eduardo Alvarez, Pedro Arnoldo Aparacio, and Freddy Delgado—who had all furiously attacked Romero, helped set him up for assassination, and boycotted his funeral. The fact that Rivera has achieved an uneasy truce with the reactionary hierarchy, bringing the institutional church back within political bounds acceptable to the ruling class, was reflected by the pope's promotion of Rivera from acting archbishop to full archbishop status when he visited

El Salvador in March 1983. And, with the radical priests, nuns and layworkers continuing to develop their christian base communities in the only parts of the country where they are not murderously suppressed—the liberated zones of FMLN control —the catholic church has faithfully reflected the explosive class contradictions tearing Salvadoran society as a whole (see ch. 5).

Class Structure of El Salvador

What is the class nature of the Salvadoran revolution? To answer this question, we must first sketch out the explosive arrangement of social classes in El Salvador, tracing the political motion into which they have been propelled by the objective logic of events.

The *landed capitalist oligarchy* has traditionally been the dominant sector of El Salvador's ruling class. The "14 families"* continue to monopolize the country's fertile land, superexploiting the rural laborers through plantation agriculture for export, and superexploiting the peasants through usurious, semifeudal leasing of land. They also monopolize the wholesale purchase of coffee, cotton and sugarcane from the mediumsized and small landowners/growers, and have traditionally controlled largescale foreign trade as well. Alongside the oligarchy's landholdings and commercial enterprises have emerged factories and enterprises set up by mostly U.S. transnational corporations, banks and conglomerates—such as Standard Oil, Texaco, B.F. Goodrich, Westinghouse, Procter and Gamble, International Harvester, Maidenform, Texas Instruments, U.S. Steel, Chase Manhattan, and Bank of America.

Intertwined with, yet in friction with the oligarchy is the *military/bureaucratic bourgeoisie*. Several military officers became wealthy landowners through their murderous extortion campaign in the course of phase 1 of the agrarian reform (see above), and still others have successfully racketeered in the U.S. aid lavished on the Salvadoran state. The upper state bureaucrats and political cliques headed by Duarte have enriched themselves through their March 1980 nationalization of banking and foreign trade—shifting the economic center of gravity in El Salvador's ruling class partially away from the oligarchy. The military

*The family names of the faceless oligarchy as are follows: Hill, Dueñas, Regalado, Wright, Guirola, Sol, Daglio, De Sola, Quiñónes, Black, Borja, García Pireto, Salaverria and Meza Ayau.[42]

'Blessed Are Those Workers Who Serve as Our Loyal Lackeys...'

(The following "bosses' psalm," written by Mario Cortés, appeared on the editorial page of the rightist San Salvador daily *La Prensa Gráfica* on 7 March 1983, on the occasion of the pope's visit to El Salvador)

LABOR'S BLESSINGS

Blessed are the workers, for theirs is the advantage or the active virtue of being workers. Of winning their daily bread with the honorable sweat of their productive and constructive brow.

Blessed are the employees, for theirs is the benefit or the circumstance of being employed.

Blessed are the workers who are employed. For someone has given them work; entrusted them with a responsibility of some sort; esteemed and protected them as golden links of goodness and progress.

Blessed are the employed workers, whether they be clerks, chiefs or subordinates. Blessed are those who do not refuse a smile, an incentive, a helping hand... Those who think time and again with a broad vision and upright judgment and who strive not to sign any layoffs.

Blessed are those workers who truly are workers. Who, both in and outside of their workplaces, are upright, disciplined and kind, and know how to love and respect that superiority which is finally gained with their own clean effort.

Blessed are those workers who, in whatever rank they serve, know how to coordinate and apply the organization of labor, because organization, in whatever field, is a harmonious ensemble of people working in accordance with a determined plan, which tries to attain life's abundance.

Blessed are those workers who, besides being workers, are happy and reflective, and understand that discipline, consideration, clerks, chiefs and subordinates are the basic components of all effective organization.

And surely, those workers who truly are workers will always be employed, and will always be busy, esteemed and blessed.

(translation by DF)

---

and state bureaucracy originally developed as direct agencies of the oligarchy. Through their crucial role in the civil war against the workers and peasants, and through lavish U.S. sponsorship, they have pried open precarious positions for themselves in the upper layers of the ruling class—partly at the expense of the oligarchy.

To be sure, the Salvadoran military/bureaucratic bourgeoisie has not achieved nearly the degree of economic and political hegemony that its Guatemalan counterpart achieved in the wake of its crushing victory over the revolutionary movement there in the late 1960's (see ch. 4). The stormy coexistence of the bureaucratic bourgeoisie with the oligarchy has occasionally erupted into violent internecine struggle—as during the agrarian reform, when the oligarchy stubbornly refused to sacrifice any of its short term economic interests for the sake of Salvadoran capitalism as a whole.

In political terms, the relationship between the oligarchy and the bureaucratic bourgeoisie, characterized here by collaboration and there by fierce competition, is expressed in the struggle between the fascist ARENA party of d'Aubuissón (closely bound up with oligarchic interests), and the rightist Christian Democratic clique headed by Duarte. U.S. imperialism, through both Democratic and Republican administrations, has shown a marked preference for the Duarte clique. This is not only because Duarte's "centrist" political image and lack of active ties to the death squads meshes with U.S. "human rights" diplomacy. More fundamentally, Duarte's bureaucratic clique is organically weaker than d'Aubuissón's pro-oligarchic clique, as it lacks any solid base of social support within El Salvador. Duarte's clique is thus bound to be more pliant to U.S. interests, eventually to a wholesale U.S. takeover of the counterrevolutionary war drive.

The oligarchy and the military/bureaucratic bourgeoisie can be grouped together as the *big bourgeoisie.* Their sectoral interests and their political tactics differ. But strategically speaking, they are united behind the aim of liquidating the revolutionary movement.

The *medium and small bourgeoisie,* such as the bus company owners, small factory and other small business owners, have seen their business prospects squashed by the rampant militarization of the economy. The grossly unequal distribution of income within the bourgeoisie makes small business owners a potential ally of the proletariat: While making up 94% of the owners of El Salvador's means of production, small business owners receive only 12.8% of total bourgeois income; middle capitalists, making up 1.7% of the bourgeoisie, receive 24.3% of bourgeois income; and the big capitalists, making up less than 1% of the bourgeoisie, receive 62.8% of bourgeois income.[43] Yet the medium and small business people, uncertain over the outcome of the civil war and frightened by the FMLN's campaign of economic sabotage, are still mistrustful of the FMLN-FDR.[44] To be sure, small factory owners are sometimes the most ruthless exploiters of the proletariat, since the meager scale of their profits compels them to resist practically any concessions to their workers, in terms of working conditions and benefits. The small business people, especially the self-employed, can be expected to vacillate between the two contending class forces in the civil war, throwing their lot in with whichever side emerges as strong and daring enough to win.

The *liberal professionals,* such as professors, lawyers, doctors, engineers and technicians, provide the ideologists and propagandists to voice the class interests of the aspiring "patriotic" bourgeoisie. They are against the oligarchy for violently hemming in their careers and their scope for prestige. But they do not want a workers' and peasants' revolution that will destroy capitalist class rule and struggle to socialize the economy. They favor a parliamentary democracy, a "pluralistic" society with a "mixed economy." Many of them are ambitious to secure for themselves cushy seats in parliament and government, in the classic bourgeois democratic tradition. The left wing of this stratum forms the leadership of the FDR. Their game plan is to lean on the mass movement of workers and peasants to crack the political and economic monopoly of the oligarchy. They do not want to destroy the existing, neocolonial state. They only want to push aside the military clique usurping that state, and replace it with a "genuine" parliamentary democratic façade. But they have no army of their own, and most of their leaders are outside the country. They are a very weak social force, vacillating between imperialism and the struggling masses. But their high level of culture and articulateness, and their international connections with liberal (and social democratic) imperialist politicians, allow them to project the aura of much more political strength than they actually have.

The *petty-bourgeois democracy* includes teachers, health workers, university students, grassroots priests and nuns, small merchants and artisans. They are closely bound up with the laboring masses: Many of them come from proletarian and peasant families, and their conditions of life and social experience hurl many of them into common cause with the revolutionary proletariat. As the unemployment rate among workers increased thanks to the capital intensive nature of El Salvador's industrial spurt, the self-employed sector mushroomed from 70,000 in 1961 to nearly 200,000 in 1975. Many of these people live under more desperate conditions than factory workers.

The *industrial proletariat* has grown up in pace with the U.S. transnational penetration of the Salvadoran economy. During the 1960's, it expanded from 3% to 11% of El Salvador's total labor force. However, it has stagnated economically since then. And it has yet to assume the political vanguard role in leading the democratic revolution, which its social position in production enables it to. In part, this is due to the fact that the urban industrial workers, while superexploited relative to comparable workers in North America, have certain privileges relative to the rural laboring masses of El Salvador: They have some legal protection in the form of minimum wage legislation, and are far less ferociously subjected to military terror than are the rural masses. But a more important reason for the relative political inertia of the industrial workers is that they have been saddled with opportunist and Christian Democratic labor union leadership, which has kept their social sights narrowed to their own wage and livelihood concerns.

The *peasantry*, which formed the overwhelming majority of the population under Spanish colonial rule, has been crushed by systematic land expropriation, sharecropping and usury. Over 60% of the rural population was totally excluded from the 1980 agrarian reform process, as treacherous as it was. Phase 1 was supposed to help the *colonos*, semipeasants and semiproletarians who lived and worked permanently on the big plantations, while hanging on to their own subsistence plots. But even if phase 1 did end up improving the livelihoods of some *colonos*— especially those politically sympathetic to the San Salvador regime—the *colonos* by then made up a tiny, relatively elite sector of the rural masses: As more and more peasants were expropriated completely from their subsistence plots, the *colono* population decreased from 55,000 in 1961 to 17,000 in 1971.[45] The semiproletariat has been more and more driven into the full-fledged army of the rural proletariat, performing the seasonal farm labor during the November to March harvest, that guarantees maximum flexibility and superprofits for the big landowners.

Migrant workers picking coffee

FMLN fighters on patrol in the liberated zone of Usulután.

U.S. military advisers at Salvadoran high command headquarters. Colonel Eldon Cummings, at right, heads up the advisory team.
(from Arnon Hadar, "El Salvador: The Struggle for Democracy and U.S. Involvement")

*The first "civilian"/military junta installed after the 15 October 1979 coup. From left to right: **Mario Andino**, a liberal engineer with ties to big bourgeois sectors; colonel **Jaime Adbul Gutierrez**, used by the CIA to infiltrate the "military youth" movement and insure that its coup not threaten imperialist interests; **Guillermo Manuel Ungo**, social democratic leader and owner of a small printing firm, now head of the FDR; colonel **Adolfo Arnoldo Majano**, the most "radical" of the ambitious young officers; and engineer **Ramón Mayorga Quirós**, rector of the jesuit university (UCA). First the three figleaf civilian leaders, then the two upstart military leaders, were swept off the stage of government as the oligarchy reasserted its power.*

LEFT: *San Salvador, Palm Sunday, 30 March 1980: Aftermath of the massacre at archbishop Romero's funeral. The Plaza Barrios, shown here, faces the metropolitan cathedral, which stands across the street from the national palace. (Barricada, 31 March 1980)*

Advertisement appearing in *La Prensa Gráfica,* the rightist San Salvador daily, in 1983: "A House of Your Own," with a "fresh climate" in a "quiet residential zone." Certain sectors of the Salvadoran upper middle classes seem to be "more gringo *than the gringos* themselves," in their social aspirations. Small wonder, then, that the revolutionary guerrillas do not mind knocking out electrical power supplies in and around San Salvador from time to time.

Meanwhile, the poorest peasants have gotten poorer. As sub-subsistence peasants hacked out tinier and tinier plots in the infertile northern zone, by 1977 about half of all farms in the country were leased or rented farms of less than two hectares. And for the poor peasants and tenant farmers, off-farm income has exceeded on-farm income.[46] Here again, we see the relentless workings of the process of fullscale expropriation of the peasant masses—a process which phase 3 of the agrarian reform was supposed to reverse, but which it in reality has accelerated. For the laboring masses of El Salvador's countryside, under the jackboot of the U.S. monopolies and a desperate oligarchic/-military dictatorship, all roads lead into the agricultural proletariat.

The *agricultural proletariat*, with its continued social overlapping with the poor peasantry and the superoppressed petty bourgeoisie, has become the majority of El Salvador's population. Buffeted by the seasonal fluctuations of the capitalist harvest and the yearly fluctuations of the capitalist world market, the agricultural proletariat is subject to brutal levels of unemployment and underemployment. It is far more mobile and volatile than the industrial proletariat, and its tendency to cross national borders in search for work helps generate an internationalist consciousness. It is easily recruitable into mass industry, in either the agrarian or urban industrial sector. Politically speaking, it is the most revolutionary social class force in the country. The agricultural proletariat played a tremendous role in the Nicaraguan revolution, and is now the mass cutting edge against the national/liberal bourgeoisie's drive to overturn the revolution there (see ch. 2). The agricultural proletariat is bound to play a dynamic political role, inspiring the industrial proletariat and other layers of the oppressed masses, in the revolution throughout Latin America, including the southwest "U.S." and Texas.

The *lumpenproletariat*, the permanently idle and/or criminal element among the masses, has swelled along with the influx of refugees from the countryside into San Salvador. The bourgeois dailies of San Salvador, which scarcely contain any coherent reportage on the civil war, are filled with stories of (nonpolitical) armed robberies and the efforts of the police forces to combat the growing "menace"—reflecting the concerns of the upper classes over the activities of lumpen elements, with regard to their pocketbooks. The most unscrupulous lumpen youths have been sucked into the political murder-for-hire racket of ARENA and the rightist death squads. Restless, always thirsting for action and easy to bribe, the lumpenproletariat is a sharply vacillating and volatile political force. It can just as easily play a combative and heroic role in the urban insurrection of the revolutionary masses, as it can serve as shock troops for the dictatorship against the revolutionary people.

The FMLN

In October 1980, the *Frente 'Farabundo Martí' de Liberación Nacional* (FMLN—Farabundo Martí National Liberation Front, named after the founder of the PCS, martyred on the eve of a mass insurrection in 1932) was formed. The FMLN eventually brought together the five political/military vanguard type organizations waging the revolutionary struggle, along with their affiliated mass organizations. A brief political characterization of the FMLN's five component organizations follows.

The *Partido Comunista Salvadoreño* (PCS—Salvadoran Communist Party), with its mass organization, the UDN, forms the right wing of the FMLN. When it finally recovered from the years of white terror following the military massacre of 32,000 peasants that crushed the 1932 insurrection, the PCS went on to accumulate decades of labor union reformism and electoral coalitioning with the christian democrats and social democrats. In the tradition of the pro-Moscow Communist parties throughout Latin America, the PCS built up a strong base among unionized urban workers, and preached the peaceful, parliamentary road to democracy and socialism. It thus functioned as a working-class wing of bourgeois-liberal nationalism. While preaching pacifism to the oppressed Salvadoran masses with respect to their oligarchic rulers, the PCS by no means preached pacifism to the Salvadoran government and military command with respect to their "foreign enemies." In the 1969 "soccer war"*

---

*The banal term "soccer war" refers to the event that precipitated the war between El Salvador and Honduras: a nationalist riot by the spectators of a soccer game between the two countries' teams. But the underlying economic and social causes of that all-round reactionary war were the sharpening contradictions between the bourgeois ruling cliques of the two countries, that brought on the breakup of the Central American common market. The military/managerial cliques ruling Honduras felt threatened by economic competition from the stronger Salvadoran oligarchy. They between El Salvador and Honduras, the PCS drifted along with the wave of bourgeois chauvinism that swept El Salvador, supporting the reactionary war aims of the Salvadoran dictatorship.

After the coup of 15 October 1979 that brought a "progressive" military clique to power, the PCS joined in the impotent civilian government which the military demagogs used as a cover for their stepped up repression against the revolutionary movement—taking several posts in the cabinet. When its functionaries, along with the social democrat Guillermo Ungo and the christian democrat Rubén Zamora, were driven out of the government at the end of 1979, the PCS finally announced that "the conditions were ripe for armed struggle."[47] Turning to the left, it joined the revolutionary mass coordinator—which later crystallized as the FMLN—and formed its first fighting units in the countryside.

PCS secretary general Schafik Jorge Handal then launched a public selfcriticism of the reformist practice and tradition of not only his own party, but of the Latin American Communist parties in general. He rejected the idea of a peaceful road to revolution, noting that "it is curiously symptomatic that the Communist parties have shown in the last decades a great ability to reach understandings with our neighbors to the right—while, in contrast, we have not been able in the majority of cases to establish relations and stable progressive alliances with our neighbors on the left." Now echoing the sentiments of those militants who had broken with his party ten years earlier to take up revolutionary struggle, Handal declared that "the machinery of repression built up over half a century cannot be brought into line even with a bourgeois democratic process. That machinery is complex and involves not only the armed forces, but thousands of people who have been trained to place their intelligence at the service of the counterrevolution, to torture and murder the people. Without destroying that machinery, there can be no process of real democratization."[48]

---

whipped up chauvinist fervor among the Honduran masses by scapegoating immigrant Salvadoran peasants for the economic woes of the Honduran peasants. The Honduran government launched a demagogic agrarian reform campaign, which involved driving immigrant Salvadoran peasants off the land they were working—for the benefit of some Honduran peasants. When the expropriated Salvadoran immigrants fled back into El Salvador, the regime there whipped up chauvinist sentiments against the Honduran people. Thus the "soccer war" broke out.

However, Handal and the PCS have continued to defend their treacherous, class collaborationist participation in the "civilian"/military government from October-December 1979. And Handal continues to portray the social democratic (really bourgeois liberal) National Revolutionary Movement (MNR) of Guillermo Ungo as a "consistent ally," praising Ungo's anti-revolutionary clique as "a sector of prestigious intellectuals who consistently stand with the people's cause."[49] Handal evidently considers fronting for a "reformed" military dictatorship to be consistent with the "people's cause." Clearly the PCS, while joining the FMLN and taking up the armed struggle, has not made a qualitative break with its traditional reformist politics, and continues to stand politically closer to the liberal bourgeoisie than to the laboring masses. The PCS is leaving the door open for it to betray again the revolutionary people's movement and join a reformist coalition government that would preserve capitalist class rule intact—in the event of a "negotiated settlement" to the civil war.

The *Ejército Revolucionario del Pueblo* (ERP—Revolutionary Army of the People) is the more popular name for the *Partido de la Revolución Salvadoreña* (Party of the Salvadoran Revolution). Its mass organization is the LP-28. The ERP was formed in 1971 by left dissident Christian Democrats, Communists, and other leftists. It was the first group to develop guerrilla warfare on a wide scale. Heavily emphasizing the armed struggle as against the electoral reformism and pacifism of the PCS, the ERP did not place strong emphasis on mass political agitation and organization, and has tended to fetishize the purely military and technical aspects of the revolutionary struggle. Since 1980, the ERP has established a powerful and extensive liberated zone centered in northeastern Morazán province, and has recruited from the aroused rural masses a regular and highly mobile army, whose units have performed boldly and brilliantly against the government army's expeditionary assaults.

The ERP's clandestine radio station, Radio Venceremos, has played an important role in communicating to the masses the progress of the revolutionary war, and rallying their support in the face of rampant military media censorship and repression. The Salvadoran army has made many, mass murderous attempts to hunt down and destroy Radio Venceremos, but all its attempts have failed; Radio Venceremos has been as tenacious and mobile as the revolutionary fighters themselves.

From the standpoint of the revolutionary intellectual and psychological training of the masses, however, Radio Venceremos leaves much to be desired. Its reports on the battles of the civil war are crudely tendentious and narrowly technical: The revolutionary fighters are portrayed as absolutely invincible, and an exhaustive inventory of all the weapons and equipment they captured from the government army is presented, to boost the morale of the listeners. The battle casualties of the counterrevolutionary army are meticulously detailed, while the casualties of the revolutionary army, if mentioned at all, are thrown in as a reluctant afterthought to the main, pep talk style reportage.*

In the subjective realm of Radio Venceremos commentary, the revolutionary fighters never seem to make any mistakes, lose any battles, or lose any arms to the government army. No serious attempt is made to develop and broadcast a scientific tactical and strategic analysis of the course of the civil war, to train the masses in the dynamic relationship between attack, defense and retreat, between guerrilla, mobile and positional warfare, between the struggle in the countryside and in the city, between proletarian and bourgeois politics in the liberation movement, and between victory and defeat. No serious reportage and analysis of international political developments is attempted.

The ERP leaders, while promoting literacy training in their liberated zones, seem to have a patronizing and contemptuous attitude towards the intellectual and moral capacity of the laboring masses. They seem to fear that frank discussion and analysis of the weaknesses and setbacks of the revolutionary

---

*Radio Venceremos' lack of rigorous objectivity and honesty in its war reportage stands in contrast to the role played by Radio Rebelde, the clandestine station of the 26 July Movement in the course of its civil war against the Batista regime in Cuba. "Whereas the government was known for its false reports on the progress of the [counterinsurgency] campaign," note Ramón Bonachea and Marta San Martín, "the guerrilla command strictly adhered to the truth... If an announcement of a government victory came from guerrilla sources, people who had refused to give financial aid through the underground in the cities would then offer it voluntarily. When the Radio Rebelde station was in operation and the guerrillas asked for large quantities of medicine, penicillin, bandages, etc., the people assumed there had been a grave defeat in the ranks of the freedom fighters, and the underground would be so overloaded with contributions that they had to ask the people not to donate so many things in such a [short] time."[50]

movement would "demoralize" the masses and play into the hands of the enemy. But it is precisely Radio Venceremos' stultifying, one-track reportage and schematic analysis that is bound to demoralize and disorient the masses in the long run. 'If our fighters are so invincible, if they always win in battle and if the government's army always loses, then why hasn't the revolution conquered power throughout the country yet?'—this is a burning question which the advanced sections of the masses must be asking themselves. Radio Venceremos, with its mindless, cheerleading style of reporting, can offer no coherent answers that would prepare the masses intellectually for the hard revolutionary struggles ahead. Politically speaking, its most glaring failing is its total lack of marxist analysis of, and agitation against the selfish, anti-revolutionary role played by the bourgeois liberals who head up the FDR.

Indeed the top leader of the ERP, Joaquín Villalobos, has wholly swallowed the treacherous, pro-capitalist military strategy espoused by the FDR liberals. In a special broadcast from Radio Venceremos in September 1983, Villalobos rejected as "totally false" the charge by the Salvadoran and U.S. governments that the FMLN aims to "destroy the national Army," i.e., the army of the oligarchy. Villalobos, trailing the bourgeois liberals and social democrats, insisted that "the FMLN is fighting for a new national army which would be made up of the present Army and the military forces of the FMLN... Within the Armed Forces there are chiefs, officers, classed ranks, and common troops who think democratically, who could form the basis of a new army together with the FMLN."[51] Such cynical talk is bound to impress the FDR gentlemen and liberal imperialists with the "political maturity" of the young Villalobos—but it is hardly likely to impress the laboring masses of El Salvador, who will surely have difficulty detecting the "democratic thoughts" of the chiefs, officers and classed ranks, behind the mortars, napalm, phosphorous bombs, machinegunnings, and bayonet thrusts ordered and executed by those hired lackeys of the oligarchy.

Villalobos then played up to the bourgeois demagogs who rule most of the rest of Latin America, assuring them that the Salvadoran revolution poses no serious threat to their exploitative interests: "It is by no means certain that one more revolution in Central America would threaten the stability of Mexico and the other nations of the continent. To the contrary: The surging forth of more nations with political and economic independence from the U.S. [sic], with stable and strong governments which foment internal transformations accelerating their economic development, would *help* the struggle for better conditions of trade between Latin America and the U.S. Better conditions would exist for the exploitation of the enormous natural resources of Mexico, Venezuela, Brazil, Argentina, etc. And this does not mean revolutions in more countries, but rather the development and gradual transformation [?] of the present capitalist economies."[52] Perhaps Villalobos considers the current genocidal assault against the indigenous peoples of Brazil's Amazon basin by colonial settler farmers, the Brazilian army and capitalist corporations to be a fine thing— since it would be a necessary feature of his muddleheaded utopia of "progressive" capitalist development in Latin America.

Resistencia Nacional (RN—National Resistance), with its mass organization FAPU, originated as a break from the ERP in 1975. A group of ERP cadres led by Roque Dalton García correctly criticized the top ERP leadership for "militarism" and insufficient emphasis on mass political agitation and organizing. Dalton, a brilliant revolutionary poet as well as political leader, was framed up by the ERP leadership as a "CIA agent," and assassinated. His followers, constituting themselves as RN, plunged into mass organizing, in both city and countryside. The RN and FAPU thus built up an active mass base among students and organized urban workers, controlling one of the largest labor union confederations in the country. RN also developed active contacts among the church hierarchy and "progressive" sectors of the military officers.

An Opportunist vs. a Revolutionary

"The FMLN does not call for the destruction of the Army, rather for the organization of a new military power built up from the present Army and the FMLN."

—**Joaquín Villalobos**, 1983.

("Why Is the FMLN Fighting?", English translation of Radio Venceremos broadcast)

"Victory cannot be considered as finally won until the army that sustained the former regime has been systematically and totally smashed ...Not even a skeleton of personnel from the former army can be retained."

—**Che Guevara**, 1959.

(cited in Edward Boorstein, *The Economic Transformation of Cuba*, NY: Monthly Review Press, 1968, p. 21)

While a world campaign was launched to vindicate Roque Dalton from the murderous slander of the ERP leaders, the RN refused political and military collaboration with the ERP. In December 1979, Ana Guadalupe Martínez publicly acknowledged that the "execution" of Dalton had been a grave mistake, and urged that it not continue to be an obstacle to the unity of the Left against the dictatorship.[53]

Despite its success in sinking deep roots among the masses, the RN's strategic perspective has been racked with petty-bourgeois pragmatism and confusion, displaying a pronounced tendency to grope for a spectacular "short cut" to the workers' and peasants' revolution. During the political struggle around the formation of the FMLN, the RN opposed the concept of building a revolutionary people's army based on the workers and peasants. Instead, it put forward a plan to coax a clique of "progressive" junior officers from the government army to form the nucleus of a "revolutionary army," which the workers' and peasants' organizations would then liquidate into.

RN's prime candidate for such a "people's savior" role was colonel Adolfo Arnoldo Majano. Majano rose to prominence in the military coup of 15 October 1979, but was later shoved aside by the most reactionary, U.S. puppet generals (headed by general José Guillermo García). Yet he ably served the cause of military counterrevolution, supporting the March 1980 announcement of the counterinsurgent agrarian reform campaign with the threat: "Since the coup of 15 October the government has been very soft on its enemies [!!], but now the party is over."[54] With his "star lit" military career fizzling at the end of 1980, Majano finally jumped ship from the junta, publicly urging the government army officers to defect to the popular forces. But he then shattered RN's opportunist fantasies by leaving the country and ostentatiously failing to join any guerrilla group.

Since they fostered illusions in the "progressive" nature of ambitious young army officers like Majano, the RN leaders seemed to feel that all the revolutionary movement needed to do was to *begin* a mass insurrection, which would then *spark* a "revolutionary" uprising by "democratic" junior officers, who would then seize the helm of the people's movement and quickly overthrow the oligarchy. RN was thus unable to develop a scientific perspective on the art of insurrection. In mid-May 1980, RN, evidently calculating that Majano & Co. were ready to bolt from the junta, called for a general strike and general insurrection. Some 30,000 to 50,000 workers responded to the general strike call, and acting archbishop Rivera voiced his support. RN units engaged in heavy fighting against the army in northern Chalatenango province, near the Honduran border. They suffered heavy casualties, and the government army carried out massacres of the local peasants, with the Honduran army lending a bloody hand. The FPL (see below), which has strong mass influence in Chalatenango, disagreed that the conditions were fully ripe for an insurrection. Neither the FPL nor the PCS rallied to RN's call to insurrection, and the isolated insurrectionary attempt was defeated.[55]

RN's sharp differences in revolutionary strategy and tactics with the other leftist organizations continued to pose an obstacle to its inclusion in a combat coalition of the Left. On 12 September 1980, RN withdrew from the unified revolutionary directorate, the forerunner of the FMLN central command. On 20 September, Ernesto Jovel and other top leaders of RN died, supposedly in a plane crash. On 10 October, the FMLN came into existence, including the FPL, PCS, and ERP. On 3 November 1980, the RN, now led by Fermán Cienfuegos, joined the FMLN.

The *Partido Revolucionario de Trabajadores Centroamericanos* (PRTC—Central American Revolutionary Workers Party), with its mass organization the MLP, is the youngest member of the FMLN. Very little information is available on the PRTC and its political program and history. One important area where it politically distinguished itself from the rest of the FMLN was in calling for a *revolutionary union of Central America*, to overcome the stifling national boundaries through the mutual revolutionary action of workers and peasants throughout the region. In its struggle to implement this crucial program, the PRTC began by organizing itself on a Central America-wide basis, and its revolutionary fighters in El Salvador included several nationals from other Central American countries. However, the PRTC has apparently retreated from this bold program and plan of action, redeploying the "foreign" revolutionaries to their home countries and quietly dropping the slogan of the Central American union in favor of the nationalistic, "purely Salvadoran" revolutionary perspective held by the rest of the FMLN. In recent years the PRTC has developed a powerful mass following and liberated zone in eastern La Unión province.

The *Fuerzas Populares de Liberación* (FPL—People's Liberation Forces) formed the left wing of the FMLN until a violent
internal struggle tore the organization apart in 1983. The FPL
emerged as a left split from the PCS in 1970, led by Salvador
Cayetano Carpio, secretary general of the PCS until he and a
handful of followers decided to break with the PCS's entrenched
electoral reformism and national chauvinism over the Salva-
doran/Honduran war. Defining itself as a "revolutionary marxist-leninist political/military organization," the FPL took up
guerrilla struggle combined with mass mobilization and organization, basing itself mainly among the agricultural laborers and
poor peasants. In contrast to the PCS's traditional urban fetish-
ism and reformist "workerism," the FPL developed a strategic
perspective of *protracted people's war*, centering on the armed
masses of the countryside. Its mass organization, the BPR,
became the largest of the popular organizations that surged to
the political forefront in the late 1970's, and the FPL itself
became the largest component of the FMLN.

The FPL's five-point political program called for "1) Destroying the bourgeois state, defeating the puppets of imperialism, the
counterrevolutionary army and other oppressive military forces
(national guard, etc.) and the paramilitary organizations such as
ORDEN. 2) Destroying as a class the bourgeois landowners.
3) Expelling the imperialist powers from our land. 4) Instating a
Popular Revolutionary Government with the hegemony of the
working class, based on an alliance with the peasantry. 5) Creating a base on which to build Socialism."[56]

Salvador Cayetano Carpio, born in 1919 into a cobbler's family, became a labor union militant and a communist from an
early age. In 1952, he was arrested and repeatedly tortured
nearly to death by the Osorio military regime. Upon his release
from jail he wrote a book, *Secuestro y Capucha* (*Abduction and
the Hood*, referring to the method of torture by strangling with a
hood), which exposed not only his own harrowing tortures, but
also the fact that the jail functionaries made of habit of murdering common criminals and prostitutes. Cayetano Carpio spent
two years in exile in the Soviet Union, where he received political training. When the FMLN crystallized 25 years later, Cayetano Carpio, popularly known as "Marcial" and widely respected as a leading veteran of the revolutionary movement,
became the logical choice for commander in chief. However,

waning health made it more and more difficult for the aging leader to participate directly in the fighting, and by 1983 he was doing diplomatic work for the FMLN in other third world countries.

The Death of Anaya Montes and Cayetano Carpio

On 6 April 1983, Mélida Anaya Montes, a 54-year-old revolutionary teacher who was second in command of the FPL, was savagely murdered in her sleep by six members of her own organization, in Managua, Nicaragua. The alleged murderers, headed by 28-year-old Rogelio Bazzaglia, a member of the FPL central command, were arrested by the police of the *sandinista* regime; they have since been held in prison in Nicaragua without a trial or even a competent investigation of the murder.

Cayetano Carpio, visiting Libya at the time of the murder, returned to deliver the eulogy at Anaya Montes' funeral in Managua on 9 April. In his eulogy, Cayetano Carpio seemed to remind his *sandinista* hosts—who were already supporting the bourgeois liberals of the FDR with their schemes for a "negotiated settlement" in El Salvador—of their internationalist duty to support the Salvadoran revolution, in deeds as well as words: "The struggle of the Central American peoples is a single struggle. When Sandino rallied the guerrillas in the mountain, he had at his side comrades from all of Central America, and the whole region vibrated against [U.S.] imperialism in the struggle and the feats of the heroic guerrillas of Nicaragua. Our main revolutionary leader, comrade Farabundo Martí, was together with Sandino..." Cayetano Carpio concluded with a prophesy: "All the Central American peoples are under the aggression of North American imperialism. We are struggling against its intervention in every worthy form that is possible. But we also know that all the Central American peoples will convert themselves into a revolutionary bonfire, if imperialism carries out its plans of aggression against Nicaragua or El Salvador."[57]

On 12 April, Cayetano Carpio wrote his last letter, addressed to "the heroic people of El Salvador, my beloved working class and the glorious FPL/Farabundo Martí." After praising his own long history of struggle against the persecution, calumny and repression of the Salvadoran ruling classes and U.S. imperialism, Cayetano Carpio lamented: "...But it is one thing to struggle against imperialism and its intrigues, and quite another to feel injustice, calumny and infamy coming from my own brothers. A black conspiracy to stain my revolutionary life and deeply damage the FPL is in progress and arriving at its culmination... I cannot stand by powerlessly and watch my beloved organization, basis of the revolutionary struggle of my people and of consistent unity, be treated this way, nor can I bear the demands that its organs, networks, members and collaborators be placed in the hands of a poorly conducted and prejudiced investigation. And I cannot bear the mockery directed against me, the infamy that seeks to involve my name, albeit indirectly, the fierce insinuation in that direction, in the painful case of the terrible loss of our comrade Ana María."[58] "Ana María" was the popular name for Mélida Anaya Montes.

At 9:23 pm on the same day, Cayetano Carpio, reportedly in the presence of top FPL and FMLN leaders as well as several leaders of the *sandinista* government and military personnel, shot himself to death.[59]

The FPL leadership, now headed by Salvador Guerra, at first publicly attributed the tragic deaths of Anaya Montes and Cayetano Carpio in Managua to "divisive maneuvers instigated by the CIA to carry out such a shameful crime through maneuver and deceit," using unscrupulous members and ex-members of the FPL.[60] Two weeks later, the FPL changed its story. "It would have been easier for us and for Nicaragua to keep blaming the CIA" for the deaths, noted FPL spokesman Salvador Samayoa.[61] Samayoa told of an internal political struggle within the FPL over revolutionary strategy and tactics, which culminated in the murder of Anaya Montes.

Which Class Is to Lead the Revolution?

The FPL had apparently functioned as a kind of "permanent opposition" within the FMLN since the latter's formation. It often voted in opposition within the unified revolutionary directorate (the FMLN's central command), on both strategic and tactical questions. The political root of the FPL's disagreements with the other four organizations in the FMLN involved the question of which class was to lead the Salvadoran revolution. Cayetano Carpio, true to the FPL's program, stressed that the proletariat must gain hegemony in the national liberation struggle, that the road to liberation had to pass through the armed conquest of power by the revolutionary people, and that the revolutionary government must be based on the worker/-peasant alliance. The other four groups in the FMLN were far more disposed to subordinate the people's armed struggle to the selfish, reformist aims of the bourgeois liberals heading up the FDR.

The FDR's "Programmatic Platform for a Revolutionary Democratic Government," first formulated and published in 1980, defines its "revolutionary democratic government" as an unprincipled hodgepodge of virtually every social and political sector in El Salvador aside from the oligarchy itself: "...This Government will rest on a wide [sic] social and political base, formed in the first place by the working class, the peasantry and the advanced [?] middle layers; intimately united with them will be all those social sectors disposed to carry out this program; small and medium industrialists, merchants, artisans, farmers and ranchers (small and medium growers of coffee and of the other items of agriculture and cattle raising). It will likewise include the honest professionals, the progressive clergy, democratic parties like the MNR [the social democratic clique headed by Guillermo Ungo], the advanced sectors of the Christian Democracy; worthy and honest officers of the Army who are disposed to serve the interests of the People, and every other sector, group, personalities or segments [?] that advocate broad democracy for the popular masses, independent development, and people's liberation."[62] This "broadbased government" formula reflects the doubletalking deception of the FDR liberals, who want to *liquidate* the revolutionary class interests of the workers and poor peasants beneath the *anti*-revolutionary class interests of the *exploiting* layers of the middle classes.

The liberals' tactical plan to carry out their anti-revolutionary strategy revolves around a "negotiated settlement" to the civil war, which would lead to some form of coalition government between the FDR/FMLN and "advanced sectors" of the bourgeois Christian Democracy—leaving the capitalist army, police and bureaucracy, and thus capitalist class rule, intact. The pressure of the bourgeois liberals, the Contadora group (see below), and liberal imperialism on the FMLN had led to a growing consensus for the "negotiated settlement" tactic as the way to resolve the civil war—with only the FPL holding out against the opportunist majority of the FMLN. A number of FPL leaders, headed by Anaya Montes, themselves began voicing the opinion that the FPL was playing a "sectarian" and "inflexible" role within the FMLN leadership by continuing to oppose the negotiated settlement plan. Anaya Montes, who felt that the 1973 Paris peace treaty between North Vietnam and U.S. imperialism had played a contributing role in the victory of the Vietnamese revolution, was struggling to popularize to the Salvadoran people what she considered the lessons of the Vietnamese liberation war and revolution. Having visited Vietnam, she had completed one volume of an intended multivolume series on the Vietnamese revolution, when she was murdered.

Rogelio Bazzaglia and other FPL leaders and cadres were apparently staunchly opposed to the Anaya Montes group's efforts to "integrate" the FPL into the pro-liberal consensus of the rest of the FMLN leadership. A bitter dispute erupted within the FPL leadership in January 1983, when the majority decided to undertake a "profound selfcriticism" of the FPL's political course inside the FMLN. The utter lack of internal democracy within the FPL, perhaps combined with the Bazzaglia clique's fear of political betrayal by the *sandinista* regime, evidently led to the dispute being "resolved" through brutal, internecine bloodshed.

Revolutionary Rift in the FMLN

Cayetano Carpio's role in this struggle—and indeed, the political content of the struggle itself—was not made known by the FPL. But the political struggle continued to rage within the FPL, inevitably engulfing the BPR as well. In the summer of 1983, the BPR split, with many of its members eventually rallying to a new mass organization called the *Movimiento Obrero Revolucionario* (MOR—Revolutionary Workers' Movement). Upholding the banner of Cayetano Carpio, the MOR declared its complete independence from the FMLN/FDR leadership, which it criticized as anti-revolutionary.

In September 1983, a sector of the FPL's army, called the *Frente Clara Elizabeth Ramírez* (FCER—Clara Elizabeth Ramírez Front), broke openly with the FPL leadership, while continuing to claim the banner of the FPL. The FCER claims to lead over 2,000 fighters, centered in the industrial belt around San Salvador. While denying any link with the MOR, the FCER denounced the current FPL leadership for pursuing "...a deviation from the strategic line [of the FPL], which departs from the true revolutionary objectives of our people. This is reflected in the impulse given to a Line of Dialog and Negotiation by the directorate of the FPL. In its content and practice, this line involves a barefaced conciliation with the bourgeoisie...since it goes along with a fundamental search to offer Yankee imperialism an acceptable way out of the war, while the FPL directorate does not concern itself with the 50,000 deaths among our people and the role which the bourgeoisie has played with its repressive apparatus; it is the bourgeoisie who are directly responsible for the exploitation, the poverty and the massacres of our people. Upon the base of this Dialog and Negotiation, they [the FPL and FMLN leaders] seek to create a Government of Broad Participation, sharing power with the abovementioned criminal bourgeoisie. Before these developments, tracing out a swerve that puts our FPL on a road separating it farther and farther from its true objectives, it was in those moments that comrade Marcial [Cayetano Carpio] maintained a constant criticism towards those deviations and weaknesses in this direction... We consider that the process of Dialog and Negotiation can proceed, always provided that it does not imply making concessions in principles..."[63] Both the FCER and the MOR have demanded a full investigation of the deaths of Anaya Montes and Cayetano Carpio.

In December 1983, the FPL leadership issued a communiqué on Cayetano Carpio and Anaya Montes, which reversed its initial position on their deaths by practically 180 degrees. Whereas, upon their deaths eight months earlier, the FPL had hailed both as "two great revolutionary leaders who have contributed to the advance of the Salvadoran revolutionary process and contributed with self-sacrifice to the development and consolidation of our organization,"[64] now the FPL denounced Cayetano Carpio as "the main organizer" of the murder of Anaya Montes. Without offering any material evidence to support this stunning charge, and without bringing to light the political dispute between Cayetano Carpio and Anaya Montes, the FPL communiqué declared that Cayetano Carpio had "clung tightly to dogmatic and sectarian schemes and plans. This, together with his obstinacy about prevailing at whatever cost, became an obstacle to the progress of the FPL/Farabundo Martí, and exercised a negative influence on the process of unification of the revolutionary forces as a whole..."[65]

Revolutionary Combatants Under the Political Lead of Liberal Noncombatants

The rump FPL's public denunciation of its late founding leader and his entire political career, reinforced the FPL's capitulation to the liberal consensus within the FMLN for a "negotiated settlement" with the ruling class as the way to end the civil war. Ironically, by this time the rest of the FMLN had largely accepted, both in concept and practice, the FPL's military strategy of a protracted people's war proceeding from the countryside to the cities. Now the FMLN leadership as a whole, trailing in the wake of the liberal FDR leaders in exile, declared its willingness to liquidate the people's war for the sake of a bourgeois coalition government.

In February 1984, the top leadership of the FMLN and FDR held a joint press conference in Mexico, where they announced "an integral program and platform of the provisional government of broad participation." This program replaced the FDR's 1980 "programmatic platform for a revolutionary democratic government," a hodgepodge of revolutionary and reformist concepts which had politically "guided" the FDR/FMLN since then.

The new program marked a distinct turn to the right. It dropped the demands for the nationalization of largescale industry and commerce. Still more dangerously, it proposed to leave the existing, capitalist armed forces intact, merely purging them of their most blatantly criminal elements: The new program calls for "the organization of a single national army made up of the forces of the FMLN and the purged government's armed forces. Until that time both sides would keep control of their arms."[66]*

*Compare the FDR/FMLN's "government of broad participation" program to the conditions for an end to the Cuban civil war publicly announced by Fidel Castro in August 1958: "The arrest and delivery of the dictator [Batista] to the tribunals of justice; the arrest and delivery of all political leaders who were responsible for the dictatorship, who in any way had helped the regime to function, or who had enriched themselves with the republic's [sic] resources; the arrest and delivery of all military personnel who had engaged in crimes of war in the cities and in the countryside, and of those officers who had enriched themselves through gambling, extortion, smuggling and all illicit means, whatever their rank; delivery of the presidency to that man appointed by all sectors fighting the dictatorship, in order that general elections might be held in the shortest time possible."[67] It is clear that Castro's "ceasefire" conditions were a rough approximation of a program for the *victorious revolutionary insurrection by the oppressed masses*—which in fact occurred some four months later. The FDR/FMLN

But as long as both the bourgeoisie and the proletariat remain armed, there can be no "single national army": One class must forcibly disarm the other, and either re-enslave or liberate the nation — according to its class interest.

The liberal jesuit *Eca* journal, politically close to the FDR leadership, approvingly noted: "...The goal of people's power based on a worker/peasant alliance has been postponed if not abandoned, and any notions of alignment with the socialist bloc or the export of revolution in the region long ago gave way to a nationalist pledge of nonalignment. Now, the FMLN/FDR offers a reciprocal security pact with the United States."[68] This would be like a bee offering a "reciprocal security pact" to a tiger—instead of boldly rallying her sister bees to sting the flailing tiger to death.

The Contadora Process of Sabotaging the Revolution

A crucial role in the triumph of liberal, anti-revolutionary politics over the entire FMLN leadership has been played by the "Contadora group" of the bourgeois governments of four key countries flanking Central America to the north and south: Mexico, Panamá, Colombia and Venezuela. Posturing as concerned friends of the embattled masses of Central America, the bourgeois gentlemen of Contadora have advanced a flurry of proposals aimed at achieving a "negotiated settlement" to the armed conflicts in El Salvador and Nicaragua. In reality, their overriding concern is to douse the flames of the Central American revolution, and prevent it from spreading into "their own" countries.

All the "humanitarian" diplomatic rhetoric of the Contadora politicians has failed to tie the hands of the fascist *somocista* counterrevolutionaries in their attacks against Nicaragua, nor has it restrained the genocidal armed forces of El Salvador and Guatemala. On the other hand, the sugary diplomacy of Contadora *has* sharply restrained the supposed revolutionary leaders of El Salvador—and with them, crucial sections of the struggling masses—from carrying the armed revolution through to its logical, victorious conclusion. The Contadora group thus functions as a Trojan horse for U.S. imperialism amidst the popular movements of Central America. U.S. president Ronald Reagan was evidently alerted to this situation by his more astute political

---

program, by contrast, is a program for *liquidating* the people's revolutionary movement into a bourgeois coalition government and a revived bourgeois army.

ESTADOS UNIDOS

OCEANO ATLANTICO

MIAMI

MEXICO

REPUBLICA
DOMINICANA

BELICE

CUBA

HAITI

PUERTO
RICO

HONDURAS

JAMAICA

GUATEMALA

NICARAGUA

EL SALVADOR

PANAMA

VENEZUELA

GUAYANA

COSTA RICA

ISLA DE CONTADORA

COLOMBIA

OCEANO PACIFICO

BRAZIL

ECUADOR

PERU

*The Contadora countries flank Central America to the north and south.
Their bourgeois rulers, like the U.S. imperialists, fear the spread of the
workers' and peasants' revolution.*

advisers shortly after Contadora formed in 1983. In an interview
geared to the upper-class readership of *Forbes* magazine, Reagan
managed to communicate his support to the "Contadora process," despite his disjointed, ranch owner's thought processes:
"The Contadora is trying to get—as they are called, those four
countries that have banded together—I will be meeting, before
too long, with some of those people. But we support them and
what they're trying to accomplish. But the thing we must recognize is that these [revolutionaries] are not just some peasants
with muskets, embattled farmers out there in the hills. These are
professionals."[69] Reagan drove the main point home again while
addressing Mexico's president Miguel de la Madrid* during the

*Miguel de la Madrid, despite his bourgeois nationalist posturing "against"
U.S. intervention and domination over Central America, has, in reality,
helped the imperialist puppet regimes of El Salvador and Guatemala more
than he has hurt them. When, in May 1984, a group of revolutionary guerrillas of the Salvadoran FCER were forced to seize hostages in the course of a
military action in a supermarket and thus gained safe passage to Mexico, de
la Madrid's regime immediately jailed them. And de la Madrid has done
nothing to protect the tens of thousands of Guatemalan Indian refugees
from murderous attacks by Guatemalan armed forces against their camps in

latter's 1984 visit to Washington: "What we disagree on are not goals or principles, but the means by which to achieve those goals."[70] Reagan is the hard cop, while de la Madrid and his Contadora colleagues are the soft cops policing the Central American revolution.

The 'Political Solution' and the Political Solution

The Contadora politicians, along with the social democratic and liberal imperialists (headed by the Socialist Mitterrand regime in France), have stressed the desirability of a "political solution" to the civil war raging in El Salvador, via the road of negotiations—as opposed to the "military solution" of having one side triumph over, and disarm the other. With their glib formula for a "political solution" that would "reconcile" the warring class forces in El Salvador, the Contadora politicians and the liberal FDR leaders aim to deceive the Salvadoran masses into thinking that the only politics they can pursue is the politics of *capitulation* to capitalist class rule.

The bourgeois gentlemen of Contadora and the FDR have "forgotten" the famous axiom by the Prussian war theoretician Clausewitz: *War is the continuation of politics by other means.* Thus the *revolutionary* war being waged by the Salvadoran masses against the oligarchy and its army is precisely the "other means," the *only means* through which a *revolutionary political solution* to the social and political crisis will be achieved. The class conscious Salvadoran workers will no doubt answer the liberals and social democrats: 'The "political solution" of Ungo, Contadora and the liberal imperialists means the abortion of our revolution and the preservation of capitalist class rule. What for them is a solution, is a *problem* for us. Here is *our* political solution: fighting our revolutionary war through to complete victory over the neocolonial regime, completely *smashing* the existing, capitalist state, expropriating the big bourgeoisie, and establishing a *workers' and peasants' government.*'

---

southern Mexico. De la Madrid's planned "solution" to this problem has been a forced relocation of the Guatemalan Indian refugees some 70 kilometers north of the Guatemalan/Mexican border—sealing them off from their ancestral homelands and their traditional livelihoods.

Revolutionary vs. Bourgeois Negotiations

As the revolutionary Frente Clara Elizabeth Ramírez (FCER) pointed out upon its public break with the opportunist FMLN leadership, the question is not whether negotiations between revolutionary combatants and their ruling class enemies are permissible: The burning question is whether the revolutionaries use negotiations as a tactical front to continue pursuing a revolutionary *strategy* aimed at overthrowing all the exploiting classes — or whether they allow themselves to be politically corrupted by the liberals and their imperialist masters, and corralled into negotiating the *liquidation* of the revolutionary struggle, for the sake of a few cozy posts in a bourgeois coalition government.

Negotiations can and should be used to make *temporary tactical arrangements* with the class enemy in the course of the struggle. Clearcut examples are temporary ceasefires to allow the wounded and dead to be removed from the battlefield, and reciprocal exchanges of prisoners of war.

Revolutionaries are sometimes compelled to make temporary tactical retreats through negotiations with the class enemy — when they are in a weak position and need time to summon mass forces for a future tactical offensive. In 1918 the bolsheviks, having led the revolutionary overthrow of the Russian bourgeois regime and established a workers' and peasants' Soviet republic, found it necessary to sign a humiliating treaty with Germany at Brest-Litovsk, ceding a huge amount of territory to German imperialism. Still, the bolsheviks gained a propaganda advantage through the course of the negotiations, as the German rulers exposed their imperialist greed for the whole world to see, and the bolsheviks used the negotiations as a platform of revolutionary agitation to the German workers and soldiers. At the end of the year, demobilizing German soldiers, radicalizing to the left, joined the insurgent workers in overthrowing the German emperor (kaiser) — at which point, Lenin and the bolsheviks tore up the treaty they had rightfully denounced as a "robber's treaty."

In the 1972 Paris peace negotiations between North Vietnam and the U.S., by contrast, North Vietnam was able to negotiate from a relative position of *strength* — since the U.S. armed forces had been virtually defeated by the revolutionary war of the Vietnamese people, and the U.S. ground troops were thoroughly demoralized, more and more rebelling against "their own" officers.

[continued on page 46]

'...That's the Life of the Green Berets'

From a former U.S. ambassador:

While I was the U.S. ambassador to El Salvador in 1964, a small contingent of Green Berets, some of whom I understood had been among the early advisers in Vietnam, came to El Salvador to supplement the training already in progress under the direction of our military mission. The Green Berets may have made the Salvadoran soldiers somewhat better prepared for later duties...

—Murat Williams, ambassador to El Salvador from 1961, under Kennedy and Johnson[71]

From a former Salvadoran government soldier:

...One day we had a welcome for the Green Berets...We got to see the Green Berets who had come to us from the U.S. The officers told us they would be teaching us some new tactics.

...Six days later, when we returned to the barracks, they began to teach us how to torture. One evening they went and got nine young people who were accused of being guerrillas and brought them to where we were.

The first one they brought was a young fellow who was around 15 or 16 years old. The first thing the Green Berets did was stick their bayonets under his fingernails and pull them out. He said all kinds of things, trying to get them to stop. But they wouldn't.

After they pulled off his fingernails, they broke his elbows. Afterwards, they gouged out his eyes. Then they took their bayonets and made all sorts of slices in his skin all around his chest, arms, and legs. Finally, they took his hair off and the skin of his scalp. When they saw there was nothing left to do to him, they threw gasoline on him and burned him.

Before they did all of this, the American Green Berets told us, 'We are going to teach you how to mutilate and how to teach a lesson to these guerrillas.' They spoke in English, but a Salvadoran officer translated it into Spanish for us.

...The next day they started the same thing with a 13-year-old girl. This time the Green Berets didn't do the torture; they only gave instructions.

First the girl was raped by all of the officers. They stripped her and threw her in a small room, then went in one by one.

Afterwards they brought her out, tied and blindfolded. Then they began the same mutilating, pulling out her fingernails, cutting off her fingers, breaking her arms, gouging out her eyes. Finally they stuck an iron rod into her womb.

The last one they killed that day suffered even more. They stripped him naked and put him out on some hot tin in midday. They made him lie

there like he was being cooked. When they took him off, he was covered with blisters. Then they took him up in a helicopter, still alive, tied him up, and dropped him out from 14,000 feet. Often the army goes and throws people out over the sea...
—Testimony from a Salvadoran watch repairer, born in 1958
  and drafted into the government army at the end of 1980.[72]

Le Duc Tho was thus able to face down Henry Kissinger's demagogic demands for a "mutual withdrawal" arrangement that would remove both the U.S. forces and the north Vietnamese forces from south Vietnam. The key substance of the treaty that was finally signed in 1973 was the phased withdrawal of the U.S. invasion force, and a reciprocal release of prisoners of war.

To be sure, the opportunist Hanoi bureaucrats, underestimating the strength of the revolutionary movement in the south, *also* agreed to a coalition government in Saigon with the bourgeoisie, including even some top officers from the U.S. puppet military dictatorship. And they tried to restrain the guerrilla fighters who were determined to continue their struggle through to complete victory. But, when the war resumed, the puppet army collapsed so swiftly and profoundly that the coalition government scheme was swept away. In April 1975, the bourgeois, neocolonial state was completely smashed, and replaced by a workers' state—even if under opportunist leadership.

It is one thing to negotiate temporary tactical arrangements, compromises and even retreats with imperialism and/or the local ruling class—while adhering to a revolutionary strategy. It is quite another to negotiate the program and social/political composition of a new *government* with the imperialists and the ruling bourgeois clique. A government means the administration of the dictatorship of one class over another. Thus the imperialists will *never* negotiate into existence a government that fails to serve their interests, the interests of the bourgeois dictatorship. The imperialists and their hired politicians know what they are doing, and what they want; their principles, strategy and tactics form a coherent, counterrevolutionary whole. It is the leaders of the revolutionary proletariat who, lacking a clear and principled grasp of which side they are on in the *international* class struggle, are vacillating dangerously between revolutionary and liberal politics, threatening to pass over to a strategic betrayal of the revolutionary movement that would allow imperialism to snatch victory out of the jaws of defeat.

Despite the FMLN/FDR's repeated offers for "unconditional negotiations and dialog" with the current Duarte regime, Duarte has insisted that the FMLN fighters lay down their arms as a precondition to negotiations. Duarte's rigid position on negotiations reflects the continuing pressure on his regime from the most principled partisans of bourgeois counterrevolution, the ARENA fascists; if he were to open negotiations with the FMLN without first extracting a suicidal concession from them, he would be furiously attacked, and quite possibly overthrown by ARENA and its allied military officers, for "selling out to communism."

But if and when "strategic negotiations" *are* opened between the Salvadoran government (whether headed by the Christian Democracy, ARENA and/or military officers) and the FMLN/-FDR, the *strategic aim* of the government and its U.S. sponsor will be the same one already stated clearly by Duarte: the *disarming of the revolutionary fighters*. A "negotiated settlement" approved by imperialism can only mean the demobilization of the revolutionary army, a violent purge of the most principled revolutionary leaders, the liquidation of the demoralized remnants of the revolutionary army into the existing bourgeois army, and a facelift of the bourgeois government that brings the traitorous ex-leaders of the revolutionary movement into a coalition with the liberals and the big bourgeoisie. This, in fact, is what happened in Zimbabwe in 1979-80.

The 'Zimbabwe Solution' or the 'Nicaragua Solution'?

When the idea of a "negotiated settlement" to achieve a "political solution" in El Salvador was first bandied about by the FDR liberals, some of the more astute imperialist analysts pointed to Zimbabwe as a practical model for such a settlement. The 1979-80 events in Zimbabwe were indeed a great and crafty victory for imperialism, and a great defeat for the Zimbabwean workers and peasants. With the seven-year civil war between the Zimbabwe African National Union (ZANU) and the Rhodesian bourgeois settler regime stalemated, British imperialism resumed its colonial authority over the country and oversaw a negotiated settlement. In negotiations held in England with rightist Rhodesian leader Ian Smith, his black puppet Abel Muzorewa, and the bourgeois liberal Joshua Nkomo, ZANU leader Robert Mugabe agreed to a government constitution enshrining private property rights and perpetuating the stranglehold of the Rhodesian capitalist farmers over the country's fertile land, which they had robbed from the Zimbabwean peasants. With elections scheduled on this bourgeois constitutional basis, a ceasefire was intitiated: The revolutionary ZANU fighters were confined to camps, while the counterrevolutionary Rhodesian army was granted full mobility to continue repressing the Zimbabwean masses. ZANU leaders who opposed the settlement as a betrayal of the party's revolutionary socialist principles were arrested and/or liquidated on orders from Mugabe. When Mugabe won the 1980 elections and became prime minister, he proceeded to *"integrate"* the tamed ZANU army into the Rhodesian army, whose white officer corps remained largely intact. Despite having won an absolute majority in the elections, Mugabe—bent on assuring the imperialists and the Rhodesian bourgeoisie of his conservative intentions— formed a coalition government with both Nkomo's party and representatives of the Rhodesian bourgeoisie.[73]

Mugabe's regime thus constitutes a black political cover for the continued class dictatorship of the white, Rhodesian bourgeoisie over the Zimbabwean workers and peasants. The results have been favorable for imperialism and South Africa, but disastrous for the Zimbabwean masses. The Zimbabwean peasants continue to be confined to the congested and barren "tribal trust lands" where they were shoved by the Rhodesian settlers, and the Zimbabwean farm laborers continue to be harshly exploited by their capitalist taskmasters. The Zimbabwean women have suffered continued police persecution, culminating in a massive roundup of supposed prostitutes. The state's armed forces under Mugabe, in their campaign to crush dissident guerrilla fighters attempting to revive the liberation struggle, have committed mass murder against "their own" people, notably in Matabeleland.

This reality of a neocolonial regime cannot be hidden by Mugabe's demagogic campaign to convert his regime into a "one-party socialist state" headed by ZANU. Mugabe has long since liquidated ZANU as a revolutionary force, transforming it into a caste of bourgeois, counterrevolutionary politicians and bureaucrats headed by Mugabe.

This is one possible fate of the Salvadoran revolution—if the FMLN leaders allow themselves to be enticed into a bourgeois negotiated settlement, and if the revolutionary workers and peasants are not strong enough to defeat the schemes of their traitorous leaders to "integrate" their movement into the bourgeois army and a bourgeois coalition government.

Another, and more likely fate of the Salvadoran revolution is that, in spite of the vacillations of its leaders and in spite of the great bloodshed it suffers, it will conquer power and destroy the bourgeois state. This is what happened in Nicaragua in 1979.

Chapter 2

Nicaragua:
The Workers
and Peasants Triumph

The first flames of the modern Nicaraguan revolution erupted in January 1978, after the dictator Somoza's thugs assassinated Pedro Joaquín Chamorro, editor of the liberal daily *La Prensa* and head of the bourgeois opposition to the Somoza dynasty.* Outraged, the working masses of Managua turned Chamorro's funeral into a fiery rebellion, burning down dozens of buildings that symbolized the Somoza and imperialist tyranny: banks and finance houses (including First National Citybank of New York), and Somoza-owned factories. The national/liberal bourgeoisie feared that the death of their leader would be transformed into the birth of a popular revolution that would leave the bourgeoisie trailing in its wake. So they called a general strike, many employers giving their workers full pay to stay at home, and raised the slogan, "peaceful resistance."

But the workers were in no mood to stay home and let the national bourgeoisie play peaceful politics with Somoza and the U.S. embassy. They took massively to the streets and continued

---

*Chamorro was head of the Conservative Party, historically rooted in family cliques of semifeudal landowners, big merchants and government bureaucrats, descendants of the Spanish colonial ruling class. Anastasio Somoza Debayle, meanwhile, was head of the National Liberal Party; his father had headed up the extreme right, militarist wing of the old Liberal Party, which had represented a more dynamic, pro-development sector of the bourgeoisie than did the Conservative Party. However, with the consolidation of the Somoza oligarchy in power, the social and political relationship between the Conservative and Liberal parties had been reversed—so that it is more appropriate to use the generic term "liberal" to describe Pedro Joaquín Chamorro, his party and the bourgeois opposition generally.

to confront Somoza's national guard. Weapons and strong organization were all they lacked to go over to a fullscale insurrection. The *Frente Sandinista de Liberación Nacional* (FSLN—Sandinista National Liberation Front), divided into three separate groups and unprepared for the lightning acceleration of events, trailed behind the spontaneous semi-insurrection far more than it led it. In February, the bourgeoisie's strike committee called off the general strike in its twelfth day. FSLN military units then launched assaults against national guard positions in the north and south, and the FSLN began to seize the initiative in the mass movement which the bourgeoisie had so fearfully dropped.[2]

February 1978: Insurrection in Monimbó

But the climax of the February upheaval was a spontaneous insurrection of the people themselves, in the Indian *barrio* of Monimbó in the city of Masaya. The people organized a series of masses and peaceful demonstrations in memory of Chamorro. One demonstration was violently dispersed by the national guard. Then the guard launched an aerial attack on a crowd marching up to the local cemetary.

This sparked a storm of streetfighting against the guard. The entire people plunged into the insurrection—men, women and children, building barricades and improvising bombs out of the materials at hand, organizing themselves block by block. In four days, the people of Monimbó took over the city. The FSLN had missed the insurrection, and Monimbó remained an isolated pocket of people's power.

Somoza sent tanks, armored cars and helicopter gunships against Monimbó. Lacking sophisticated weapons, the people defended themselves heroically, and some national guardsmen crossed over to their side. After killing over 200 people, Somoza's forces reconquered Monimbó.[3]

The national bourgeoisie, in calling its general strike, had aimed to *lean on* the mass movement to pressure U.S. president Jimmy Carter into easing Somoza out of office and opening the way to a regime in which the bourgeoisie would share more equally in the spoils of exploitation. But the stormy acceleration of the people's revolutionary movement had outstripped the bourgeoisie's game plan, and the defeat of the Monimbó insurrection found the bourgeois opposition in disarray.

The Masses Prepare for Revolution...

And now, a revolutionary mass movement raised its head boldly throughout Nicaragua. The FSLN initiated a United People's Movement to embrace practically all of the country's opposition parties and mass organizations. This led, in turn, to the formation of hundreds of local *Comités de Defensa Civil* (CDC— Civil Defense Committees), which conducted clandestine political agitation and military preparation in workingclass and oppressed people's *barrios*. In May, hundreds of peasant families in the north launched land seizures, backed by strong political and military organization.

"Nobody in Nicaragua now is talking or thinking about anything but politics," declared women in Masaya in July. Everyone knows what is going on, everyone is conscious... Yes, we're afraid, because we know our task won't be easy...but we're confident. Look at the walls here in the city. All of them are covered with pro-FSLN slogans. The people paint them, the guard come along and wipe them off, next day they're back again. We're going to be all right, we're organizing. It's only a matter of time."[4]

...and the FSLN Reunites

Under the pressure of the mass movement demanding unity of the revolutionary vanguard, the three tendencies of the FSLN moved into operational unity. The FSLN had split in 1975, when the sharpening differences over revolutionary strategy and tactics could be neither contained nor resolved under conditions of ferocious Somoza repression and physical dispersion of the FSLN's cadres. Three tendencies had emerged back then: The leftist "proletarian" tendency, headed by Jaime Wheelock, Luis Carrión and Carlos Núñez, emphasized political work among the urban masses and agricultural laborers in preparation for mass insurrection. The centrist "prolonged people's war" tendency, headed by Tomás Borge, Henry Ruiz and Bayardo Arce, called for a prolonged war of liberation based among the peasantry, gradually liberating rural territory and thus surrounding the cities. The right-opportunist *"terceristas,"* headed by Daniel Ortega, Humberto Ortega and Edén Pastora and becoming the majority tendency, stressed the need for an alliance with the national bourgeoisie and pursued a course of spectacular military insurrections and actions by the vanguard fighters, with the aim of "sparking" the masses to rise up. Now all three tendencies reunited in the preparations for mass insurrection.

In August 1978, U.S. president Carter dashed the national bourgeoisie's fond hopes of a "democratic opening." He sent a letter to Somoza *praising* the dictator's "human rights" record, and approved a new U.S. aid grant to his regime. Cornered, the national bourgeoisie had no choice but to lean on the masses again. They called a new general strike on 25 August, one day after the end of a spectacular *tercerista* attack on Somoza's national palace. The *tercerista* fighters had held Somoza's cronies hostage until winning the release of 58 FSLN prisoners; Somoza was also forced to acknowledge that 27 other FSLN prisoners whose release had been demanded were dead—having already been murdered in his prisons.

The September 1978 Revolution

This time, the general strike went over to *nationwide* mass insurrection. The people of Matagalpa were the first to rise, and within days they had conquered power in several workingclass *barrios*. But like Monimbó in February, revolutionary Matagalpa —arising spontaneously from below—was isolated from the rest of the country. It was crushed by national guard terror by 3 September, as two-thirds of the population fled to the surrounding hills.[5]

On 9 September, the FSLN issued a proclamation for a nationwide people's insurrection. Within 24 hours, revolutionary war engulfed both the cities and countryside, climaxing in the departmental capitals of Masaya, León, Estelí and Chinandega. Seasonally unemployed farmworkers and aroused peasants joined the urban poor in the fierce urban battles to destroy police stations and defend the fledgling people's power against the national guard's white terror.*

The FSLN armed forces, which had started the month with only a few hundred fighters, were growing by the thousands as the September insurrection spread. But the FSLN's military capacity had not yet developed to the point where they could engage the national guard in a fluid war of movement from countryside to city and from city to countryside, to disperse and destroy it. The FSLN remained locked in a war of *positions* to defend

---

White terror refers to counterrevolutionary terror—whereas *red terror* refers to revolutionary terror.

the liberated cities from Somoza's calculated counterassault. Somoza thus enjoyed all the advantages of mobility. Concentrating his dreaded elite national guard forces against the departmental capitals, he reconquered them one by one.[6] Somoza's U.S. equipped and advised military machine resorted to saturation aerial bombardment of the liberated *barrios*, napalm burning of peasants' crops, and summary mass executions of youths from the age of 10 and up—killing over 10,000 people out of a population of 2.8 million.

Somoza's national guard, touted as the strongest army in Central America, seemed all powerful. But it had less than ten months to live. Already its gravediggers were in motion: Thousands of youths, workers and peasants fled Somoza's white terror to join the FSLN units in the mountains.

From Revolutionary Defeat to Revolutionary Victory

A wave of rebellion in January/February followed by a bigger wave of revolution in September, in the face of Somoza's white terror, counterrevolutionary maneuvering by U.S. imperialism, and selfish jockeying for position by the national bourgeoisie—this single year of intense revolutionary experience transformed the Nicaraguan people into the most revolutionary, the most politically enlightened people in the world. By the end of 1978, they were fully confident that the 42-year Somoza dynasty would before long be buried by their own efforts. The fresh recruits who had flooded into the FSLN now plunged into military training and political education. The CDC's, driven further underground by the white terror, *intensified* their preparations for a new wave of insurrection, passing on their revolutionary experience to new CDC's just awakening to political life. The CDC network also forged links with christian base committees and local consciousness raising groups built by radical priests and nuns to rally the masses for social justice.

The FSLN's "proletarian" tendency proved to have the most correct vision of the strategy and tactics of the revolution (a vision which was later blurred by the victorious FSLN's attempts to develop its *tactical* alliance with the national bourgeoisie into a *strategic* alliance). Yet the successful reunification of the three tendencies in the very midst of the revolution proved that *all* of them had grasped *part* of the richly complex social and political truth that was the Nicaraguan revolution. The urban masses *did* play the key role in the insurrection, and the agricultural proletarians spearheaded the mass revolutionary upheaval in the countryside. Yet they could not have conquered and held power without the lightning mobile campaign of the FSLN army, which had sunk fairly deep roots among the peasantry. And the tactical alliance with the anti-Somoza bourgeoisie, though its importance was grossly overestimated by the *"terceristas"* (and later by the entire FSLN), did play a useful role in strengthening the national insurrection and cutting down on Carter's room for counterrevolutionary maneuver.

The crude political division of labor which had assigned urban work to the "proletarian" tendency, rural work to the "prolonged people's war" tendency, and military work to the *"terceristas"* was now broken down. The FSLN as a whole began profoundly grasping the dialectical relationship between the urban struggle and the rural struggle, between the military action of the masses and the military action of the vanguard. In March 1979, while their guerrilla fighters, actively supported by the mass movement, were engaged in a campaign of harassment against the national guard, the FSLN's three tendencies formally reunified.

The fruition of this persistent mass activity and organic unity of the vanguard was not long in coming. In a revolutionary resurgence unprecedented in world history, the Nicaraguan masses, *less than a year* after the white terror had defeated their September 1978 revolution, rose up in a still more powerful nationwide insurrection. And this time, the FSLN was in the lead from the start. FSLN guerrillas harassed and demoralized the overextended national guard units. FSLN regular, larger units outmaneuvered the national guard in a brilliant campaign of mobile warfare between countryside and city, repeatedly encircling the guardsmen in their barracks and forcing their surrender or headlong flight. Agricultural laborers of the *Asociación de Trabajadores del Campo* (ATC—Association of Rural Workers) ambushed guardsmen and cut their communication lines, setting up supply lines for the FSLN units. The urban masses role up with heightened selfconfidence and heroism. The role of women fighters was stunning: In León, Nicaragua's second largest city, the victorious insurrection was led largely by women, headed by commander Dora María Tellez. A number of radical priests and nuns broke with christian tradition to take up arms in the insurrection. The national bourgeoisie again threw its puny weight behind the mass anti-Somoza upheaval. On 19 July 1979, the Somoza dynasty was destroyed, and the red and black flag of Sandino raised throughout Nicaragua.

Workers' State, Petty-Bourgeois Government

The social revolution had triumphed; a new class was in power. The neocolonial, bourgeois state, centered on Somoza's national guard (which had functioned both as an army and police force), had been *completely smashed* through revolutionary civil war. An *entirely new* state had risen to take its place, centered on the FSLN army—a proletarian/peasant army—as well as the people's militias which had emerged in the heat of the revolution as the masses spontaneously seized arms left behind by the fleeing national guardsmen. The national bourgeoisie was unarmed.

The new state was a *workers' state*. It immediately expropriated the vast capital holdings of the Somoza dynasty, including all of Nicaragua's commercial banks and Somoza's substantial industrial and landholdings, and established a state monopoly on foreign trade for the country's key agricultural exports.

However, the FSLN leadership did not recognize—or rather, refused to recognize—the objective, proletarian class transformation that had taken place. Instead of creating a *workers' and peasants' government*, it established—without consulting the masses—a coalition government between itself and the national/-liberal bourgeoisie. To be sure, the FSLN held majority control in this coalition government from the start, and controlled the key levers of state power, such as Tomás Borge's ministry of the interior. But the coalition with the national/liberal bourgeoisie, who had sacrificed practically nothing in the course of the struggle against Somoza while the masses fought and died, meant making

---

FROM ONE CLASS CONSCIOUS WORKER TO ANOTHER...

A: Just before he was overthrown by the revolution, the dictator Somoza went on countrywide U.S. television and moaned that the youth of Nicaragua were acting like the youth of the south Bronx.

B: Amazing! What was the butcher trying to do, slander the revolutionary youth of Nicaragua?

A: Of course. But his words had precisely the opposite effect.

B: What's that?

A: To praise the revolutionary potential of the youth of the south Bronx.

an unprincipled compromise with those selfish, "patriotic" exploiters, and slamming the brakes on the revolutionary movement of the workers and peasants.

Enshrining the right of private property in the new constitution, the FSLN leaders refused to take the elementary, revolutionary step of *nationalizing all the land*, and instead guaranteed ownership rights to all "anti-Somoza" landowners. Even in the many cases where agricultural laborers and poor peasants had occupied large estates owned by "anti-Somoza" landowners and begun tilling the land on a cooperative basis, struggling to bring fresh land under cultivation to feel their starving families, the government balked at expropriating the liberal landowners.

The FSLN leaders were bent on maintaining an economic alliance with the national/liberal bourgeoisie and their U.S. imperialist sponsors who, under Somoza, had come to provide the key spare parts and infrastructural inputs needed to keep the underdeveloped Nicaraguan economy running. At the time Somoza fled his fortified bunker under the hammer blows of the revolution, he had left the country with a mammoth foreign debt of $1.6 billion, swindling the central bank to the point of leaving only $3.5 million in foreign exchange. Instead of boldly *renouncing* that bloodsoaked debt piled up by Somoza, the FSLN government proceeded to *renegotiate* it with the U.S. imperialist banks and lending institutions—cancelling only Somoza's debt to fascist Argentina and Israel for arms purchases.

As long as the FSLN leaders resign themselves to the bleak scenario of Nicaragua remaining encircled and isolated by bourgeois, neocolonial regimes in Central America (and Latin America) for the indefinite future, Nicaragua, with its "micro-economy" distorted by agro-export trade geared to service North America, has no chance of breaking the bind of underdevelopment. Given the current reality of such a scenario, their policy of begging more loans from the imperialists on the basis of the same kind of economic structure contains a certain pragmatic logic. But it is a selfdefeating logic, which leads inevitably to Nicaragua, despite being under proletarian rule, sliding back into the same old pattern of neocolonial dependence on imperialism.

It was not long before the new Nicaragua was devoting over 20% of its foreign exchange payments to paying off the compounded debt service on Somoza's debts to the imperialists. In 1981, Nicaragua made interest payments of $121 million against the foreign debt; in 1982, the interest payments amounted to $154.4 million. By June 1983, the country's foreign debt had swollen to $3.34 billion.[8]

There has thus been a sharp *contradiction between the Nicaraguan state and the government sitting on top of that state.* The state is a *workers' state*; the government is a *petty-bourgeois government*—originally a coalition government between the proletariat (represented by the opportunist FSLN leaders) and the national/liberal bourgeoisie. This contradiction is antagonistic. It can be resolved in only one of two ways: Either the *purging* of the bourgeois representatives from the government under the pressure of the revolutionary masses, bringing the government into correspondence with the class foundations of the state and clearing the way for the complete expropriation of the big bourgeoisie—or the *smashing* of the new, workers' state by the bourgeoisie through counterrevolutionary civil war combined with imperialist attack.

Class Struggle Sharpens

Contrary to the FSLN leaders' petty-bourgeois fantasies that, now that the revolution was in power, the whole country could and should just "settle down" for peaceful consolidation and national economic reconstruction, the class struggle continued, and in fact sharpened. On 17 February 1980, over 30,000 farm laborers and peasants of the ATC, furious that the government had announced the return of land they had occupied to its capitalist owners, converged from all over Nicaragua, brandishing their machetes, to the plaza of the revolution in Managua. They marched by ATC billboards reading, "Only the workers and peasants will go all the way to the end." ATC head Edgardo García, speaking before the assembled crowd, demanded that "not one inch of land be returned" to the large landowners.[9] In response, the government nationalized the disputed land—but offered the old owners compensation through state bonds, thus further strapping the workers' state with debts to the bourgeoisie.

In the heat of the revolutionary insurrection and following its victory, Nicaragua's mass organizations had expanded and radicalized enormously, provoking the near hysterical anxiety of the bourgeoisie. The ATC, the factory workers' confederation, the *sandinista* defense committees (CDS) which had emerged from the insurrectionary CDC's as neighborhood committees of selfdefense and self-government, and the women's association (AMNLAE) which had evolved from its middle-class, urban origins to strike a tremendous chord of response among rural laboring women—all began to put their class and social imprint on the revolution and demand that the government serve their interests.

The Coalition Government Is Wrenched

The original plan for an unelected "council of state," drawn up by the FSLN in collaboration with the national/liberal bourgeoisie ten days before Somoza's overthrow, had projected that roughly half of the seats would go to bourgeois parties and organizations, with *no* seats going to the mass organizations. The mass organizations, outraged over this undemocratic buffoonery, began taking to the streets and exerting pressure on the FSLN leaders to reverse the extremely *narrowly* based government composition. In response, the FSLN leaders announced in April 1980 that the council of state would be expanded by 14 seats, with most of them going to the mass organizations.

The bourgeoisie reacted furiously. Alfonso Robelo, a liberal industrialist with a determining influence over the bourgeois daily *La Prensa** and an original member of the five-person "revolutionary" junta set up after Somoza's overthrow, resigned

---

*During the same week, a political struggle within *La Prensa* itself ended in the fullscale takeover of the paper by the increasingly counterrevolutionary bourgeoisie. As *La Prensa*'s news coverage was moving heavily to the right under the impact of the employers' council and the bourgeois parties, Xavier Chamorro and his progressive colleagues had continued to write pro-*sandinista* editorials, under tightening pressure from the paper's management, held by conservative members of the Chamorro family. On 19 April, *La Prensa*'s workforce, fed up with the rightward drift, demanded a collective bargaining agreement with management and union representation on the paper's editorial board. Xavier Chamorro supported the workers' demands, and was dumped by management the next day. The union immediately went on strike and occupied the *La Prensa* facilities, demanding Xavier's reinstatement. The workers denounced the newly appointed editorial board members as "people who never wrote a word against Somoza and now furiously attack the revolution."[10] Violeta Barrios, widow of *La Prensa* editor Pedro Joaquín Chamorro, resigned her post from the national junta a few days before Robelo, and sided with her counterrevolutionary son Pedro Joaquín Chamorro Barrios against Xavier Chamorro in the dispute in *La Prensa*—calling on the *sandinista* security forces to intervene against the striking workers. The dispute ended when 95% of *La Prensa*'s workforce joined Xavier Chamorro in creating a new daily, *El Nuevo Diario*, on a cooperative basis with worker participation in editorial decisions. *El Nuevo Diario* has pursued a line of critical support to the *sandinista* regime.

CIA sponsored mercenaries training in Miami, aiming to lend a helping hand to the somocista counterrevolutionaries based in Honduras.

Sandinista soldiers searching for counterrevolutionaries near the Honduran border.

A peasant (left) confronts agricultural minister Jaime Wheelock (right). "Children's stomachs cannot wait," insisted the farmworkers and peasants in the face of the government's legalistic delays in expropriating idle land held by "anti-Somoza" landowners.

Barricada

February 1980: Farmworkers and peasants of the ATC march to Managua to demand that the government nationalize the land they have occupied. Their banner reads: "We are not birds to live from the air, nor fishes to live from the sea—We are men to live from the land."

Barricada

May Day 1980: FSLN and government leaders lock arms. From left: Henry Ruiz, Sergio Ramírez (a junta leader close to the FSLN, today vice president), Carlos Núñez, Jaime Wheelock, Tomás Borge, Bayardo Arce, Luis Carrión, Humberto Ortega, and Moisés Hassan.

his government post. Robelo denounced the expansion of the council of state as a "totalitarian scheme." True to bourgeois democratic principles, Robelo views the political monopoly of a minority of exploiters over the working people as real democracy —whereas the rule of the majority of working people over the exploiting minority is "totalitarian." Three bourgeois parties, including Robelo's Nicaraguan Democratic Movement (MDN), refused to take their seats in the council of state. The private enterprise council (COSEP), representing the major business associations, accepted its five seats only after much vacillation and sharp protest.

Revolutionary Democracy vs. Counterrevolutionary Liberalism

The bourgeoisie and the catholic church hierarchy began stridently denouncing the creeping "communist influence" on the *sandinista* regime. Thousands of young volunteer workers were enthusiastically going out to the countryside on the weekends to help pick cotton and prepare fallow land for fresh planting on the newly collectivized and state farms. The bourgeoisie and the bishops denounced this as "destroying familial traditions."

In the summer of 1980, 120,000 young people—one-third of them from middle class families—were mobilized to spearhead a mass literacy campaign in the countryside under impoverished and dangerous conditions, as some were subjected to murderous attack by *somocista* ex-guardsmen. They succeeded in reducing the illiteracy rate from over 50% to 20%.* When the government followed up this successful campaign with a universal work/-study program requiring students to supplement their studies with productive labor in the fields and factories, *La Prensa* raved that "man is reduced to a simple monkey who works and produces."[12] Actually, the problem was that the cultured gentlemen of *La Prensa* had reduced themselves to simple monkeys chattering the line of U.S. imperialism.

In May 1980, a mass rally was held to honor a young literacy *brigadista* murdered by counterrevolutionary thugs near the

---

*The regime has claimed that the campaign reduced the illiteracy rate to only 13%. But this figure tendentiously excluded the 9% of the population who were judged unteachable, due to physical or mental blocks, in the course of the literacy campaign. These "incorrigible" illiterates had, on the other hand, been *included* in the 50% illiteracy figure from before the campaign.[11]

Honduran border in the north. Tomás Borge declared: "It is no coincidence that the *somocista* groups, concentrated at the Honduran/Nicaraguan frontier, have substituted Alfonso Robelo for Anastasio Somoza as their leader." Robelo had just made an anticommunist speaking tour of the northern region. Yet Borge, ultrasensitive lest he be accused of violating "human rights," Jimmy Carter style, continued to give Robelo full freedom to organize the counterrevolution.

On 9 November 1980, Robelo called for a mass antigovernment demonstration. The government, receiving information that the demonstration would coincide with armed attacks from Honduras, banned it. Three days later, 11 bourgeois opposition delegates, led by COSEP, walked out of the council of state to protest the ban. On 17 November, COSEP vice president and plantation owner Jorge Salazar was shot to death when his armed band opened fire on police attempting to arrest them for plotting a counterrevolutionary coup.[13] The next day, COSEP denounced the shooting of Salazar as a "political crime," and *La Prensa* proclaimed that his death "should be avenged."

Meanwhile, the bourgeoisie was going over to economic sabotage, diverting much of its capital abroad and sabotaging production on the plantations and factories it still held. While the anticommunist, AFL-CIO sponsored CUS labor union confederation as well as some labor unions led by leftist economist* groups

Economism, in leninist terminology, refers to those currents in the workingclass movement which focus the workers' attention mainly on their own, economic interests and demands at the point of production—as opposed to training the workers to actively discuss, denounce and struggle against *every* act of social and political oppression by the ruling classes, championing the democratic aspirations of *every* oppressed layer of society, above all those masses who are *even more oppressed* than the workers, such as the poor peasants. Lenin denounced "economism" as a form of bourgeois liberal ideology within the workingclass movement, which effectively leaves "the political struggle" in the hands of the liberal bourgeoisie. (See Lenin's *What is to be Done?*). At least 95% of the U.S. leftist groupings today are economist.

In Nicaragua, the question of to what extent leftist groups like the anti-*sandinista* Nicaraguan Communist Party and the pro-Albania People's Action Movement/Marxist-Leninist were playing into the hands of the bourgeoisie by inciting the workers to economic strikes after Somoza's overthrow, is complicated by the lack of objective, thorough and reliable information on the actual strike struggles that took place beginning in early 1980. It is also complicated by the fact that the FSLN leaders, by leaving several large factories in the hands of the "patriotic" capitalists and establishing joint state/private ventures with other such capitalists, had produced many situations where capitalist exploitation of the workers was continuing—thus played into the bourgeoisie's hands by inciting the workers in both state and privately owned factories to strike for massive wage hikes, the class conscious factory workers proceeded to *occupy* the privately owned factories and implement *workers' control of production*, energetically combatting the bourgeoisie's sabotage. But even in these cases, the FSLN government balked at expropriating the factories.

On 13 March 1981, as Robelo was making a renewed bid to rally a "democratic" counterrevolution, fighting broke out in Tipitapa, 25 kilometers east of Managua, between supporters of Robelo's MDN and members of the *sandinista* defense committee militia. One person on each side was killed, and streetfighting erupted in several other cities. The next day, the outraged revolutionary masses surrounded several bourgeois radio stations and the office of *La Prensa*, and blocked the roads leading to the site of a scheduled MDN demonstration. Robelo had to call it off. The government, frightened by the revolutionary selfmobilization of the masses, dispersed 300 occupiers of a bourgeois radio station with army units. Borge lamented, "We do not have at our disposal enough policemen to contain 5,000 demonstrators if this continues." But the class struggle does and will continue, no matter how much the minds of the FSLN leaders lag behind the struggle.

Agrarian Revolution, FSLN Reform

The FSLN leaders failed to realize that the revolutionary conquest of power could not mean the *end* of the agrarian revolution, but only its great *extension* and *acceleration*. In the first weeks after the victory over Somoza, the FSLN leaders were far too busy scrambling to divvy up the Mercedes Benz's and sumptuous houses left behind by the Somoza clique, to pay serious attention to the agrarian problem. The new government initially assumed that, in expropriating the economic dynasty of the Somoza clique, it had taken over 60% of Nicaragua's agricultural land into its hands. Three months later, it was amazed to discover that it held, in fact, only 20% of the country's farmland.[14] And the FSLN's government coalition with the national bourgeoisie meant

---

fertilizing the soil for leftist economist agitation. One thing is clear: The FSLN regime's repression against the "ultraleftist" groupings has been a lot harsher than its treatment of bourgeois liberal counterrevolutionaries like Robelo, archbishop Obando and *La Prensa*.

that any and all landowners who could not be legally proven to have had ties to the Somoza clique could continue owning as much land as they pleased—no matter how much they were exploiting the farmworkers and peasants.

"We are militants in a revolutionary cause who knew little about the process of an agrarian reform, in theory or in practice," declared FSLN leader Jaime Wheelock, who was to become head of the ministry of agriculture.[15]* But where ignorance of revolutionary necessity creates a political vacuum, opportunism** inevitably steps in to fill the vacuum: Right after the revolutionary victory, the FSLN tried to slam the brakes on peasant and farmworker land seizures, to placate the "patriotic" landowners at all cost. "I don't understand it at all," complained a peasant in Chinandega just days after the victory. "One minute seizing the land is revolutionary, then they tell you it's counterrevolutionary."[16] Clearly, this simple peasant was far more qualified to head up the agricultural ministry than was the petty-bourgeois muddlehead Wheelock.

By 1981, the continued bourgeois framework of landownership was bursting at the seams, as the farmworkers and peasants insisted that the new regime uphold their revolutionary class interests. The landowners were more and more going over to economic sabotage—"decapitalizing" their estates in preparation for flight from the country. About 30% of the normally cultivated land was being left idle.

As the second anniversary of the revolution approached, and with it the government's long awaited agrarian reform decree, the rural laboring classes stepped up their struggle. Land seizures

---

*Wheelock was a remarkably well informed ignoramus: The son of a rich cotton grower, he had written a statistical study of the economic and social impact of Nicaragua's cotton production before the revolution.

**Opportunism, in marxist terminology, means *the politics of the bourgeoisie in the workingclass movement*—or, with regard to the underdeveloped countries, the politics of the bourgeoisie in the national liberation movement. Characteristic features of opportunism are the concept of the peaceful transition from capitalism to socialism; the slogan of "preserving world peace" as opposed to struggling for world revolution; adherence to bourgeois and imperialist dominated "international" bodies such as the "United Nations" and "nonaligned nations movement," as opposed to the struggle to build a revolutionary International; preaching the existence of a "progressive, anti-imperialist" bourgeoisie and pursuing a strategic alliance with such bourgeois forces; and accommodating to *exploiting* sectors of the middle classes under the guise of "broadbased" politics and coalitions. Opportunism and reformism are basically synonymous. Economism is one form of opportunism.

increased; they were led by the ATC, often in collaboration with the *Unión Nacional de Arrendatarios y Ganaderos* (UNAG — National Union of Farmers and Ranchers). The ATC and UNAG militants demanded the government legalize their seizure of land which the exploiters refused to cultivate. "Children's stomachs cannot wait," they insisted.[17] Where coffee estate owners had fired workers or left fields untended, the ATC was moving in to complete the harvest. And in June, large numbers of peasants once again converged on Managua. "We have been forced to farm small plots of marginal land, trying to grow enough food," declared one of them to the press. "And now we see the gentlemen farmers letting hundreds and hundreds of acres of good land go idle."[18]

On 8 July 1981, less than two weeks before the second anniversary, a fresh demonstration of farmworkers and peasants converged in front of the government house in Managua. They were demanding that the government move sharply against the landowners' decapitalization campaign. "*Contra la descapitalización —confiscación*," chanted the rural masses again and again.[19]

Although this longwinded slogan did not have the catchiest rhythm, it drove to the heart of the revolutionary solution to the agrarian problem—as against the legalistic and "pluralistic" tomfoolery of the FSLN-led government. According to the "decapitalization" law implemented on March 1980, the government had to prove in court that a landowner had decapitalized before it could take decisive action against him; and the court system, which had yet to be revolutionized, moved slower than a bloated donkey chasing a predatory coyote. The law required documented proof that assets had been taken out of the country—which was usually impossible, since the landowners, following in Somoza's footsteps, had grown adept at hiding the tracks of their swindles. The legal process thus "took so long that by the time the courts decided against the owner, it was literally too late."[20]

"Yes, against decapitalization—confiscation," declared ATC head Edgardo García at a news conference. "But *timely* confiscation—not when there's nothing left but ruins, debts and a bankrupt farm." The existing law also required the government to pay the landowner the value of anything expropriated, regardless of the economic condition of the estate he had abandoned. "...This was tantamount to a financial incentive to decapitalize."[21]

On 19 July 1981, FSLN and government leader Daniel Ortega read the text of the proposed agrarian reform law to the half million people gathered in the capital. When the law was made official a month later, it formally codified the regime's balancing act between the large landowners and the rural laboring masses.

All abandoned land, along with idle or underused land on very large holdings, was declared subject to confiscation and redistribution. Lands whose titles had been shifted to other members of the same family were defined as part of the same holding, to prevent legal evasion of the reform. Absentee landownership was curbed by decreeing that, on farms larger than 35 hectares in the prime Pacific coast area and larger than 70 hectares elsewhere, any lands being sharecropped, or rented for cash or labor can be expropriated. Peasants receiving new land titles through the redistribution pay nothing for the land, which is urburdened from debt. The new titles cannot be sold; they can be inherited, but the heirs cannot divide up the land. The land received can also be transferred to a cooperative. An earlier decree setting a low ceiling on land rent was retained.[22]

Such were the anticapitalist aspects of the agrarian reform law. But the same law package made land seizures by farmworkers and peasants illegal. Reaffirming the government's pledge to protect private property rights, the law placed no limit on landholdings, as long as the owner did not abandon his estate, leave good land idle or underused, of decapitalize (sell off machinery or cattle). Scorning the protests of ATC and UNAG, the farmworkers' and peasants' organizations, the new law allowed for compensation to owners for all idle or underused land expropriated—unless the owners are caught decapitalizing.[23]

And even the progressive provisions of the law were saddled with a heap of bureaucratic lard: Final authority in deciding whether to expropriate land was given to the national junta (governing council)—thus restraining the revolutionary initiative of the rural masses in the localities.

The Women's Struggle

Another major front in the struggle between proletarian socialism and bourgeois reaction in Nicaragua has been the women's liberation struggle. Passionately roused by their major role in the liberation war and by the agitational and organizing work of the women's association (AMNLAE), thousands of working women of all ages began clamoring to be fully incorporated into both the people's militia and the army reserve. The FSLN leaders were reluctant, but the aroused masses of women pressured them into opening the doors of military training to women.

As working women flooded into the people's militia, the bourgeoisie and church hierarchy whipped up an hysterical propaganda campaign against the project as a plot of "Cuban communism" to undermine christian traditions. But a 26-year-old woman who sews and sells clothes for a living and had just joined the militia declared: "...All the women's morale is high. The rumor campaign the Right has going, is what keeps some women from entering the militia. But my brother joined up and he told me what it was really like. He encouraged me to come. I left my six-month-old baby with my mother, and didn't ask permission from my husband. We'll see what happens when I get home, but if he doesn't like it I guess we'll have to separate. Because I'm not giving this up for anything...!"[24]

This revolutionary sentiment clashes not only with the social program of the bourgeoisie and the bishops, who desperately want to re-enslave women beneath the patriarchal tyranny of man and his family, boss and his enterprise, and god and "his" church. It *also* challenges the narrow, petty-bourgeois social horizons set for Nicaragua's women by the male chauvinist FSLN leaders.

In particular, the "law of maintenance," proposed by the AMNLAE leaders and eagerly passed by the FSLN-led government, requires every father to financially support his woman (whether wife or unmarried lover) and children (whether the couple is living together or not). This law was intended by the AMNLAE leaders as a road to equality between man and woman in the family. But it is really patronizing and utopian, since, instead of *challenging* the patriarchal, nuclear family as the cellular unit of bourgeois society, it attempts to *salvage* the same old structure under "liberating" conditions. It assumes that individual parents (in reality, individual mothers) will continue having to shoulder the enormous burden of childrearing, and that women will continue to be economically dependent on men (see ch. 6). The "law of maintenance" thus lends a helping hand to the reactionary tendency for the bourgeois nuclear family to re-entrench itself. And any talk of equality between women and men under such conditions would make about as much sense as talk of equality between slaves and slavemasters, without the overthrow of the slave system.

Yet at the same time, AMNLAE has agitated for, and partially implemented, collective kitchens and childcare programs. This points the way to the progressive, proletarian task of *socializing housework and childrearing*. The modest beginnings made in this field can only be carried to liberation through the complete overturn of the patriarchal family and the legal structure supporting it, including the law of maintenance. Otherwise a revived patriarchal family structure, supported by a conservative state bureaucracy, will heavily stifle and truncate women's efforts to liberate themselves from domestic slavery.

Under Somoza, the right to divorce formally existed, but in the event of divorce the man was routinely granted custody of the children. Now, the woman routinely wins custody in the event of divorce. Birth control materials, while scarcely accessible in the first several months after the revolution, are now both legal and available free in health clinics.[25]

But abortion is still *il*legal. The FSLN government wants to keep conciliating the church on this burning question, and to increase Nicaragua's tiny population by preaching to women that childbirth is their "patriotic duty." So Nicaraguan women—like poor women in the U.S., who have the legal right but not the economic means to clinical abortion—continue to be mutilated, and even killed by amateur abortion attempts.

In the summer of 1983, the unresolved question of women's military role in the ongoing revolutionary struggle emerged once again, in the national debate over the government's new compulsory military service law. The law, proposed by defense minister Humberto Ortega on 10 August and approved by the council of state a month later, requires military service—either active or reserve—for all *males* between the ages of 18 and 40,* with service for women in the same age group being purely voluntary.

The proposed law met with a storm of demagogic criticism by the bourgeois political parties and church hierarchy, forces which by no means want to strengthen the nation's military defense against the ongoing counterrevolutionary threat orchestrated by U.S. imperialism from both north and south. The rightist Social Democratic Party declared that the law "attacks the emotional

*The law allows for several categories of exceptions to compulsory service, including for men who are the sole breadwinners of their households.

stability of the Nicaraguan family and lays the basis for a holocaust which will bring mourning to the nation." The Nicaraguan
bishops conference declared that the law "follows the general
lines of totalitarian legislation."[26] According to the bourgeois gentlemen and bishops, when the broad masses are mobilized and
armed to defend their revolutionary conquests against the armed
thugs of imperialism, that is "totalitarian" and tending towards a
"holocaust"—whereas, when the bourgeoisie conquers the
masses, disarms them and suppresses them with its own special
armed forces, that is "freedom."

While the bourgeois parties and bishops criticized the proposed
law *from the right*, the revolutionary women criticized it *from the
left*. In the hundreds of neighborhood meetings held to discuss
the proposed law, politically advanced women consistently took
issue with its sexist double standard of making military service
compulsory for men, but voluntary for women. They demanded
that compulsory military service be *extended equally to women*.
As AMNLAE representative Angela Rosa Acevedo argued, wom-
en, through their participation in the revolutionary insurrection
and economic reconstruction, "have won the right to be more
broadly included in the law."[27] But the all-male FSLN leadership
disagreed.

The five bourgeois parties and economic organizations sitting
in the council of state, expressing their rightist opposition to the
proposed law, boycotted the council's debates on it, and were
absent when the final vote was taken. AMNLAE, which has one
seat on the council of state, thus cast the only dissenting vote.

Bureaucratically Deformed Workers' State

The new Nicaraguan state created in 1979 was *bureaucratically deformed* from the start—owing to the country's economic
backwardness and the massive destruction wrought by Somoza's
clique, *combined with* the opportunist strategy pursued by the
FSLN in power: conciliation with the bourgeoisie as opposed to
direct reliance on the revolutionary masses. Instead of transferring *all power to the sandinista defense committees (CDS)* and
letting the revolutionary masses run their own state through
their directly elected and recallable representatives, the FSLN
leadership set up an unelected national junta and council of state
coalition with the bourgeoisie, resting on a traditional bureaucratic apparatus.

While the desperate economic and cultural conditions of post-war Nicaragua did not allow for the *complete* elimination of bureaucracy, a revolutionary democratic structure of government centering on the CDS could exert revolutionary *control* over the bureaucracy, and organize an ongoing mass struggle against its reactionary aspects. As matters stand, the CDS movement today embodies a *truncated* form of revolutionary democracy: It conducts mass discussions and debates on important national and local issues, and mobilizes its members for vital social and economic campaigns (literacy training, neighborhood patrols, mass innoculations against polio and malaria, campaigns against hoarding and price gouging merchants, etc.). But its political decisions are in no way binding upon government policy, and it has no say over the crucial questions of *foreign policy*. The opportunist government thus has a free hand to sabotage the revolution in El Salvador and elsewhere in Central America, under the selfish and shortsighted signboard of "national security for Nicaragua."

FSLN Leaders Abandon the Salvadoran Revolution

"If we had to arrest everyone in Nicaragua who supports the Salvadoran revolution, we would have 2½ million people in jail!" sighed FSLN leader Tomás Borge in 1981.[28] A remarkable self-confession, revealing a profound psychological truth: Borge wants to erect a kind of jail around "his" revolution, instead of boldly *unleashing* and consciously *developing* the revolution regionwide and worldwide. Under the merciless military and economic pressure of U.S. imperialism, the FSLN leaders have swallowed whole the honeytongued tenets of bourgeois "international law" that mutual "noninterference in the internal affairs of sovereign states" is the "normal" way civilized nations can and should behave.

For the U.S. imperialists, the doctrine of "noninterference" has always been a hypocritical sham, which has *never* restrained them from invading and conquering weak countries, dictating economic policy through their private banks and "international" lending agencies like the IMF, penetrating and advising "friendly" police forces and military cliques throughout the third world, conducting torture and murder on a grand scale to crush popular opposition to friendly dictatorships, overthrowing unfriendly governments, etc. "Noninterference" for *them*—in addition to protecting them from unwanted intrusion by rival imperialist powers (the Monroe doctrine)—means no *revolutionary intervention* by the class conscious proletariat of a given country *in favor of* the struggling, revolutionary masses of another country. Thus when the U.S. government gives millions of dollars of military and economic aid to the Salvadoran oligarchy, sends military commanders and advisers, Green Beret torturers, etc., that is not interference—since, after all, all this has been duly requested by the elected government of a "sovereign" nation. But, if revolutionary Nicaragua dares to provide material aid to the embattled *workers and peasants* of El Salvador, dares to send generous revolutionary volunteers to fight side by side with their Salvadoran class brothers and sisters *against* the oligarchy—why, *that* is outrageous interference, which must be punished with U.S. battleships, economic blockade, and possibly invasion.

Instead of boldly renouncing this murderous imperialist logic and legalistic hypocrisy, the FSLN leaders have capitulated to it utterly. If they were revolutionary internationalists, the FSLN leaders would be responding to Reagan's mouthfoaming charges that they are sending massive military aid to the Salvadoran revolutionaries, by proudly pleading "innocent as charged!", and urging the North American workers to overthrow their own criminal government. Instead they have slavishly—and truthfully—*denied* giving any material support to the Salvadoran revolution. Selfishly viewing the struggle of the Salvadoran and Guatemalan revolutionaries as a prickly obstacle to their utopian dreams of peaceful national development in Nicaragua and peaceful coexistence with U.S. imperialism, the FSLN leaders have forbidden the FMLN to set up a revolutionary radio station on Nicaraguan territory, and even pressured representatives of the Salvadoran and Guatemalan revolutionary organizations to pack up and leave Nicaragua.*

Like the reformist Cuban leadership group of Fidel Castro, the FSLN leaders support *not* the revolutionary workers and peasants of El Salvador, but rather the anti-revolutionary bourgeois liberals like Guillermo Ungo (whom Daniel Ortega escorted into the UN's general assembly as his grand "comrade" in 1981) and

---

*Point 20 of Contadora's 21-point program for "peace in Central America" calls for "preventing the use of one's own territory and not giving or permitting military or logistical support to persons, organizations or groups that intend to destabilize the governments of the Central American countries."[29]

the bourgeois leaders of the Contadora group. Fervently assuring the imperialists and their Contadora lackeys that they are absolutely innocent of "exporting revolution," the FSLN leaders have had few qualms about *deporting revolutionaries*. In late 1983, they sent over a thousand Cubans—mostly teachers and technicians—home, apparently to reassure the Contadora gentlemen that there are no "foreign military advisers" in Nicaragua. And FSLN leader Daniel Ortega has repeatedly offered to set up a "joint military patrol" between the U.S. and Nicaraguan armies in the Honduran/Nicaraguan border region, with the dual aim of preventing further *somocista* invasions of northern Nicaragua and guaranteeing that no military supplies are reaching the Salvadoran revolutionaries from Nicaragua. This would be like a cat offering to set up a "joint patrol" with a tyrannosaur, with the dual aim of preventing further tyrannosaur invasions of the cats' forest, and preventing vulnerable offspring of the tyrannosaurs roaming the area from being wiped out by overly aggressive packs of cats. Naturally, the North American tyrants have scornfully ignored Ortega's grovelling proposals; since the FSLN leaders have *already* liquidated all their support to the Salvadoran revolution, the U.S. imperialists have nothing to gain by going through the motions of restraining their *somocista* attack dogs.

Bureaucracy or Revolutionary Democracy?

The contradiction between Nicaragua's anti-revolutionary state bureaucracy and its revolutionary democratic movement is

---

Two Leading 'Exporters' of Opportunism Speak Out

"The idea of exporting a revolution is nonsense. Every country if it wants one will produce a revolution, and if it doesn't, there will be no revolution. Thus, e.g., our country [sic] wanted to make a revolution and made it..."

Josef Stalin, 1936 interview with Roy Howard—attempting to justify dragging the USSR into the counterrevolutionary League of Nations and converting the Communist International into a reformist pressure arm of Soviet state diplomacy.

"You cannot export a revolution. Each people has to make their own revolution in their own way. This was a Nicaraguan revolution..."

Fidel Castro, 26 July 1979 speech in Havana—attempting to justify his failure to militarily support the Nicaraguan revolution in the face of Somoza/U.S. genocide, while massively supporting the counterrevolutionary Ethiopian military junta's genocidal wars against Eritrea and the Ogaden Somalis.

an antagonistic one: In the last analysis, one force must eliminate the other. And the economic trend in Nicaragua since the revolution's victory has run clearly in favor of the rising state bureaucracy. While the unemployment problem has festered and even worsened (the unemployment rate increased from 15.9% in 1981 to 19.8% in 1982[30]), the only sector of the workforce which has experienced significant growth has been the bureaucracy.

Due to the FSLN leaders' halfbaked agrarian reform policy, which has not attacked the foundations of private landownership, it has been impossible to mobilize the masses of former peasants and farmworkers now languishing in the cities for want of job opportunities, to return to the countryside to gainful employment on a collectivizing basis. And as long as agriculture stagnates and vast sources of human labor power continue to be squandered, there can be no question of seriously developing industry. Thus, despite the great strides of the literacy campaign and the cultural ferment embodied in the mass poetry and drama workshops, the basis for an allround cultural and educational revolution which can eliminate the social need for a stratum of professional "experts" (i.e., a bureaucracy) to administer society, is still far from being laid.

But, while the economic trend of festering underdevelopment under the heel of a capitalist world market favors the parasitic state bureaucracy, the political trend of revolutionary struggles in Central America favors the revolutionary democratic movement. The conquest of power by the Salvadoran and Guatemalan workers and peasants would give a tremendous moral boost to the Nicaraguan masses, encouraging them in their struggle to take over the reins of their own state. And the victorious extension of the revolution throughout Central America and into the rest of the Americas would break Nicaragua's economic isolation, allowing the regional pooling of economic and social resources on the basis of socialist construction. But ironically, one of the chief internal obstacles to such a permanent revolutionary development, which could bring enormous benefits to revolutionary Nicaragua, is the foreign policy of the current Nicaraguan government.

Revolutionary Youth, Senile Leaders

The contrast between the youthful exuberance of the Nicaraguan revolution and the premature senility of the FSLN leaders is remarkable. In Cuba, it took some ten years following the revolutionary victory, before the leadership "consolidated" itself as an *obstacle* to the spread of the Latin American and world revolution. In Nicaragua, the FSLN leadership emerged *within months* of the revolutionary victory as an obstacle to the Latin American revolution. Not surprisingly, their premature senility was praised by the opportunist Castro as "political maturity."

The FSLN leaders' openness to admitting their own mistakes (at least in *domestic* policy), and their continued closeness to the working masses in their daily political life, has been enthusiastically noted by many recent visitors to Nicaragua. These healthy qualities of the leadership reflect the fact that the contradiction between the state bureaucracy and the revolutionary democratic movement has yet to be resolved one way or the other.

But if the victorious spread of the Central American revolution is long delayed and the Nicaraguan bureaucracy tramples revolutionary democracy underfoot, it is certain that the FSLN leaders will extinguish what remains of their revolutionary candor and close links with the mass movement, "consolidating" themselves as a clique of cynical frontmen for the parasitic bureaucracy— using their former revolutionary credentials as a flashy cover for a profoundly conservative, anti-revolutionary policy. Such a development is precisely what occurred in Cuba in the late 1960's, when the bureaucracy triumphed over the revolutionary democracy and Castro and his colleagues were transformed from relatively honest and revolutionary leaders, into anti-revolutionary scoundrels and charlatans.

On 8 January 1959, a victorious young Fidel Castro was addressing a jubilant crowd in Havana, when he posed a provocative question: "Who can now become the worst enemies of the revolution?" His startling answer has long since been forgotten by his supporters, and by Castro himself: "The worst enemies of the revolution in the future are we, the revolutionaries."[31]

Chapter 3

The Miskitu Question in Nicaragua

"...I objected to this and spoke about their [the *sandinistas'*] duty, as revolutionaries, to give a positive example of their treatment of Indian peoples, because all the Indian peoples of Latin America were watching Nicaragua..."

—**Armstrong Wiggins**, a young Miskitu leader who fled Nicaragua in 1981, and now works with the International Indigenous Human Rights organization in Washington DC.[1]

"...I keep thinking about this Reagan and what kind of a person can he possibly be? He's either a brute or a horse's ass."

—**Indira Brigette Zacharias**, a 22-year-old Miskitu woman, living in Nicaragua, who has joined her local *sandinista* defense committee, people's militia, medical brigade and the *sandinista* army — after describing the anguish of having to fight against her fellow Miskitu.[2]

The Nicaraguan revolution took place in the western part of the country, facing the Pacific. The vast, sparsely populated territory of Nicaragua's eastern half felt the echoes of the revolutionary upheaval in the west. But it did not become embroiled in the revolutionary civil war, nor did it suffer the systematic white terror of the Somoza dictatorship. When the *sandinistas* conquered power and extended their authority to the Atlantic coast, they faced a whole array of social, cultural and political questions which they had not bothered to confront in the course of their struggle for power.

The Atlantic coast, whose population of about 300,000 makes up just over 10% of the total Nicaraguan population, contains some 75,000 Miskitu Indians, 5,250 Sumu Indians, 570 Rama Indians, and 25,000 African descendants (the latter concentrated in Bluefields). The 186,000 *mestizo* Nicaraguans—i.e., those of Hispano-Indian origin, who predominate on the Pacific coast—make up around 60% of the Atlantic coast population[3]*. The *mestizos'* eastward migration to the Atlantic coast under Somoza's reign was often resented by the Indian and African populations, who felt disadvantaged in the competition over land and jobs with the "Spanish" newcomers, who—to them—represented a foreign and domineering culture.

The Atlantic coast region, abysmally underdeveloped, was largely neglected by Somoza, who contented himself with making plump concessions to U.S. fruit, mining, lumber, and fishing companies. These companies would ravish the indigenous people's lands, natural resources and labor power while creating a heady economic prosperity that drew the people into the sticky network of commodity exchange—and would later pull their facilities out when the resources they were exploiting became exhausted, leaving the people desperately poor, more and more cut off from their communal social organization and subsistence economies. To maintain control over the Atlantic coast, Somoza established a patronage network of local bosses (*caciques*), who kept the people pacified by dispensing consumer goods regularly shipped in by Somoza.

When the Somoza administration collapsed under the impact of the revolution, the victorious *sandinistas* confronted a serious gulf in social formations, culture and religious values between the Pacific and Atlantic coast dwellers. The Miskitu, whose attempts to organize themselves into a political cooperative had been squelched by Somoza in the mid-1970's,[5] were ambivalent towards the victorious revolution, whose partisans began arriving from the Pacific coast. "The Atlantic coast people didn't feel they had won anything, because they hadn't been involved in the fighting; it was like a change without knowing why," notes Myrna Cunningham.[6] On the other hand, "our people were very positive toward [the *sandinistas*]," according to Armstrong Wiggins. "In fact, they went to get them in the mountains, to bring them to Puerto Cabezas, the city, because we had heard them express

*These statistics are open to dispute. Norman Bent, a Miskitu pastor, set the total number of Miskitu, Sumu and Rama Indians living in Nicaragua at about 120,000.[4] The contradiction between these figures and the Nicaraguan government figures citied above might be only an apparent one, explainable by the fact that not all of the Indians in Nicaragua live along the Atlantic coast.

on the clandestine radio that they were fighting a revolution of the poor, and who is more poor than the Indian?"[7]

Instead of struggling to *bridge* the cultural gulf through free and voluntary initiative on *both* sides, the FSLN leaders, with their rude, ignorant and bureaucratic drive to "integrate" the Miskitu into the new Nicaragua, managed to *widen* the gulf violently, driving thousands of Miskitu youths into the camp of the armed counterrevolution. This has led to a fratricidal civil war among the Miskitu people, strengthening the hand of U.S. imperialism in the region and sharply setting back the revolutionary movement throughout the Americas. The partial corrective actions taken by the FSLN regime, in a selfcritical spirit, since 1983 have lessened the regime's isolation from the Miskitu people and helped win a number of young Miskitu who have remained in Nicaragua, over to the side of the revolution. But the underlying presumptions and practices of cultural chauvinism towards indigenous peoples have yet to be uprooted.

Historical Background to the Conflict

The Spanish and Portuguese colonial invaders of the Atlantic (Caribbean) coast region considered the area economically worthless. So they massively enslaved the indigenous peoples and shipped them off to toil in the mines of Perú and elsewhere in South America. The Atlantic coast region was thus depopulated by around 90%. When colonial settlers later began establishing large plantations in Central America, they had to import African slave labor to fill out their workforce in the now sparsely populated land.[8]

At the time of the Spanish colonial invasion, the Miskitu were organizing their society along the lines of the *village community*. They lived through hunting, fishing, and slash and burn agriculture—clearing small plots from the tropical rain forest, which they planted for up to three years and then let go fallow and return to its natural state. Their land was held in common by the entire village. The whole village worked together at agricultural tasks, and in constructing huts for individual families. The fruits of the hunting and fishing expeditions were shared out equally among the villagers. There were neither rich nor poor, nor money, nor prisons, nor church, nor state. The people governed themselves through democratic councils of elders, rather than hereditary chiefs.

But the traumatic and demoralizing experience of the colonial invasion and massive enslavement they suffered must have imposed upon the Miskitu a cruel new ethic: Enslave or be enslaved. Towards the end of the 17th century, Miskitu men began launching widescale slavehunting expeditions, first into the territory of their indigenous neighbors, the Sumu.* The women and children captured in these expeditions were either kept as domestic slaves, or sold into slavery to Jamaican traders who occasionally arrived at the coast. The slavery which the Miskitu imposed on their indigenous neighbors was mild and humane, compared to the chattel slave system organized by the European colonialists. Slave boys working in the Miskitu communities were allowed, once reaching the age of puberty, to take a Miskitu wife; the children of such marriages grew up as free members of the tribe.[9]

To counteract Spanish colonial power, the Miskitu made an alliance with French and English pirates, who lived by preying on Spanish commerce in the Caribbean. Many Miskitu served for three or four years on the pirates' ships, fishing and hunting sea turtles to feed their crews. Learning either French or English through the experience, these Miskitu were paid in iron tools for their service.[10] They also gained access to guns in the process.

The worldly wise Miskitu now had a decisive edge over the other indigenous peoples, and were growing into a threat to the Spanish colonial settlements as well. Their territory was expanding at the expense of other indigenous peoples, and their population was growing rapidly thanks to the capture of Sumu women and children. Led by their allies the pirates, Miskitu warriors launched incursions deep into Honduras and Nicaragua by ascending the larger rivers in fleets of canoes, each carrying 20 or more armed men. They surprised and plundered the nearest Spanish settlements, capturing their women and children. Penetrating south into Costa Rica, they disrupted and ruined Spanish cacao plantations. Their armed expeditionary raids along the Caribbean coast ranged as far south as Panamá, and as far north as Mexico's Yucatán peninsula. These expeditions against the Spanish colonists became a source of boastful storytelling by older men in the Miskitu communities, and thus an integral part of Miskitu cultural psychology.[11]

---

*The Miskitu and Sumu were evidently once a single people; the Miskitu emerged through an intermingling with other ethnic groups thrust together along the Atlantic coast, such as the Creoles and Chinese immigrants.

As England gained the upper hand over Spain in the slave trade and established a fabulously profitable "sugar and spice empire" that included several Caribbean islands, a strategic alliance with England became a logical (if not natural) choice for the Miskitu in their efforts to deter Spanish settlements pressing eastward from the Pacific coast region. England had wrested Jamaica from Spain in 1655, taking over its sugar plantations with the intention of preserving and extending the slave system. But the slaves had other plans. They rose in revolt, many of them fleeing to the mountains to form breakaway communal societies where they could live in freedom. These rebellious descendants of enslaved Africans, who became known as the Maroons, posed a mortal threat to the system of colonial slavery; realizing that they could not long remain free while their brothers and sisters remained enslaved, they periodically came down to the lowlands and attempted to rally the remaining slaves to rise up and over-throw their colonial owners for good.

The British colonial rulers, in their struggle to crush the maroon revolt, made handy use of their alliance with the Miskitu. In 1697 in Jamaica, the British crowned a Miskitu king to rule over Nicaragua's Atlantic coast region—the first in a series of 15 Miskitu kings to be recognized by the British monarchy over the next two centuries. In 1720, the British governor of Jamaica signed a counterinsurgent agreement with the Miskitu king Jeremy. Two hundred Miskitu soldiers were shipped into Jamaica, organized in companies under their own officers. They were paid 40 shillings a month and a pair of shoes to hunt down maroon rebels. Remaining in Jamaica for several months, they "rendered valuable services to the English."[12] A few years later, a fresh maroon rebellion broke out, and the British shipped in 100 Miskitu soldiers to help suppress it. In 1738, a new maroon rebellion brought 200 Miskitu soldiers to Jamaica. White guides were assigned to each Miskitu company, to lead them to the maroons' places of refuge. "...The maroons were soon pressed on all sides, cut off from their provision grounds, and compelled to make peace" with the slaveowners.[13]

The imposition of a Miskitu king, as a puppet of the British colonial empire, over the indigenous peoples of the Atlantic coast region climaxed the erosion of Miskitu selfgovernment since the Miskitu were swept up into the European slave trade and mercantile capitalism. The Miskitu king extracted tribute from the Sumu and Rama peoples in the form of canoes, cattle, etc. "The rule of the Miskitu 'king' was absolutely despotic. His orders were carried out by his quartermasters. Every Indian was compelled to render him assistance, lodge him, sell him food, and furnish him with the means of continuing his journey, against reasonable pay. That the Indians of the interior did not pay much attention to such commands need hardly be told."[14]

The British policy of "indirect rule" over the Atlantic coast peoples contrasted with the Spanish policy of widespread military invasion, aggressive colonial settlement and overturn of indigenous societies in the Pacific coast region. "The conquest of the Pacific coast by the Spanish and by the catholic church was nearly complete," notes Wiggins. "As a result, it was passed down to us by the grandparents that the catholic church had destroyed Indian cultures there. Traditionally, the principal enemies that we [Miskitu] identified were the Spanish and the catholic church."[15]

Thus, by the time Central America declared independence from Spain in 1821, the social and cultural division between Nicaragua's Pacific and Atlantic coasts was pronounced. Neither the Spanish language nor the catholic church had taken hold on the Atlantic coast, where natural (subsistence) economy was still the rule. The Atlantic coast peoples spoke their native languages or English, which was spoken by the African descendants living in Bluefields.* The Atlantic coast region, continuing to support a Miskitu monarchy under British sponsorship, remained politically separate from the rest of Nicaragua until 1894, when the Liberal government of José Santos Zelaya militarily invaded the headquarters of the Miskitu reserve in Bluefields and announced the "reincorporation" of the Atlantic coast region into Nicaragua.[16]

U.S. Monopolies Invade, Proletariat Emerges

With the rise of U.S. imperialism to hegemony over Central America by the beginning of the 20th century, U.S. companies established enclaves of largescale production of cheap raw materials and foodstuffs amidst the jungles of the Atlantic coast:

---

*Some of the Atlantic coast blacks live in isolated communities which are ethnically and linguistically distinct, and number at least five. Their historic origin is still a matter of speculation. At least some of them are likely descended from Africans who revolted on the slave ships where they were confined, took command of the ships and sailed them to the Atlantic coast and freedom.

mines, lumber harvesting and sawmills, and banana plantations. This created the first modern proletariat in Nicaragua, laboring under desperate conditions reinforced by a racial caste system: The Indians were at the bottom, *mestizos* in the middle, and whites on the top. The early 1920's saw a wave of strikes against the U.S. fruit, lumber and mining companies; some of the strikes ended in massacres of the workers. In 1926, plantation workers struck against every U.S. banana company on the Atlantic coast. This strike went over to an armed uprising. And just at that time, Augusto César Sandino returned to Nicaragua from his oil-worker's job in Mexico.[17]

The Miskitu and Sandino

The uprising of the largely Indian proletariat paved the way for the revolutionary people's war led by Sandino, a Liberal general, against the U.S. marines starting in 1927. Sandino, himself of Indian origin, found a powerful base of support for his movement among the Indian communities near the Rio Coco. The Miskitu contributed a number of military leaders to Sandino's movement; their most famous was Adolf Cockburn, whose struggle ended in assassination by the national guard headed by the traitor Anastasio Somoza García. Miskitu prostitutes servicing European contract laborers on a Standard Fruit plantation turned the tables on their imperialist pimps; organizing themselves, the women plunged into the guerrilla struggle of the *sandinista* movement and liberated Puerto Cabezas in 1929.[18] So tenacious and daring was the popular resistance inspired by Sandino's movement in the face of genocidal assaults by the U.S. armed forces, that in 1933 the marines were withdrawn from Nicaragua.

Decline of the Atlantic Coast

But the subsequent annihilation of Sandino and his partisans by the U.S. puppet Somoza—a cruel defeat greatly helped along by Sandino's own political vacillations—caused the Atlantic coast region to sink into deep political and economic decline. With the world price of Nicaragua's agro-exports plunging due to the world depression, and a plant disease ravaging the banana plantations, many of the Atlantic coast's big capitalist enterprises shut down completely. The combative Indian proletariat was thus dispersed. The dynamic growth in capitalist agriculture (especially in cotton) which was to sweep the Pacific coast under the Somoza dynasty, passed the Atlantic coast by.

Men and Women in Miskitu Society

To be sure, the Miskitu still maintained strong links with their subsistence, semicommunal social organization. While land plots were now owned individually, men of the whole community would work together to clear them from the jungle. Women, while long ago deprived of their selfgoverning status and subordinated to the social power of men, continued to play a highly active and respected role in social and family based production.

After the men cleared the forest and prepared family plots for cultivation, women planted, weeded and reaped the harvests. Women also fished with hooks; all other methods of fishing (using spears, nets, etc.) were reserved for men, who manufactured the fishing and hunting implements. The carrying of heavy loads was usually left to women, who used backstraps attached to their foreheads for that purpose.[19] This shows that the sexual division of labor in Miskitu society had nothing to do with any biological difference in physical strength between the sexes. The key to the prime "male" functions was that they guaranteed the men a monopoly over *weapons* (machetes, spears, guns) and practice for warfare. This prevented the women from rising up to overthrow the patriarchal order.*

Cooking and most other domestic industries were pursued by women. But tailoring was often done by men, some of whom even made the clothes for their wives. Men also barbecued the game they had hunted. Remnants of women's social autonomy still existed, as when a woman going through menstruation would seclude herself form men for three days, in a temporary hut built by her husband. Divorce was available by mutual consent, and the children remained with their mother. But a widow continued in the status as property of her husband, becoming the property of his relatives.[20]

*I have not come across any information—either in objective anthropological findings or in the mythological tradition of the Miskitu—that casts a direct light on the primordial women's society (matriarchy) and its armed overthrow by men, which paved the way for later Miskitu society. However, I am inferring this sequence of events from general considerations based on "primitive" peoples' creation myths (especially the historic transition from nature worship, to goddess worship, to polytheistic god worship, to monotheistic god worship), and on such world anthropological data as has filtered through the sexist biases, neglect and distortions of the "mainstream" anthropologists.

The Moravian Church and Capitalism

Amidst the traumatic ups and down of capitalist enterprise in the Atlantic coast's extractive and agroexport industries, capitalism had a steady ideological implant among the Miskitu in the form of the Moravian church. Moravian missionaries, evangelical protestants whose church originated in eastern Europe at the onset of the bourgeois reformation, first arrived at Nicaragua's Atlantic coast in 1849. They soon established a permanent mission among the Miskitu, and translated the bible into the Miskitu language (which already had a written form). Preaching and teaching in both English and Miskitu, the moravians established mission schools in Puerto Cabezas and Bluefields, as well as a modern hospital in Bluefields.

Over the generations, the moravians made deep inroads into the spiritual and cultural life of the Miskitu. Their message was one of bourgeois sobriety, selfrestraint, thrift, and humility before earthly and heavenly authority—just what was needed to convert the Miskitu into a productive and docile labor force for the invading capitalist enterprises. Threatening the Miskitu with the burning punishment of hell in their daily sermons, the moravian missionaries declared dancing and liquor drinking banned. Earthly joys were allowed only in the afterlife. To the moravians, it made no difference that dancing *enhances* sensual pleasure and exerts a socially *binding* force—whereas heavy alcohol drinking *dulls* sensual pleasure and provokes violent conflicts among the people (notably the men). Both customs were lumped together as "evil" and declared prohibited. There was, to be sure, a definite social logic behind this: In banning dancing the moravians were undermining the Miskitu's communal traditions, while in banning liquor they were shaping the Miskitu up for disciplined labor—all to the benefit of capitalist penetration and profit. Over time the moravian preachings were fairly effective—although the "evil" customs persisted.[21]

One of the main reasons for the moravians' success among the people of the Atlantic coast has been their training of Miskitu and Creole lay pastors, who now form the majority of the moravian pastors in Nicaragua. These lay pastors have been trained in the conservative ideology of North American "democracy." But they stand fairly close to their own people, and are thus (potentially) capable of voicing truly democratic and progressive aspirations coming from the people of their neighborhoods and communities. The position of the white moravian *hierarchy* is quite another matter. The moravian mission leaders, whose headquarters are in Bethlehem, Pennsylvania, do no productive labor, nor have they integrated themselves into the Atlantic coast's indigenous communities. They live in luxury in Yankee style settlements, in houses prefabricated in England and assembled on the Atlantic coast, sporting swimming pools and the other trappings of civilized parasitism. They employ indigenous people as their servants in both their homes and the mission schools.

The two main mission schools in Bluefields and Puerto Cabezas give instruction only in Spanish and English, not in any of the indigenous peoples' languages. They impose stiff tuition and strict rules upon the students. If a student is late for class, s/he is fined 25¢; if late by more than 15 minutes, s/he is fined $1 for the day—a hefty sum for most youths living on the Atlantic coast.[22]

The Trauma of Dependent Capitalism

Following world war 2, the Somoza regime granted a huge lumber concession to a U.S. company in the far northeastern region of Nicaragua. The company levelled vast tracts of forest, driving many Indians from their ancestral lands. When it pulled out of Nicaragua in 1966, Somoza decided to revive the lumber industry by "nationalizing" the Indians' forest lands. With the collaboration of the UN's Food and Agricultural Organization, Somoza created a state institute which aimed to develop the Atlantic coast region without the consent of, and at the expense of its indigenous peoples.[23]

The Miskitu people were further wrenched from their traditional lives by the border dispute between the bourgeois/military cliques ruling Nicaragua and Honduras. Before 1960, the border between Nicaragua and Honduras lay north of the Rio Coco, so that most of the Miskitu communities, which lie along both sides of the river, fell within Nicaragua's state territory. However, a 1960 World Court decision of the border dispute between Nicaragua and Honduras—a decision provoked and argued by lawyers representing competing U.S. agribusiness firms operating in the region—moved the border south, to become the Rio Coco itself. This virtually split the Miskitu communities into two, with over 100,000 Miskitu living north of the Rio Coco now falling under

Honduran sovereignty. The arrangement also allowed Somoza to forcibly relocate thousands of Miskitu south of the Rio Coco, into Nicaragua.

The coastal Miskitu, meanwhile, were being drawn into a network of world commodity economy that was finer still than the nets they used to catch the great sea turtles. Turtle fishing, providing protein rich meat throughout the year, traditionally formed the backbone of their subsistence diet, along with the starchy foodstuffs cultivated by the women. "Agriculture, hunting, fishing and gathering were organized seasonally according to weather and resource availability and provided adequate amounts of food and materials without overexploiting any one species or site."[24] That was before commercial fishing and hunting took hold. The Miskitu began selling a portion of their turtle catch to processing plants, which in turn exported the meat to gourmet markets in Europe and North America, providing turtle soup for the leisure rich.

Once the Miskitu became accustomed to money exchange, they bought more consumer items in town. These consumer goods, mostly produced in the big capitalist countries, eased some of their domestic chores, but also tempted them to abandon key aspects of their subsistence livelihoods. The ready availability of canned food and processed flour caused them to stop planting many subsistence crops. Commodities they had once considered luxuries now became necessities, and the race for cash earnings was on.

The turtle hunters sold more and more of their catch for cash, sharing out fewer and fewer turtles among their fellow villagers. Communal generosity was assailed by selfish lust for cash. "Kin expect gifts of meat, and friends expect to be sold meat. Besieged with requests, turtlemen are forced to decide who will or will not receive meat... The older Miskitu ask why the turtlemen should have to allocate a food that was once available to all. Turtlemen sell and give to other turtlemen, thus ensuring reciprocal treatment for themselves, but there are simply not enough turtles to accommodate other economic and social requirements."[25] By the time of the revolution, the Miskitu were selling between 70% and 90% of the turtles they caught.

The Miskitu diet thus suffered terribly, both in quality and quantity, and the health conditions of the people worsened. Hardest hit were those people too old or too sick to provide for themselves, who could no longer count on receiving meat or money from their relatives. Infant mortality increased; 40% of Miskitu babies died before reaching the age of two. The Miskitu (semi)communal villages fragmented and hardened more and more into nuclear family units, each enmeshed in the selling and buying of commodities at the losing end of the world market. Under the lash of capitalist demand, the sea turtle population has declined catastrophically. So have the populations of sea otters, crocodiles and leopards, which the Miskitu have also been driven into overhunting by the capitalist north's demand for luxury items. Capitalist shrimp enterprises would destroy their massive fish catches scooped up along with the shrimp—since the fish were not nearly as profitable to them as the shrimp.

As the capitalist threat to their livelihood and cultural identity intensified, the Miskitu began to awaken politically. In the mid-1970's, after Somoza had suppressed their attempt to build a political cooperative, they reached out to their former antagonists the Sumu, to form the Alliance for the Progress of Miskitu and Sumu Indians (Alpromisu). It was a unique attempt at Indian self-organization, going beyond the narrow scope of local tribal governments and the conservative fatalism of the moravian church. Somoza refused to give legal recognition to Alpromisu, and moved to coopt its leaders by offering them cushy government jobs.[26]

The Miskitu and the Revolution

By now, the social and political consciousness of the Miskitu was sharply contradictory. Some Miskitu, especially those most actively and successfully participating in commodity exchange, were locked into a cash/export mentality; since they viewed capitalist penetration as a boon, they were not the least bit hostile towards the neocolonial Somoza regime. Other Miskitu, grasping the devastating impact of foreign capitalism on the Miskitu communities, favored a return to communal traditions, and may well have been sympathetic to the anti-imperialist aims of the *sandinista* liberation front.

But practically all the Miskitu, along with the other Atlantic coast dwellers, were isolated from the revolutionary agitation, upheavals and organization, and the counterrevolutionary terror, that convulsed the Pacific coast region as it moved through its lightning pre-revolutionary epoch. While the catholic church had some influence on the Atlantic coast, it scarcely felt an echo of the liberation theology movement that was sweeping the base of the church in the Pacific coast region. The catholic church on the Atlantic coast thus solidly remained its old, reactionary self. And the Miskitu still maintained their historic distrust towards the "Spanish" intruders from the west; for many, this ethnic distrust clouded over any political distinction between the revolutionary *sandinistas* and the counterrevolutionary Somoza clique. Since the *sandinistas* had done nothing to overcome this ethnic/cultural barrier in the way of developing an indigenous revolutionary movement among the Atlantic coast peoples—instead confining their activities to the western half of the country—the only Miskitu who were sharply aware of the revolutionary struggle against Somoza were those living in the Pacific coast region.

In 1978, prior to the September insurrection in western Nicaragua, the "broad opposition front," a coalition of the bourgeois opposition parties and labor unions (in loose tactical alliance with the FSLN), invited Alpromisu to join the anti-Somoza coalition. But the leadership declined the offer. Steadman Fagoth Mueller, a Miskitu university student in Managua who was ardently pro-*sandinista* (at least outwardly), denounced the Alpromisu leaders for selling out to Somoza.

The Situation After Somoza's Overthrow

The overthrow of Somoza brought the fate of the Atlantic coast peoples to a crossroad: On the one hand, it opened up exciting possibilities for the regeneration of Miskitu and the other native cultures on a revolutionary basis, making them available to the people of all Nicaragua and the world. On the other hand, it opened the possibility for reactionary elements at the head of the native peoples to rally them demagogically against the new regime in Managua—taking advantage of the added material hardships brought on by the collapse of the old regime which the Atlantic coastdwellers had not played an active part in destroying. The region's fragile commodity network collapsed overnight, as the Somoza clique's merchandise ships pulled out (or were destroyed by the national guard), and the Chinese merchants, widely resented by the Indians for their exploitative commercial practices, fled in fear of expropriation. The road which the Miskitu people would take depended, above all, on the policy of the *sandinista* leaders.

After the revolution's triumph in 1979, the Alpromisu leaders, discredited by their nonopposition to Somoza, were pushed out and replaced by Steadman Fagoth, Brooklyn Rivera and Hazel Lau, all expressing strong support for the *sandinista* revolution.[27] At the same time, the Miskitu began reclaiming their tradition of selfgovernment from decades of corrosive moravian church influence, organizing a council of elders in every village.

In the Name of Sandino...

Instead of uniting with this progressive development among the Indian people, the FSLN leaders at first tried to *oppose* it.* They insisted that the Indians dissolve the mass organization which they had created, and join the *sandinista* mass organizations established in the Pacific coast region. In November 1979, FSLN leader Daniel Ortega appeared at an assembly in Puerto Cabezas, which was attended by 900 delegates from all the Atlantic coast villages. Refusing to recognize the delegates as genuine leaders of the Atlantic coast peoples, Ortega demanded the dissolution of Alpromisu into the *sandinista* organizations. He was told at meetings around the region that the Indian people supported Alpromisu as their organization. Ortega returned to Managua and backed off from his collision course with Alpromisu. But when he came back to the Atlantic coast, he showed that he had not grown much in wisdom or tact: While haughtily "allowing" the organization to continue as the mass organization of the Indian villages, he now demanded that it change its name so as to incorporate the word *sandinista*.[28]

Although there were some objections to this, "the people accepted the name change and reported to *comandante* Ortega that it was an honor to include *sandinismo* in their organization,"

*Supporters of the FSLN leadership have since claimed that the councils of village elders organized during this period were set up as traditionalist rubber stamps for the personal ambitions of Steadman Fagoth. It is not clear to me, from the information and accounts available, to what extent there was truth to this charge. One thing, however, is clear: The FSLN leaders did not understand the social and historical background of the councils of village elders, and dogmatically rejected them as a "backward" and "counterrevolutionary" form of local government. They should have worked patiently to bring the democratic aspirations of the Miskitu people (especially the Miskitu women) to bear on the revived elders' councils, to purge them of any subservience to treacherous leaders like Fagoth, and— when the people *themselves* decided—to replace them with new forms of local selfgovernment that would better reflect the people's desires and needs.

relates Norman Bent, a Miskitu moravian pastor who sympa-
thized with the revolution. "They had defended Sandino against
the U.S. marines in his early days, and he was very meaningful to
them."[29] Thus Alpromisu changed its name to *Sandinista* Unity
of Miskitu, Sumu and Rama Indians (Misurasata).

...a Chauvinist Policy is Imposed

Ortega's "commandist" approach towards the Indians' organization was symptomatic of the fact that the FSLN leadership
maintained a chauvinistic, paternalistic attitude towards the
Indian peoples. The program of the "united people's movement,"
a coalition of mass organizations which the FSLN had built in
preparation for the September 1978 revolution, had called for "a
development and integration program for the Atlantic coast
region."[30] No mention was made of the need for the integration to
be *voluntary*, nor for the development program to be worked out
and implemented by the Atlantic coast peoples themselves, on
the basis of *territorial autonomy* for the culturally distinct region.

During their struggle against Somoza, the FSLN cadres had
never bothered to build strong roots among the Atlantic coast
peoples, learn their languages nor study their cultural traditions,
history and psychology. Now the FSLN leaders, compounding
their ignorance with the heady arrogance born of a fresh revolutionary triumph, raised the rude slogan of "complete integration"
of the Atlantic coast region. While the FSLN leaders intended
unilaterally to integrate the Atlantic coast into Nicaragua, they
had no intention of integrating the Atlantic coast peoples' representatives into their "revolutionary" government in Managua.
Misurasata was given a token seat in the legislative council of
state. In the national junta, the governing body, there was room
for ambitious bourgeois politicians like Alfonso Robelo and a
potbellied bourgeois lawyer like Rafael Córdova Rivas (who continues to sit on the national junta to this day). But there was no
room for the Indian and Creole peoples' representatives from the
Atlantic coast. To the Miskitu, the "integration" they were promised by Managua must have appeared as a new campaign of
"Spanish" colonial domination.* The FSLN leaders, lacking any
grassroots organization or base of popular support among the
Miskitu, counterposed their internal state security organs and

*And the Miskitu word for Spaniard means "our enemy."

military commanders to the "backward" councils of village elders organized by Misurasata.[31]

Contradictions of the Literacy Campaign...

The 1980 *sandinista* literacy campaign, which was so liberating and effective among the Spanish speaking people of western Nicaragua, ran into sharp obstacles on the Atlantic coast. Despite the fact that, according to a Misurasata survey, scarcely over 5% of the Miskitu spoke Spanish, the FSLN leaders insisted on conducting the literacy campaign among the Miskitu in Spanish.[32] This led to mass resentment, and two successive waves of literacy brigades sent to teach Spanish to the Miskitu left the region without accomplishing their goal. The people were demanding literacy training in their own language.

A dispute over the question took place between the Misurasata leaders and the FSLN leaders. Finally the FSLN reversed its policy, allowing literacy training to be conducted in the Miskitu language, whose written grammar was further developed in the process. The new campaign began in October 1980, at the end of the Spanish literacy campaign.

...and State Industrial Policy...

Misurasata also began protesting the discharge of chemical wastes from a nationalized gold mine into the river Bambana, along which most of the Sumu communities are located. The people, lacking wells, were accustomed to drinking their water straight from the river; the polluting chemicals, including arsenic, could be deadly. According to Wiggins, in a single day over 20 Sumu children died from drinking the polluted water. And the chemicals were also destroying the fish and other wildlife which the Sumu needed for subsistence.[33]

When the Misurasata leaders raised their criticisms over this situation, the FSLN leaders reacted like callous bureaucrats. Insisting that there was no proof of chemical poisoning, they went on to explain that the gold mine was too important to the national economy to be shut down: It was necessary for generating foreign exchange, especially U.S. dollars. Paying off Nicaragua's monstrous foreign debt to the imperialists, which the FSLN had slavishly inherited from the Somoza swindlers, was thus considered more important than the lives of Indian children.

Such were the flesh and blood consequences of that pragmatic, "nondoctrinaire" policy for which muddleheaded apologists of the FSLN have praised the Managua regime.

...and Heavyhanded Bureaucracy...

Unwilling to deal with Misurasata as a fraternal organization enjoying autonomous governing powers, the FSLN leadership set up a bureaucratic apparatus, the "Nicaraguan Institute of the Atlantic Coast," which sought to bypass and isolate Misurasata. It was headed by William Ramírez, a Pacific coaster unfamiliar with the Indian societies and cultures. The FSLN then tried to coopt the Misurasata leaders into bureaucratic posts under Ramírez. The Indian leaders refused, considering Ramírez hostile to their interests.[34]

Nervous over the possibility of a U.S./*somocista* invasion and occupation of the sparsely populated Atlantic coast region, the FSLN leaders were, above all, interested in militarily "securing" the region. Crude military considerations came first, and the indigenous people came second. In January 1981, a young Miskitu fisherman was killed by the FSLN military. It was a "wanton overreaction—and for three days the Indian people held mass demonstrations. They were angry because the military had hidden the body and had, again, tried to cover up the incident..."[35]

...and Land Rights Policy

Meanwhile, Misurasata was conducting a comprehensive land survey of all the Indian villages, to demarcate Indian land claims to be negotiated with the Managua government. The date set for Misurasata to deliver the land survey results to the FSLN leadership was 28 February 1981.

But just a few days before the date arrived, FSLN police arrested the entire top and middle leadership of Misurasata (including Steadman Fagoth, Brooklyn Rivera, Armstrong Wiggins, Hazel Lau, and others), along with some Miskitu and Sumu youths who were just winding up the literacy campaign—33 people in all.[36] The charge levelled against them was "separatism." Sergio Ramírez, a member of the national junta politically close to the FSLN and author of *The Living Thought of Sandino*, publicly stated, "We are going to destroy Misurasata."[37] Hundreds of Miskitu men and youths, having lost all confidence in the government, began fleeing into Honduras. Two weeks later, the government dropped the charges and released all the jailed Indians, except Misurasata head Steadman Fagoth.

The Case of Steadman Fagoth

Fagoth, a university student fluent in both Spanish and Miskitu, had become the most popular leader among the Miskitu, who elected his as their representative to the council of state. Energetic and articulate, Fagoth had not only defended the *sandinista* revolution against *somocista* elements on the Atlantic coast, but had aggressively agitated and mobilized the Miskitu masses to protest the chauvinist policies of the FSLN leadership —whereas the more cautious Misurasata leaders preferred to bargain quietly with the FSLN behind closed doors.

Soon, however, it became clear that Fagoth's struggles were based not on a coherent principle, but on personal ambition. "When he would return to the coast [from Managua]," relates Myrna Cunningham, "he told people that everything they received from the government, the vaccines and doctors, were his doing, and people believed him. He also told people that if anything were to happen to him, it was because the government was communist, and made them swear by tribal law to fight against communism..."[38] Shortly before his arrest, FSLN security officers had tracked Fagoth's movements in Managua, as he met with the U.S. embassy and rightist political parties.[39] Now, the FSLN leaders announced they had unearthed police documents proving that Fagoth had been an undercover agent for Somoza and, while studying at the university of Managua, had fingered students and professors working with the *sandinista* underground, leading to the death of four people at the hands of Somoza.*

The FSLN leaders did not bother to explain why these documents linking Fagoth to the Somoza intelligence apparatus, which ought to have been in their hands for the 1½ years since the overthrow of Somoza, were only being exposed now that the government had declared war on Misurasata. After all, on two occasions Fagoth had been chosen by delegated assemblies of the Miskitu people as their political leader with FSLN leaders pres-

*According to Roxanne Dunbar Ortiz, Fagoth, while under arrest, publicly admitted his secret work for Somoza. But I have not seen this assertion corroborated by any other source, and Dr. Dunbar has taken a tendentiously pro-FSLN position on the Miskitu question.

ent, and the FSLN had raised no objections: in November 1979, when Fagoth was chosen as general coordinator of Misurasata in the presence of Daniel Ortega and culture minister Ernesto Cardenal, and in the spring of 1980, when he was elected representative of the Atlantic coast to the council of state.[40] So it seems that either the FSLN leaders had been sitting on the evidence of Fagoth's *somocista* treachery all that time, or they simply fabricated the evidence.

At any rate, even documents proving that Fagoth was in the *somocista* camp could not save the FSLN's Miskitu policy now. Instead of isolating Fagoth from the Miskitu people, the maneuver only backfired, revealing how dangerously isolated the FSLN regime had become from the Miskitu people. "...The reaction in the communities by that time was, 'If Fagoth is a *somocista*, then we are *somocistas*.'"[41]

The Turning Point

And the FSLN regime was by no means ready to end its campaign of arrests of Miskitu leaders. It ordered the arrest of Elmer Prado, a Miskitu leader in the mining sector. FSLN soldiers attempted to carry out the arrest in the midst of a meeting in a moravian church, where 600 youths had assembled to celebrate the end of the literacy campaign. The following account of what happened next is given by Norman Bent, a Miskito moravian pastor generally sympathetic to the FSLN regime and its progressive achievements*:

"...Four military men armed with machineguns walked into the church, and five others surrounded the building. While the minister was preaching, one of the military men stepped up to the pulpit and asked to speak. He said he was looking for the young Miskitu leader [Prado]. The young man lifted his hand and said, 'I am he.'

*Norman Bent, tragically trapped between his sympathy for the *sandinista* revolution and his loyalty to his own Miskitu people, described his position in these words: "I...have a political, ideological conviction. I don't believe in capitalism as a system. I think it's finished. What I hope for in Nicaragua is a model for the third world. Therefore, I believe in the struggle of the revolution. Already I can see that this revolution has benefitted the poor.

"But I have a personal problem. The revolutionary leadership does not trust me because I am a church leader of the Indian people. Neither am I trusted by my own people, because of my revolutionary approach to interpreting the scripture. So you see where I am: I am the meat of the sandwich."[42]

"The military man asked, 'Will you follow me?'

"The young man replied, 'We are in the midst of a religious ceremony. Can you wait until the ceremony is over? Then I will willingly follow you.'

"Another military man who was at the door shouted, 'Why wait? Shoot him!' and opened fire. At that, the young people in the church jumped on the military men. Four civilians and four of the military were killed. The military men outside the church dropped their guns and ran."[43]

That was the turning point in the relationship between the FSLN and the Miskitu. The Managua government was hellbent on sliding down the inclined plane which it had greased with the blood of both Miskitu youths and FSLN soldiers. Sergio Ramírez frothed that the four Indian literacy teachers killed in the church incident had been "subversives," and the FSLN launched a propaganda campaign denouncing Misurasata as a counterrevolutionary, separatist, and racist (!!) movement.[44]

A General Strike against the FSLN

The Miskitu began holding mass demonstrations and vigils of prayer and fasting in the churches, demanding the release of Fagoth, freedom to organize for Misurasata, and public recognition by the government that it had been at fault in the death of the eight people in the church incident. But the government responded with still more military repression, driving the protesting Miskitu out of a church at gunpoint on at least one occasion.[45] As hundreds of more youths fled into Honduras, the Miskitu remaining in Nicaragua, furious at the government, stopped sending their children to school and refused to do farming or accept any medical aid.[46] Miskitu miners and factory workers laid down tools, and the Atlantic coast economy was paralyzed.

FSLN military units were sent to confront some of the Miskitu demonstrations. A large demonstration in the town of Prinzapolka was shot up, with several people killed.[47] Young Miskitu men began capturing weapons from the FSLN military and going off to the mountains, beginning an armed resistance which had wide popular support in the local communities. The Managua government placed the Miskitu communities under direct military supervision. "The presence of military people in their area was very much a shock to the Indians," says Norman Bent. "Even Somoza had not had an army there."[48]

Fagoth Bolts to Honduras

In mid-May 1981, the Managua government, piling one folly on top of another, released Fagoth, but on the following three conditions: 1) Fagoth was to spend at least five days restoring industrial activity on the Atlantic coast, convincing Indian parents to send their children back to school and accept medical services once again; 2) he was to go to Honduras and convince those Miskitu who had fled there to return—"which was a dangerous task since the *somocistas* were already there as counterrevolutionary forces making use of the Miskitu."[49]; 3) he would accept a scholarship to study in a Soviet bloc country for a year.

Intelligent people throughout Nicaragua—of which there are many—must have been asking themselves: What is the point of sending out a supposedly proven *somocista* agent to defuse his own people's militant hostility towards the FSLN government, and then expecting him to spend a year studying in the Soviet bloc (presumably there to assimilate the collected speeches of Leonid Brezhnev on peaceful coexistence, *détente*, noninterference in the internal affairs of sovereign states, etc.—and the Soviet bloc bureaucrats would no doubt have deeply appreciated having a *somocista* agent in their university system). As it turned out, Fagoth fled quickly into Honduras, made contact with the U.S. puppet military dictatorship there, and joined the counterrevolutionary forces.

Fagoth had been Misurasata's undisputed leader. Now, in broadcasts in Miskitu from the powerful *somocista* radio station established in Honduras with CIA sponsorship, Fagoth urged his followers to disband Misurasata and join him in Honduras. In strident anticommunist agitation over the airwaves, he warned that the Miskitu would be massacred by the FSLN army if they remained in Nicaragua. He also echoed the Reagan administration's claims that the Cuban Communists had "taken over" Nicaragua—adding that Cuba was "colonizing" the Atlantic coast. And this radio station soon became the most listened to station on Nicaragua's Atlantic coast.* As the FSLN regime pressured the Miskitu

---

*Propaganda of this sort, conducted along the lines of CIA psychological warfare, also made a profound impact among the African descendants (Creoles) living in the Atlantic coast city of Bluefields. With the people increasingly insecure over the worsening economic conditions brought upon their region by the collapse of the Somoza regime, rightist elements whipped up anti-Cuban, anticommunist feelings among them—claiming that Cuban

to openly dissociate themselves from Fagoth, several Misurasata leaders, struggling to continue their work in Nicaragua, put out a press release condemning Fagoth's action. But under the increasingly polarized conditions, Misurasata ceased functioning as a mass organization.

Chauvinism Assumes Legal Form

It could come as no surprise to the Miskitu to find that the FSLN regime had disregarded Misurasata's land claims in drawing up the agrarian reform law in the summer of 1981. Article 31 of the law provided for the splitting up of the Indians' communal lands, "with the resulting loss of much of the territory and...in complete opposition to our culture and traditions."[50] The agrarian reform law was thus more accommodating to the bourgeois landowners—who were not faced with any limit on landownership, nor with expropriation as long as they used all their land productively—than to the indigenous peoples.

After two years of riding roughshod over the democratic cultural and political aspirations of the indigenous peoples, it was only logical for the FSLN to give its chauvinist practice a formal, legal expression. This came in the "Declaration of Principles of the Sandinista Popular Revolution in Relation to the Indigenous Communities of the Atlantic Coast of Nicaragua," released on 12 August 1981. As usual, the declaration was a unilateral fiat emanating from Managua; no attempt was made to solicit a declaration of the principles of the indigenous communities of the Atlantic coast in relation to the *sandinista* popular revolution.

Point 1 of the declaration established the "principle" of Hispanic chauvinism: "The Nicaraguan nation is one, single territory politically and cannot be dismembered, divided, or cut up in its sovereignty and independence. Its official language is Spanish."[51]

---

volunteer teachers, technicians and medical personnel were hellbent on taking jobs away from the people of Bluefields. This agitation culminated in anti*sandinista* demonstrations and riots in October 1980, involving some 10,000 out of Bluefields' 25,000 people. The riots were put down militarily by the FSLN army, with several people killed. FSLN leaders then travelled to Bluefields and held mass public meetings in which the people aired their grievances against the government. The FSLN leaders criticized themselves for their insensitive policy towards the local people. While the FSLN's policy towards the English speaking Creoles has been bound up with its chauvinist policy towards the Atlantic coast in general, it has not had as devastating consequences as has its policy towards the Indians.

The writers neglected to add that the FSLN, through its antide-
mocratic denial of *territorial autonomy* to the Atlantic coast peoples, so deeply antagonizing them, had given a tremendous boost
to the counterrevolution and U.S. imperialism—thus *opening
wide the danger* of the reactionary dismemberment of Nicaragua.
Point 6 hammered home the fact that the Indians had no say over
the use of their land and natural resources: "The natural resources of our territory are the property of the Nicaraguan people,
represented by the revolutionary state which is the only authority
able [!] to establish their use rationally and efficiently..."[52]

Lenin vs. the FSLN

It is ironic that the FSLN's hamhanded policy towards Nicaragua's Indians has been viewed by the Indians themselves as a
result of the *sandinistas'* adherence to "marxism-leninism"—
thus deepening the conviction of many American Indians that
both marxism-leninism *and* capitalism, as world outlooks promoting industrial development, are fundamentally hostile to the cultural identity and democratic aspirations of indigenous peoples.
In fact, the FSLN's policy has had *nothing in common with
Lenin's approach to indigenous peoples and ethnic minorities.**

Most selfstyled marxist-leninists have completely "forgotten"
Lenin's actual views on the subject of national and ethnic minorities (if they ever bothered to study them in the first place);
instead they select only those of Lenin's writings on the national
question (e.g., his polemics against the narrow nationalism and
cultural aloofness of workers' organizations basing themselves on
ethnic minority groupings within a multinational state) which
they can use, in a distorted way, to prop up their own, *oppressor
nation* chauvinism.

A bolshevik resolution dealing with the rights of national/-
cultural minorities in Russia, passed in 1913, called for "...wide

---

*The FSLN policy has, on the other hand, had much in common with the
stalinist perversion of leninism on the national question: Stalin's trampling
on the rights of the non-Russian nations of the Soviet Union, a chauvinist
policy which has been continued by Stalin's successors in power. To be sure,
the FSLN leaders had no need to consciously "imitate foreign models" in
order to fall into a stalinist mold in their national policy; stalinism is, in
essence, bourgeois ideology and policy grafted onto the proletarian dictatorship, and as such tends to manifest itself quite spontaneously among the
upper strata of a workers' state.

regional autonomy and fully democratic local selfgovernment, with the boundaries of the selfgoverning and autonomous regions *determined by the local inhabitants themselves* on the basis of their economic and social conditions, national make-up of the population, etc."[53] In the same set of resolutions, and in several articles published by Lenin the same year, Lenin and the bolsheviks denounced the idea of *any* language being imposed as the compulsory official language, and called for public school instruction in *all* the native peoples' languages. Lenin stood for the right of every child (and youth) to receive *general* education in the language of his or her choice, within the public school system. He was also for the right of all people to use the language of their choice in daily public life—whether in the factories, universities, professional institutions or in dealings with the government.

Positive Aspects of FSLN Policy

The 1981 FSLN declaration on the indigenous communities did state, to its credit, that "The government of national reconstruction supports the rescue of the different cultural expressions, granting to the Miskitu, Creole, Sumu and Rama communities of the Atlantic coast the means necessary to promote their own cultural traditions, including the preservation of their languages." (point 3).[54] There has since been a cultural renaissance among the Atlantic coast peoples. Teams of young cultural workers have gone out to the village elders, collecting folklore and the peoples' history, reviving their dances, music and languages.[55] The first dictionary of the three dialects of the Sumu language is being compiled by a Sumu leader, Ronas Dolores. The Rama Indians' population, by the time of Somoza's overthrow, was down to 570, only 25 of whom spoke their native language. Yet their language has been developed into written form under the FSLN regime. Ernesto Cardenal, head of the cultural ministry which has guided this linguistic work, also inspired the creation of a university of the indigenous peoples of the Americas.

Indian schoolchildren are now supposed to receive education in their native languages up to the fourth grade, at which point the general curriculum switches to Spanish. For adults, however, education in Miskitu has lapsed since the violent end of the literacy campaign in February 1981. Hazel Lau has had to continue struggling with Hispanic chauvinist bureaucrats over the need for bilingual and bicultural education.[56] Both in its conception and practice, the FSLN's language policy has fallen well short of the leninist, consistently democratic language policy, according to which the Atlantic coast peoples should *not have to* learn Spanish if they do not want to—just as the non-English speaking nationalities in the U.S. will not have to learn English, once the revolution abolishes English as the official language.

The 'Red Christmas' Plot

In December 1981, Miskitu fighters headed by Fagoth launched an intensive campaign of assaults against FSLN soldiers, health workers and teachers along the Nicaraguan side of the Rio Coco. It was coordinated with terroristic raids by *somocista* ex-national guardsmen upon Nicaraguan border villages, and undoubtedly directed by CIA covert operations based in southern Honduras. At the same time, the U.S. mass media floated false stories that the FSLN army had massacred hundreds of Miskitu civilians. The "red christmas" plot to provoke a secessionist uprising among the Miskitu, dynamite the Managua oil refinery and ultimately overthrow the FSLN regime was on.

Had all or most of the Miskitu crossed the Rio Coco to join Fagoth's forces in Honduras, that would have been a tremendous psychological victory for the U.S./*somocista* counterrevolution, which could then have launched a fullscale invasion of eastern Nicaragua behind the banner of avenging the FSLN's "genocide" against the Miskitu. But, while Fagoth retained much sympathy and support among Miskitu remaining in Nicaragua, their positive response to his calls for mass flight across the river had been far from unanimous. Fagoth now attempted to force the issue. His fighters occupied several Miskitu villages within Nicaragua and tried to strongarm their residents into joining forces with them.

As with the *somocista* thugs attacking border villages farther west, Fagoth's forces soon selected health workers and teachers —vanguard workers for the revolution—as special targets for their terror. Myrna Cunningham, the only Miskitu doctor, has organized a campaign of mass vaccination of the Miskitu against rampant malaria, tuberculosis and measles, in collaboration with the Nicaraguan government. She was kidnapped, along with other health workers, by Fagoth's men at the end of 1981. The women were driven into Honduras, tortured, raped, and threatened with execution before finally being released back in Nicaragua.[57]

Mass Relocation of the Miskitu
from their Ancestral Home

Faced with this tense military and social situation, the FSLN decided to relocate 33 Miskitu border villages *en masse* into the Nicaraguan interior. Beginning in January 1982, over 10,000 Miskitu were thus moved out, on foot, from the region where they had lived for centuries. Their homes, crops and livestock were destroyed, "to prevent use by the counterrevolutionaries." The Miskitu were given the choice of moving to Honduras—which some 10,000 others did[58]—or elsewhere in Nicaragua, if they did not want to move to the designated settlement areas some 100 kilometers to the south. The relocation march, while well organized, was very traumatic for the Miskitu. According to the FSLN, two Miskitu died during the relocation—one of a heart attack, the other of hepatitis.[59]

So far had the FSLN slid down the road to antagonizing the Miskitu and driving them towards an alliance with the *somocista* counterrevolution, that the Miskitu had become a *part* of the "security problem" along the eastern Honduran border, and had to be cleared away like so much troublesome undergrowth. Had the FSLN pursued a correct policy towards the Atlantic coast, the Miskitu would eagerly have organized and armed themselves *against* the *somocista* thugs and Miskitu traitors such as Fagoth. They would then have become a part of the *solution* to the security problem, and their continued location along the border would have been an *advantage* to the revolution. A correct policy would have helped the Miskitu become revolutionary *subjects* of history. But the false policy made them hapless *objects* of history, chafed between the chauvinist Managua government and the counterrevolutionary CIA/*somocista* bloc.*

*Predictably, U.S. imperialism leapt at the opportunity to score easy propaganda points against the *sandinista* regime. Addressing a senate subcommittee on western hemisphere affairs, U.S. ambassador to the UN Jeane Kirkpatrick seized on the Miskitu question to denounce Nicaragua as "the worst violator of human rights in Central America."[60] Kirkpatrick "forgot" to consider the genocidal slaughter of Indians by the U.S. allied military dictatorship in Guatemala—or, for that matter, the U.S. government's paramilitary campaign to expel over 8,000 Navajo and Hopi people from their traditional lands in the Big Mountain region of the "U.S." southwest. At the same time, Ronald Reagan had a field day brandishing a photo published in the French magazine *Le Figaro*, supposedly showing FSLN cadres burning Miskitu corpses. It was soon revealed that the photo actually showed the corpses of

[continued at bottom of page 107]

*Brooklyn Rivera (left) returns to Nicaragua on 20 October 1984, for a ten day visit. At right is Hazel Lau, who, along with Rivera, was a leader of Misurasata until the organization was wrenched apart by the traumatic events of 1981 and Rivera fled to Honduras and pursued armed resistance against the FSLN regime in the Atlantic coast region. At right center is Fernando Cardenal, jesuit priest and minister of education. (*Barricada Internacional, *25 October 1984)*

Claudia Gordillo

Residents of a Miskitu resettlement village in northeastern Nicaragua.

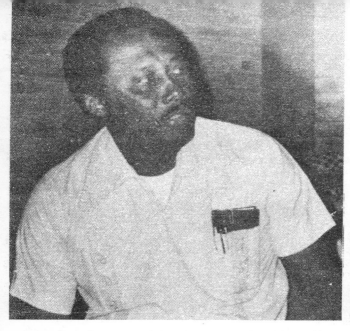

Norman Bent, the Miskitu moravian pastor who is sympathetic to the sandinista revolution. "...So you see where I am: I am the meat of the sandwich." *(Sojourners magazine).*

Loren Tapahe/Navajo Times

Myrna Cunningham. The only Miskitu doctor, she has organized a mass vaccination program in collaboration with the FSLN government.

A Heavy Hand against the Miskitu, a Light Hand against the Somocistas

Starting in January 1982, the FSLN army arrested some 500 Miskitu in the border area, accusing them of either carrying out counterrevolutionary activity or sympathizing with it. "It is a case again of racism, overreaction, and mistrust," noted Norman Bent.[62] Meanwhile, the Miskitu refugees in Honduras have been living under terrible conditions, their squalid camps policed by Honduran soldiers and armed *somocistas*, who ruthlessly crush any sign of opposition and pressgang young Miskitu men into fighting the FSLN.[63] Thus some Miskitu returned to Nicaragua, hiding out in their former villages. They, along with other Miskitu bringing food to them, were viewed as "counterrevolutionary" by FSLN security officers, and many of these people were swept up in wanton arrests.

The FSLN's jailing and imprisonment of several hundred beleaguered Miskitu, often on spurious charges of counterrevolutionary activity and with no right to a trial, formed an ironic contrast to Tomás Borge's "good will" release of 3,000 captured national guardsmen right after the revolutionary victory in 1979—despite the fact that those professional counterrevolutionaries were deeply hated by the Nicaraguan masses who had suffered their official terrorism.[64] The remaining 5,000 arrested guardsmen were all brought to public trial. Typically, they defended themselves by insisting that they had been strictly "noncombat" personnel, serving as cooks, chauffeurs, etc. Many of these cynical war criminals were acquitted for lack of eyewitness evidence against them.[65] And many of the released guardsmen immediately set up camp in southern Honduras, renewing their terror attacks against the Nicaraguan people.

Here are the bitter fruits of the FSLN's vaunted "pluralistic" regime, a regime that showed generosity towards the *oppressors* (the bourgeoisie and national guard), and chauvinist hostility towards the *most oppressed* (the Indians): The FSLN succeeded not only in building the *revolutionary* army that destroyed the Somoza regime and brought the proletariat to power, but *also*

Nicaraguan victims of Somoza's white terror being burned by the Red Cross (for hygienic reasons) during the 1978 revolution and counterrevolution.[61] Even so, Reagan continued bullheadedly spouting his slander against the *sandinistas*.

virtually built up the *counter*revolutionary army now assaulting Nicaragua, by giving thousands of *somocista* guardsmen a free ticket to Honduras and then driving thousands of Miskitu youths into their arms.

From the christian standpoint, this would perhaps be considered charity to the counterrevolution. From the marxist standpoint, it has been opportunist sabotage of the revolution. The fact that the counterrevolution, despite its ferocity, has yet to make any serious headway in its campaign to destroy the new class regime, shows that the revolutionary activity and consciousness of the Nicaraguan masses is still stronger than the opportunism of their leaders.

Miskitu Leaders Choose Up Sides

In the course of the traumatic events of 1981-2, practically the entire leadership of Misurasata fled to Honduras or Costa Rica. A notable exception was Hazel Lau, who has remained with her people in Nicaragua, adopting a position of critical support towards the FSLN regime. The fact that Lau was also the only woman among the main leaders of Misurasata can scarcely be accidental. The Miskitu women stood closer to their people's communal traditions than did the men; they felt more keenly the brutalizing impact of capitalist penetration and the chase for personal profit—upon themselves, their children and the elderly. They were thus less likely to be enamored of U.S. capitalism and its dazzling offers of a military alliance against the FSLN regime. Lau has had to continue struggling against the chauvinist aspects of the FSLN's Indian policy, while facing the continual danger of kidnapping and/or assassination at the hands of the Miskitu warriors based in Honduras, who consider her—along with all other Miskitu who have worked with the FSLN regime— a traitor to the Miskitu cause.

Brooklyn Rivera, who fled Nicaragua in mid-1981, set up an anti-FSLN military organization while ironically maintaining the name Misurasata, and formed a bloc with Edén Pastora's Democratic Revolutionary Alliance (ARDE), based in Costa Rica. Steadman Fagoth, joined by several rightist moravian pastors,*

---

*According to Roxanne Dunbar Ortiz, the *official* moravian church on the Atlantic coast *denounced* the Miskitu's flight to Honduras. This probably had nothing to do with any sincere opposition to the counterrevolutionary forces based in Honduras, and everything to do with the moravian hierarchy's parasitic instinct for selfpreservation.

formed a new organization, Misura—an acronym for the Miskitu, Sumu and Rama Indians (but without the *"sandinista* unity" which Daniel Ortega had foisted onto the Indian organization's name in 1979). Misura works closely with the *somocista* Nicaraguan Democratic Forces (FDN), and its combat units are reportedly commanded by ex-national guardsmen and foreign mercenaries on a regular basis. Rivera's Misurasata, not wanting to be openly associated with *somocismo* and the CIA, has publicly distanced itself from Fagoth's Misura—just as Pastora's ARDE has publicly distanced itself from the FDN. But, while Pastora's "independence" from the FDN/*somocista*/CIA bloc is demagogic and selfserving, Rivera's independence from Fagoth's counterrevolutionary movement seems sincere.

Fagoth's Misura has failed to put forward a coherent program for the social and political liberation of the Miskitu people. His warriors seem to be fighting, above all, out of a desire for blind revenge against the FSLN for having trampled Miskitu aspirations in 1979-82. But if the Misura fighters lack a positive program, their U.S. imperialist sponsors do not: *They* are consciously striving to reimpose capitalist class rule and U.S. hegemony over Nicaragua. These Miskitu warriors are thus being cynically used as cannon fodder by U.S. imperialism in its war aims against the Nicaraguan revolution—just as Miskitu warriors were used as cannon fodder by British imperialism in the 18th century, in its war against the revolutionary maroons of Jamaica.

FSLN's Amnesty and Self-Criticism

On 1 December 1983, as the Miskitu and counterrevolutionary attacks against the FSLN regime were intensifying and the U.S. was mounting a huge military buildup in Honduras, Daniel Ortega proclaimed a general amnesty for Miskitu, Sumu and Rama Indians who had clashed with the government over the previous two years. Over 300 Miskitu prisoners were released, many of them having spent up to two years behind bars without charges being brought. Ortega criticized the forced relocation of Miskitu villagers as an "error," and Tomás Borge portrayed the conflicts on the Atlantic coast as the result of "stupid errors on our part."[66] "We have become the victim of our own mistakes," said Borge. "We have driven the Miskitu into the arms of the CIA."[67]

[continued on page 112]

The Miskitu Question as Viewed by North American Indians

The conflict between the FSLN and the Miskitu Indians has led to a painful split within the North American Indian movement: Some groups have defended the Miskitu unconditionally, denouncing the FSLN policy as oppressive and unjust. Other groups, in their desire to defend the Nicaraguan revolution against U.S. imperialism and its counterrevolutionary campaign, have supported the FSLN with little or no criticism.

Perhaps the most vocal partisan of the pro-FSLN camp has been Roxanne Dunbar Ortiz, a professor of Native American studies at California State University who works with the International Indian Treaty Council, edits the excellent bilingual paper *Indigenous World/El Mundo Indigena*, and has spent a great deal of time among the Miskitu of Nicaragua's Atlantic coast. Dr. Dunbar Ortiz has done valuable work in exposing the CIA's propaganda slanders against the *sandinista* regime and Reagan's deceptive hypocrisy in "championing" the Miskitu cause. But she has publicly tended to apologize for the FSLN's chauvinist Indian policy, uncritically supporting the forced relocation of Miskitu of early 1982.

An expression of this tendency can be seen in Dr. Dunbar's sympathetic formulation of the FSLN's approach to Nicaragua's ethnic minorities: "...In the sandinista view,...within the revolutionary process it is necessary to develop a goal of emancipation for the *historically subordinate* ethnic minorities on a level of respect, *equality* and friendship."[68] (emphasis added). How the ethnic minorities can be at once "historically subordinate" to, and "equal" to the ethnic majority, Dr. Dunbar did not bother trying to explain. She has raised no public objection to the FSLN's imposition of Spanish as the official language over Nicaragua, or to the FSLN's steamrolling of the Miskitu's land claims, which denied them territorial autonomy (see above).

On the other side, *Akwesasne Notes*, a bimonthly newspaper and official publication of the Mohawk Nation in New York state, has strongly defended the Indian peoples against the FSLN regime—while demarcating its position from that of the counterrevolutionary U.S. government. *Akwesasne Notes* ran a long and remarkable interview with Armstrong Wiggins in its autumn 1981 issue, and has since published a number of thoughtful articles on the Miskitu/FSLN conflict. But it did not interview Hazel Lau or any other Miskitu willing to work with the FSLN regime, and dogmatically closed its pages to North American Indians supporting the FSLN position. Worse still, *Akwesasne Notes* uncritically published an article on the conflict by Bernard Nietschmann, a geography professor at the University of California/Berkeley who, despite his excellent fieldwork among the Miskitu in the 1970's, has taken a reckless and irresponsible political stance since the conflict between the Miskitu and the FSLN regime broke out into the open. Nietschmann has sweepingly character- ized the conflict as a fullscale counterinsurgency war by the FSLN military against the Miskitu people, whose warriors, he claims, are waging an "autonomous revolution" whose goals are in no way determined by the tactical "marriages of convenience" they have made with "antisandinista groups."[69] Nietschmann has made public accusations of war atrocities by the Nicaraguan military against Miskitu civilians—namely, aerial bom- bardment of Miskitu villages in the zone of conflict. But he has provided no documentation for his claims, and visitors to the villages in question have reported no evidence of bombardment. Nietschmann has dishon- estly "overlooked" the fact of CIA/somocista military support and gui- dance of the Miskitu warriors based in Honduras—as well as the trend of politically conscious Miskitu who are working with and supporting the FSLN, despite its chauvinist policy of the past.

Some American Indian Movement (AIM) leaders, such as Vernon Belle- court, have sided with the FSLN regime, while voicing mild criticisms of some of its erroneous policies towards the Atlantic coast Indians. Belle- court has pointed out that *Akwesasne Notes* used to be the principal organ of AIM and the International Indian Treaty Council. "But now," he adds, "it's controlled by people who have never been to Nicaragua, and only accept the viewpoint of people on the anti*sandinista* side of the issue... We've sent them volumes of documentation, but they've generally chosen to ignore it."[70]

Roxanne Dunbar Ortiz, despite holding some critical views of the FSLN's Indian policy, has chosen to confine these criticisms to closed door discussions with FSLN leaders; in public, she maintains a position of 100% support to FSLN policy, not even acknowledging the FSLN leaders' sharp selfcriticism of their Indian policy at the end of 1983. Evidently, Dunbar Ortiz feels that any public criticism of the FSLN would play into the hands of U.S. imperialism and its psychological and military campaign against Nicaragua.

I do not believe that the Nicaraguan revolution is so fragile that it cannot withstand frank public criticism by its supporters; it it were that fragile, it would have been overthrown a long time ago. *Revolutionary* criticism of the revolution's errors, to the extent that it reaches and edu- cates the working masses, can only *strengthen* the revolution in Nicaragua *and worldwide*—no matter how much such criticism grates against the nerves of the *opportunist misleaders* of the revolution.

The FSLN/Miskitu conflict holds crucial lessons for North American marxists. And, to put things in proportion, one must admit that, compared with the approach of most U.S. leftist groups towards the Native American struggle, the FSLN's Indian policy has been positively *enlightened*.

In the "model" Tasba Pri resettlement village, the Miskitu have begun taking command of their own lives. They have made big increases in rice production since the village was established. As in much of the Nicaraguan countryside, they have made advances in nutrition, health care and education. The Hispanic directors of the four Miskitu resettlement villages have now been replaced by Miskitu directors. In three of the villages, the Miskitu residents carry arms and have formed local defense militias.[71] Still, the resettled Miskitu are clamoring to return to their homeland along the Rio Coco.[72] And for those Miskitu who have attempted to maintain a more traditional and autonomous lifestyle in their war torn land, conditions have been far worse, including hunger.[73]

As the FSLN partially corrected its chauvinist Indian policy, and the armed incursions by Miskitu fighters based in Honduras became increasingly antipopular and repressive, the political sympathies of the Nicaraguan Miskitu shifted away from Steadman Fagoth, towards a cautious willingness to work with the FSLN regime and its grassroots social movements. Some 200 Miskitu who had fled to Honduras—both civilians and fighters— took advantage of the FSLN's amnesty program and moved back into Nicaragua with citizenship rights.[74]

Repression of Miskitu by Honduran Army

The slowing down of this stream of repatriation seems due not to a lack of desire to move back, but to increasing bureaucratic and military repression against Miskitu refugees by the Honduran government. In January 1984, a Latin American human rights organization touring the area denounced the massacre by the Honduran army of some 200 Miskitu men who were attempting to move back into Nicaragua. The massacre was confirmed by a Honduran Miskitu leader, Baltimore Kumi, who added that such repression by the Honduran army occurs frequently.[75]

Brooklyn Rivera's Return

In their approach to Brooklyn Rivera and his armed partisans (as well as to the majority of Fagoth's supporters), the FSLN leaders have made a "standing offer" for them to lay down their arms, return to Nicaragua with a full guarantee of their safety, and work for the Miskitu people in a nonantagonistic way.[76] But they have refused to open unconditional negotiations with Brooklyn Rivera and his fighters, considering that prospect an unacceptable "surrender" of Nicaraguan "sovereignty."

It would be quite wrong to politically *equate* Brooklyn Rivera with his counterrevolutionary ally, Edén Pastora. Pastora was a *sandinista* leader who, due to his political sympathies with the liberal bourgeoisie and his unbridled personal ambition, betrayed the revolution and launched an unprincipled armed insurgency against it. Rivera and the other Misurasata leaders were representatives of the poorest people in Nicaragua; they were rudely disregarded, shoved aside, falsely arrested, threatened and humiliated by the FSLN regime, in the context of a chauvinist campaign of forced assimilation of their peoples. Rivera and his supporters' uprising against the FSLN regime was initially based on just historical and political grievances—even if it has taken on a dangerously reactionary momentum.

But, if the FSLN leaders did not draw a clear political distinction between Rivera and Pastora, Rivera himself made the distinction clear when he partially accepted the FSLN's amnesty offer and returned to Nicaragua on 20 October 1984. After meeting with top FSLN leaders to secure safe passage, Rivera visited Indian communities and Miskitu resettlement villages, "with the aim of speaking with the brothers, listening to their concerns and trying to find a solution to the problem of the separation of the Miskitu people." Recognizing the improvements in the FSLN's Indian policy and the need for peace, Rivera rejected the notion that the interests of the Miskitu stand in contradiction to the positions of a people's revolution. "Indeed, I believe they are complementary: The aspirations of the indigenous peoples have to be fundamental pillars of the revolutions of Latin America. The *sandinista* government, or any other one, must give a just response to the land claims and recognize a territory within which the indigenous peoples can govern their own lives and communities, within the framework of the Nicaraguan state."[77]

A New Miskitu Organization

In June 1984, a new organization of Nicaragua's Miskitu people formed, calling itself Miskitu Aslatakanka Nicaragua. Its declared aims are: 1) reunification of the Miskitu family (torn apart by the war conditions and militarization of the border); 2) government recognition of the Miskitu language as an official national language; and 3) a call upon the government to "pay more attention to the indigenous communities and...respond to their problems."[78]

The formation of Miskitu Aslatakanka Nicaragua, which the FSLN has formally welcomed, shows both the FSLN regime's fresh willingness to tolerate peaceful opposition organizing among the Miskitu, and the fact that the historic injustices committed against the Miskitu are far from having been overcome. At the same time, the organization's formation on a strictly Miskitu basis marks a step back from Alpromisu's and Misurasata's efforts to unite all the Indian peoples (see above). And the organization's response to the FSLN's Hispanic chauvinist language policy—calling for Miskitu to be added as another "official" language of Nicaragua—is ill considered, failing to challenge the whole bureaucratic conception of language policy. There should be no official language, so that all the people can freely use the language of their choice.

The FSLN's Indian policy has improved considerably since the tragic events of 1979-82 which paved the way for the present armed conflict. But, for there to be a chance of a revolutionary resolution to the traumatic conflict, the FSLN leaders would have to go far beyond their pragmatic selfcriticism of their pragmatically chauvinist Indian policy—which has led to only partial corrective actions. If revolutionary theory (dialectical materialism) is indispensable for sustained and systematic revolutionary action, then pragmatism (a superficial bourgeois outlook which defines truth as that which is useful for the given moment) is an inevitable intellectual product of bureaucracy. And the FSLN leaders are sitting atop an increasingly bureaucratic political structure which—out of its parasitic self-interest—requires the subordination of the weaker nationalities. Since the FSLN leaders have shown no revolutionary inclination to struggle against the bureaucracy, it is unrealistic to expect a fundamental transformation of their Indian policy.

The task of reclaiming the honor of revolutionary socialism in the eyes of the indigenous peoples of the Americas now falls to those revolutionaries who have passed through painful defeats and regroupment, to fruitful fusion with the struggling Indian majority of their country: the revolutionaries of Guatemala.

Chapter 4

Guatemala and the Fate of the Americas

"...Night falls. Today the quetzal bird which has visited the *guerrilleros* at this hour for the past two days has missed the appointment. His red breast and gorgeous plumage had glided into the center of the patch of the sky left visible above the camp by the mountains. The quetzal is the national symbol of Guatemala. He is said to have lost his voice when the Mayas were defeated by the Spaniards. Others say he never lost his voice but since then has refused to sing. The fact is that when he is caged, he dies."[1]

The contrast between large landed estate (*latifundio*) and tiny land parcel (*minifundio*) sums up the four and a half centuries of race and class oppression that the peoples of Guatemala have lived through. In the mid-16th century the Spanish rulers, fresh from their bloody conquest of Guatemala in the face of intense but divided Indian resistance, seized the lion's share of the country's fertile lowlands and distributed them to a clique of large owners who established *latifundios* to cultivate cocoa and raw materials for the world market. The Indians were left with tiny fragments of their communally held land in the infertile highlands of Guatemala's interior. Hard pressed to live from the meager harvest of their *minifundios*, the Indians had to labor seasonally on the *latifundios* for pittance pay. To guarantee themselves a regular labor supply, the big colonial landowners instituted a system of forced labor.[2]

The shaded strip shows the franja transversal del norte, *northern transverse strip.* The "Ixil triangle," *strategic for both the revolutionary people's movement and the counterrevolutionary army campaign, is demarcated by the towns of Nebaj, Chajul, and San Juan Cotzal.*

(NACLA)

Spanish colonial rule ended in 1821, but the oppressive social structure remained. The feudal type contrast between the *latifundio* and *minifundio* was invested more and more with a capitalist economic content, and the immiseration of the indigenous peoples deepened. In the 1870's, a liberal bourgeois regime, spurred on by the demands of the world coffee market, expropriated more of the Indians' lands. Debt peonage was made legal. The peasants were required to carry workbooks recording any debts they owed to the landowners, whose agents would enter Indian communities and force all those saddled with debts to work on the *latifundios* to pay them off.[3]

At the beginning of the 20th century, U.S. monopolies headed by the United Fruit Company invaded Guatemala, building a railroad and port specially geared to deliver bananas and other crops for export. In the 1930's a vagrancy law imposed by the rightist Ubico dictatorship required Indians to work on the *latifundios* at least 150 days per year, and to carry cards showing how many days they had actually worked there.

The Partial Revolution of 1944

In June 1944, the students of Guatemala City went on strike against the pro-nazi regime. Ubico's forces fired on one of their demonstrations. This triggered a general strike against the government. Ubico resigned, but appointed a governing clique that continued to serve as a pawn of the coffee oligarchy and its military apparatus. In October, armed workers and students joined a group of radical military officers to overthrow the rightist regime.[4]

As the mass movement spread from the radicalizing petty-bourgeois democracy of the capital city to deeper sections of the laboring masses, government power shifted to the left. An interim military junta called elections in 1945, and philosophy teacher Juan José Arévalo was elected president with over 80% of the votes; only 4.5% of the electorate abstained from voting.[5] A new constitution issued the same year abolished the vagrancy laws and all forms of forced labor. As labor organizations sprang into the light of day following decades of military repression, Arévalo issued a new labor code in 1947 defining workers' basic rights, including the right to organize and strike. His administration greatly increased government spending on education and health programs. The vote was granted to everyone except illiterate

women, who then made up 75% of the total female population and
95% of Indian women. A petroleum law aiming to exert Guatemalan sovereignty over the country's oil industry virtually closed the
ports to U.S. oil trusts.

Arbenz Is Elected

In the 1950 elections, colonel Jacobo Arbenz, a radical army
officer who had played a key role in the revolution of 1944, was
elected president with 63% of the vote; 31% of the electorate
abstained. While the elections were fair and Arbenz' victory convincing, the drop in Arévalo/Arbenz' Revolutionary Party's vote
percentage since 1945 reflected a growing class polarization in
the country. Both the coffee oligarchy and the new agroexporting
capitalists holding sugar, cotton and cattle estates were getting
alarmed over the rising workingclass mobilization and the government's attempts to advance national economic development and
workers' rights against the domination of U.S. imperialist capital.[6]

In 1951, Arbenz legalized the pro-Moscow *Partido Guatemalteco del Trabajo* (PGT—Guatemalan Labor Party). The reformist PGT, which had no intention of rallying the broad laboring
masses to destroy completely the old regime, uncritically supported the democratic reform program of the Arévalo/Arbenz
administration. Its cadres played a key role in labor union organizing and in the mass mobilization to implement Arbenz' agrarian reform program which began the next year.

Arbenz' Agrarian Reform

Arbenz, like Arévalo, was a bourgeois nationalist. He publicly
declared that his three prime goals were: 1) economic independence for Guatemala; 2) "to transform our backward nation, with
a predominantly feudal economy, into a modern capitalist country," and 3) "to bring about this transformation in a way that
will bring the highest possible living standard to the large
masses of the people."[7] His plan was to create an internal market
for national industrial development by a partial land redistribution from the *latifundios* to the desperate peasant masses. He
also struggled to break the U.S. monopolies' stranglehold over
Guatemala's economic infrastructure by building a state hydroelectric plant, a Caribbean coast highway and a new Atlantic
seaport.

The agrarian reform law, passed by Guatemala's congress in June 1952, went into motion at the beginning of 1953. It allowed for the expropriation of fallow lands on farms larger than 90 hectares. Poor peasants received such land in parcels up to 20 hectares, which were to be paid for over 25 years through low-interest state loans. Through the 1½ years of the agrarian reform campaign, 1.2 million hectares were redistributed to about 100,000 peasant families.[8]

The land reform campaign was moderate in its goals, by no means threatening the foundations of private property. Yet it threw the big landowners into a panic. The campaign was conducted through a mass mobilization from below: Peasant leagues sprang up, and growing numbers of Indian peasants were drawn into political action. The big bourgeoisie naturally saw red, and launched a ferocious campaign of anticommunist agitation against the Arbenz regime. The catholic church chimed in to denounce communism and Arbenz. U.S. imperialism orchestrated the counterrevolutionary mobilization. Arbenz' greatest crime, from the standpoint of the U.S. government, was to expropriate 160,000 hectares—all of them lying fallow—of United Fruit Company's 220,000 hectare holdings. Giving United Fruit a taste of its own medicine, Arbenz announced that he would compensate the company for the expropriated land according to its declared taxable value—which the company had set scandalously low to evade taxes.

Arbenz Is Overthrown

In June 1954, an army of mercenaries in the pay of the CIA invaded Guatemala from Honduran base camps. The peasant supporters of Arbenz clamored for arms to fight the invading "*contras*." But the military high command issued Arbenz a secret memorandum ruling out the arming of the people and demanding a purge of "communist and hostile elements" from the government.[9] When Arbenz refused to carry out the purge, the military withdrew its support, forcing his resignation. The unarmed masses were defeated almost without a struggle.

The U.S. puppet colonel Castillo Armas, head of the fascist *Movimiento de Liberación Nacional* (MLN), seized the state and imposed a reign of terror upon the peasants, workers and urban democratic forces roused by ten years of political freedom and mass mobilizing. All the democratic reforms of the Arévalo/-

Arbenz regime were trampled underfoot. Those sections of the "modernizing" bourgeoisie which had stood to gain from Arbenz' campaign to promote national capitalist development capitulated to the neocolonial coup. "When the crunch came, most of the new growers, urban industrialists and state bureaucrats were easily seduced into an alliance with the United States and the revitalized oligarchs."[10]

Guatemala 1954 vs. Nicaragua Today

Many radical and liberal commentators have drawn an historical parallel between the current CIA/*contra* campaign to overthrow the *sandinista* regime in Nicaragua, and the CIA sponsored coup that toppled Arbenz in Guatemala. From the standpoint of U.S. foreign policy and strategic doctrine (anticommunism, domino theory, east/west confrontation, etc.), the similarities between the two counterrevolutionary scenarios are indeed striking.

But the similarities end there. Nicaragua today is a *workers' state*, the product of a revolutionary civil war and armed insurrection of the workers and peasants who completely *smashed* the old, bourgeois state. Thus the *sandinista* regime has not been afraid to arm the people against the counterrevolutionary invasions; the arming of the people strengthens the foundations of the new workers' state. Guatemala under Arbenz was *still a bourgeois state*, as the old bourgeois army, police and bureaucracy inherited from the Ubico regime had remained intact. For Arbenz to arm the people would thus have been to *challenge* the very foundations upon which his regime rested. The arming of the Guatemalan people in 1954 could only have been a prelude to a fullscale civil war whose logical, revolutionary outcome would be the complete destruction of the bourgeois state by the laboring masses. Arbenz, like Chile's Allende in 1973, feared such a civil war more than he feared a counterrevolutionary coup. That is why his regime could be toppled so easily.

The imperialists, the big bourgeoisie and rightist officers did not need to smash the Guatemalan state in 1954: All they needed to do was to reassert their control over a state whose governing summits had gone "renegade" by pursuing a radical, bourgeois democratic course. The *sandinista* regime in Nicaragua, by contrast, cannot be "toppled." For the imperialists to overthrow it, they would have to organize and win a fullscale, *counter*revolutionary civil war, combined with direct invasion. And they are very far from achieving that. In Guatemala, meanwhile, the *revolutionary* civil war, so tragically crushed in the egg in 1954, was postponed for 25 years.

Guevara's Contradictory Legacy

A young Argentinian adventurer, trained as a doctor, witnessed the overthrow of Arbenz, and was stunned by the brazen intervention of U.S. imperialism to put the counterrevolution in power. The terrible events were to awaken in Ernesto Guevara a desire for revolutionary struggle. Joining Fidel Castro's revolutionary movement in Cuba, "Che" Guevara played a crucial role in the victory of the 26 July Movement over the U.S. puppet Batista in 1958-9. A passionate revolutionary internationalist, he then inspired the formation of the "tricontinental" grouping of national liberation movements in Latin America, Africa and Asia, and personally participated in several of their armed struggles. The Guatemalan revolutionary movement which raised its head in the 1960's to avenge the terrible defeat of 1954 was inspired, above all, by Guevara's practice and theory.

But history has its ironies within ironies. A false generalization from the experience of the Cuban revolution was to prove inadequate to the tasks of the revolution in Central America, and in the rest of the underdeveloped world. Guevara's *"foco"* concept held that small groups of guerrilla fighters, acting autonomously in selected rural zones, would engage the government army in "exemplary" combat and thus inspire the oppressed masses to join in the armed struggle. *Foquismo* ("foco-ism") assumed implicitly that the oppressed masses were spontaneously revolutionary, merely requiring a psychological trigger from without to embark on the armed struggle for power.

Lessons of the Cuban Revolution

Even as a summary of the tactics that had guided the Cuban revolution to victory, the *foco* theory was wrong. The revolutionary insurgency embarked upon by the 26 July Movement was far more than the work of Castro's and Guevara's heroic band of guerrillas ensconced in the Sierra Maestra mountains. In order to survive in those rugged mountains and have any chance of spreading the insurgency to the plains, the guerrillas had to build a lasting base of support among the local peasantry. Destroying the old, corrupt and exploitative rural order of Batista, they built a new, revolutionary order which upheld the interests of the poorer peasants against the local propertied classes. In the Sierra Cristal guerrilla zone headed by Raúl Castro, the movement sank still deeper roots among the oppressed masses, carrying out the beginnings of a radical agrarian reform and bringing several workers and peasants into leading positions in the guerrilla army.

Moreover, the 26 July Movement's *urban* underground network, with its links to vital workingclass sectors, played an indispensable role in sustaining the rural insurgents and supporting their triumphant campaign towards the cities. Not only did the urban underground supply desperately needed material support in the form of arms and medical supplies, but it also formed the backbone of a nationwide revolutionary intelligence service—strongly rooted among the communications workers—that alerted the rural fighters to every move Batista's army was making.[11]

The Cuban peasants and farmworkers were not spontaneously revolutionary. They were propelled onto the road of revolutionary action by the persistent agitation of Castro's Radio Rebelde, and above all by the *revolutionary social program* which the movement's fighters carried with them in practice. The truly popular agitation, organization and military actions of the 26 July Movement had a devastating impact on the ranks of Batista's army, whose peasant recruits surrendered or defected in droves to the side of the rebel army. By the time of its victory over Batista's forces at the end of 1958, the 26 July Movement army had transformed itself from a band of isolated guerrilla adventurers into a *"workers' state on wheels,"* a mass insurrectionary movement which contained within itself the social content of the new, proletarian regime.[12]

The False Foco Theory

The *foco* theory overestimated the importance of guerrilla fighters engaging in isolated combat against the government forces, and underestimated the importance of the laboring masses, through systematic and allsided revolutionary work by their vanguard, becoming conscious of their revolutionary historic mission and taking up arms for a genuine *people's war*. The Cuban revolution had triumphed with relative ease, thanks to the extraordinary cowardice of the Batista clique and the equivocations and political confusion of U.S. imperialism at the time. This led to a romantic exaggeration of the historic role of the guerrilla fighters, and to subjective hopes that the revolution could be spread throughout Latin America without a rigorous summing up of the experience and sociopolitical lessons of *all* the major workers' and peasants' revolutions of the 20th century.

The *foco* theory was also a reflexive response to the hidebound reformism of the Latin American Communist Parties (CP's). Typically based among the more privileged, unionized workers of the urban centers, the CP's strove to become permanent political fixtures within bourgeois society by slavishly supporting bourgeois nationalist demagogs like Perón in Argentina, and even neocolonial dictators like Batista and Somoza. Since the opportunist CP's bombastically defined themselves as the "marxist-leninist vanguard parties of the working class," the revolutionary *foco* adherents rejected the concept of the vanguard party altogether, and attempted to *bypass* the urban—and, for that matter, rural—workingclass movement by direct actions against the government army, usually based in the countryside.

The tricontinental attempts to implement the *foco* theory led to a series of disasters for the young revolutionary movements in Latin America, Africa and the Middle East. In Venezuela, Colombia and Bolivia, rural *foquista* insurgencies were annihilated by the government forces directed by U.S. counterinsurgency advisers; in Bolivia, Guevara's guerrilla band, isolated from the local peasants and cynically betrayed by the Bolivian CP, was easily crushed, and Guevara himself captured and murdered. In Brazil and Uruguay, attempts at urban insurrectionary warfare, *foco* style, were likewise crushed. While the young revolutionaries of Latin America were being politically disoriented by the false *foco* theory, U.S. imperialism, confronting a fullscale people's war in Vietnam, was becoming ever more vigilant and ruthless against revolutionary stirrings all over the world, and more sophisticated and varied in its counterinsurgency tactics.

The FAR and Foquismo in Guatemala

In Guatemala, the pro-Moscow PGT, engaging in endless electoral coalition maneuvering with various bourgeois opposition parties, spawned a militant left wing under the impact of the Cuban revolution in the early 1960's. First forming the armed wing of the PGT, the young revolutionaries eventually broke from the PGT to form the *Fuerzas Armadas Rebeldes* (FAR—Rebel Armed Forces). The FAR guerrillas charged that, in the midst of a severe military/police repression which cost the FAR several dead, the PGT's "top party clique" had served the government as an intermediary to set up trade relations with the Soviet bloc countries, thus escaping repression itself.[13] They declared that the PGT's "work in the Indian peasant sector amounted to nothing; taking off from the false premises that the Indians are 'reserves of reaction,' the party's national leaders have dedicated themselves to shuffling papers and politicking in the city, and to working with the artisans and trade unions."[14] Meanwhile, North American missionaries and Peace Corps cadres, trained to fluency in the Indian languages, were pouring into the country to immunize the rural Indian masses against revolutionary ideas, preaching peaceful acceptance of, and passive submission to oppression.*

A Ghost from the Arbenz Regime
Fronts for Military Dictatorship

The newly formed FAR, despite its correct criticism of the PGT's opportunism, was ill prepared to tackle the enormous and complex tasks confronting its tiny revolutionary movement. For one thing, it was saddled with the subjective *foco* theory; this hindered it from conducting the patient and systematic rural mass work necessary to free both the Indian and Ladino (*mestizo*) masses from selfdefeating modes of thought and action, and develop them into a conscious movement for people's war.

---

*There were rare but notable exceptions to the reactionary trend among the North American missionaries. One was Thomas Melville, a priest of the catholic Maryknoll order who worked among the Indian peasants of Quetzaltenango, helping them organize a farming cooperative and preaching liberation theology in the face of murderous repression. "We began teaching the Indians," wrote Melville, "that no one will defend their rights, if they do not defend them themselves. If the government and oligarchy are using arms to maintain them in their position of misery, then they have the obligation to take up arms and defend their God-given right to be men."[15] Accused of communism and collaboration with the guerrillas, Melville and his colleagues were expelled from Guatemala by their religious superiors and the U.S. ambassador. Melville courageously went on by expose the reactionary role of the U.S. catholic church—including his own maryknoll order leaders —in propping up the parasitic, antipopular church hierarchy in Guatemala. He also denounced U.S. military intervention, revealing that "This past year, 1967, salaries, uniforms, and vehicles for 2,000 new policemen were paid for by the Alliance for Progress."[16]

Worse still, the FAR, failing to draw the scientific lessons of the rise and fall of Arbenz, had yet to free *itself* from PGT style illusions in the radical bourgeois politicians. In the 1966 elections, Julio César Méndez Montenegro, a liberal catholic lawyer who had been involved in the Arévalo and Arbenz regimes of the 1944-54 "revolutionary" period, took the field against two military candidates. Highly popular among urban workers, professionals, and propertied Ladino peasants, Méndez Montenegro promised a return to the social reforms of the Arbenz regime, and offerred to negotiate with the guerrillas. Trailing behind the masses' illusions in bourgeois reformism, both the PGT *and* the FAR endorsed Méndez Montenegro. Méndez won the election easily, and promptly signed over most of his power to the army, behind closed doors.[17]

The PGT and FAR had fallen into a deadly trap. Far from preparing a regime of Arbenz style reformism (which would have been dangerous enough for the masses), Méndez Montenegro was preparing to front for a Castillo Armas style dictatorship on a grand scale. During the election campaign, Méndez accepted U.S. support in exchange for an agreement to open Guatemala up more fully to Alliance for Progress programs—i.e., to further enmeshing Guatemala in the U.S. economic empire and enabling stepped up U.S. military aid under the cover of economic aid. On election eve, a high level PGT meeting was invaded by armed men, who seized 28 PGT leaders. "They were tortured, murdered, and their bodies dumped into the ocean."[18]

Even so, when Méndez Montenegro assumed the presidency and gave the demagogic impression that he was "humanizing" the counterinsurgent army, the FAR dropped its guard. Playing for time, Méndez offered the guerrillas an amnesty, and the army pulled back from the guerrillas' base areas in the northeast for several months. The FAR, while rejecting the amnesty offer, demobilized and relaxed its security measures. The army now donned a liberal counterinsurgent mask, aggressively competing against the FAR and other guerrilla groups for the minds and loyalties of the peasant masses. Appearing before the peasants with projects for social reform and schemes to "protect" them against the "communist menace," army counterinsurgency units organized groups of peasants into armed "civilian patrols," to combat the guerrillas. So dramatically had the FAR lost the political initiative in the countryside to the army, that in some cases its cadres found themselves being lynched by the same peasants who had previously been active supporters of the guerrilla movement.

The Revolutionary Movement Is Crushed

By the time the FAR leaders realized the terrible mistake they had made, it was too late to revive the revolutionary movement. At the end of 1966, the army shed its liberal mask and launched an all-out assault against the guerrilla zones. U.S. military advisers were in charge of the overall strategy, U.S. airforce planes provided napalm bombings, and Green Berets participated in combat actions. The most ferocious assault was directed against the peoples of the eastern mountains. Between 1966 and 1968, the military campaign under colonel Carlos Arana Osorio, dubbed "the butcher of Zacapa," killed 8,000 peasants, wiping out the guerrilla movement in the process.

Under the cover of the military's terror campaign in Zacapa, the already entrenched, rightist National Liberation Movement (MLN) aggressively expanded beyond its natural base among rich peasants to recruit masses of poorer peasants who were swayed by more than anticommunist propaganda: All peasants who did not support the MLN were assumed to be communist sympathizers, and thus fair game for the MLN's death squads. The resulting mass based fascist movement destroyed the possibility of a revolutionary revival for many years to come.[19]

Economic Boom, Growth of Dependent Capitalism

While the forces of revolution were being destroyed, the forces of dependent capitalism were growing chaotically—transforming Guatemala's traditional social structure so as to pave the way for a more profound revolutionary upheaval in the future. The Central American Common Market, established in the 1960's to pool Central America's local industrial and agricultural resources for the sake of smoother profiteering by the U.S. corporations, greatly favored Guatemala at the expense of the economically weaker members of the "community" (Honduras and Nicaragua). Foreign investment poured into Guatemala, led by the Bank of America and a cabal of U.S. corporations. World prices for coffee were high, and the sugarcane and cotton* industries expanded on a

*As in Nicaragua, the implantation of a modern cotton industry in a hostile climatic zone was accompanied by enormous capital inputs of pesticides to battle tropical insects. The massive aerial spraying of these pesticides (inclu-

modern agribusiness basis. The expropriation of peasants' land increased.

Now it was less possible than ever before for the peasant masses—especially the Indian highlanders—to eke out a year round subsistence from their tiny family plots. The system of debt peonage places a crushing burden on the peasants, and the debt is passed down from father to son, without end. Before the three-month seasonal harvest of coffee, sugar cane and cotton, the large landowners of the southern coast sent their recruiters to the highlands to lend money to the desperate peasants—in exchange for the peasants' obligation to harvest the coastal crops. Under the whip of wage labor, Guatemala came to have the highest migrant labor force (49% of the total rural labor force[20]) of any country in the world.

Capitalism Recruits Its Gravediggers

The Indian peasant was wrenched decisively from his closed-in world of the highland *minifundio*, and there was no road back. "The traditional *patrono/colono* relationship, involving mutual obligations between landowners and workers, as well as the belief that the situation was fated and unchangeable...gave way to a modern, wage relationship."[21] Economically, the Indians were now more downtrodden than they had ever been since the days of colonial slavery. But the very same conditions which were driving them to the depths of economic despair were also opening up new horizons of social and political consciousness and action. The seasonal plantation labor brought together not only the many different groups of Indians historically separated from each other by barriers of geography and language; it also brought Indian and Ladino workers together under the same cruel conditions. The longstanding mutual distrust between Indians and Ladinos began breaking down.[22]

What the revolutionary movement of the 1960's had failed to accomplish, was now being accomplished by the blind greed of capitalist agriculture: the unity of Indian and Ladino laborers. And this was to impact on the revolutionary movement of the 1970's.

---

ding DDT, which had been banned in the U.S.) has had disastrous effects on the health of the farm laborers and peasant families living around the region.

Onslaught of the Military/Bureaucratic Bourgeoisie

Meanwhile, the military officers commanding the state, their appetite for power whetted by their victorious counterinsurgency campaign, decided it was time to go in for bigger spoils. They were no longer content to serve as the mailed fist of the traditional ruling classes; now they wanted the lion's share of the country's wealth and social privileges for themselves. In collaboration with U.S. imperialism, the generals and their technocratic cronies launched a breakneck campaign of economic expansion, centering on the *Franja Transversal del Norte* (northern transverse strip). The Franja, a vast strip of land stretching from the Mexican border on the west to Guatemala's narrow Caribbean coast on the east, contains rich deposits of oil and nickel. The region was sparsely populated with some 120,000 people, most of them Indians—the Ketchí, Quiché, Mam, Ixil, and Pocomchí—whom the generals were already accustomed to trampling underfoot.[23]

The government, now headed by the "butcher of Zacapa" Arana Osorio in the form of an elected president, dished out fabulous tracts of land in the Franja and the vast northern El Petén region to military bureaucrats and businessmen closely linked with them. Cattle raising and agribusiness enterprises sprang up, and huge fortunes were made overnight in land speculation. Roads to the new estates were built by rank and file army soldiers. A vast hydroelectric dam, funded by the International Development Bank, was built in Chixoy, to power the extraction of oil and nickel, a vital element in the imperialist military industry. The army established its own bank and insurance company to further grease the financial machinery and provide a handy plumb pie for graft.

The military officers generally came from lower middle class families—which explains their aggressive "get rich quick" mentality and their upstart brashness about pushing traditional industrialists out of the picture (as in cement production). Driving to lure popular participation in their selfserving "development" projects, the generals doled out land parcels to landless peasants in a colonization scheme in the Franja and Petén. But the peasants received the worst land, and soon slipped into the exploitative net of the all-powerful monopoly capital. The real reason for their relocation to the "development" zones was to serve as a cheap labor force on the generals' estates and in the transnational corporations' mines. To make way for the nickel mining operations and agribusiness estates, entire villages of Indians were evicted from their ancestral lands. Thus were the social contradictions of neocolonial Guatemala reproduced in the Franja, on a still more explosive level.

Transformation of the Revolutionary Movement

In 1971, the FAR made a painful assessment of the lessons of its six defeats at the hands of the army, the last occurring in the remote Petén region. The FAR decided to move its base of organizing and struggle to Guatemala City and the agroexport plantations along the southern coast. Striving to build a mass based workers' party, it set to work clandestinely in the labor unions, which had been battered by the long years of military rule. This brought the FAR back into tactical alliance with the PGT, which, while muleheadedly sticking to a semi-open method of work which made its leaders easy targets for the regime's death squads, was beginning to pay lip service to a prolonged revolutionary war.[24]

The ORPA

But now the FAR, which five years earlier had sharply criticized the PGT for its backward neglect of the Indian question, was met with a similar criticism by its most dedicated rural cadres. FAR militants working among the Indian masses of the densely populated regions of San Marcos and Quezaltenango formed a new nucleus of revolutionaries, 95% of whom were Indians. In the fall of 1971, they withdrew into the Indian mountains of the Sierra Madre. But this was no rerun of the bankrupt *foco* strategy of the 1960's. These revolutionaries, influenced by the brilliant African revolutionary theoretician Frantz Fanon, planned to sink deep roots among the indigenous laboring masses, preparing the basis for a genuine people's war of liberation.

To be sure, they tended to downplay the urban working class as a serious factor in the revolutionary struggle, feeling that the urban workers were too exposed to, and beaten down by the repression of the military regime. Yet their Sierra Madre base gave them active access both to the *minifundio* peasants of the highlands and the laborers of the hilly agricultural belt between the highlands and the coastal plains. For eight years, these revolutionaries patiently rooted and expanded their organization among the laboring masses in complete clandestinity, without firing a single shot. In 1979, their organization publicly announced its existence as the *Organización del Pueblo en Armas* (ORPA—Organization of the People in Arms). Today, the ORPA is one of the two most powerful political/military organizations in the Guatemalan revolution.

The EGP

The other was originated by a group of 16 men, survivors of the defeated guerrilla struggles of the 1960's. In early 1972, they crossed from Mexico into northwest Guatemala, establishing their base in the rugged mountains and rain forests of Ixcán—a zone they had chosen after long debate. They reasoned that economically backward Ixcán formed the weakest link in the chain of domination by the regime and imperialism —a link which, moreover, was ripe for breaking, as the Ixil peasants populating the area had been driven into the bitter whirlwind of seasonal labor migration to the southern coast more than any other of Guatemala's 22 Indian groups. Within three years, they found a mass base of support among the Ixiles.[25]

These revolutionaries, also breaking from the *foco* adventures of the 1960's (while upholding Che Guevara as their prime inspirational figure), saw the need to organize among the migrant laborers of the southern coast, and the working masses of Guatemala City. As their organization became the dynamic hub of a resurgent people's movement using a rich variety of methods of struggle against all the big exploiters, they were eagerly joined by many young layworkers (cathechists) of the catholic base community movement, who came to embrace armed revolution as the only road to social justice. In 1975 the new organization, the *Ejército Guerrillero de los Pobres* (EGP—Guerrilla Army of the Poor) consisted of only 50 armed fighters. But behind those 50 stood hundreds of politically aroused peasants clamoring for arms. The first shot fired by the EGP, after three years of painstaking preparatory work, took the life of the most hated landowner in Ixcán.

A New Mass Movement Raises Its Head

By the mid-1970's, the social, cultural and psychological conditions were ripe for the upsurge of a mass movement more united, more deeply rooted yet uprooted, and more combative than Guatemala had ever seen before. The logic of breakneck economic growth geared to the profit needs of a tiny clique of monopoly capitalists

and imperialist concerns had led to a deepening mass immiseration: While in 1965, 42% of the country's population consumed less
than the daily caloric intake needed to maintain basic health, by
1975 this percentage had risen to 70%; and by 1980, to 80%.[26]

The economic upheaval had created a dynamic new proletariat,
in both city and countryside. The young urban factory workers,
while small in number, had to struggle from the start against
ruthless exploitation and military supervision and terror in their
factories. Removed by at most one generation from peasant life,
they were not bound by any labor aristocratic tradition,* and they
took a broader view of the workers' social and political role than
did the older generation of urban workers and artisans.

In 1973, a vigorous strike wave broke out for the first time since
the labor movement was crushed in 1954. Major strikes were
launched by public sector employees, in defiance of antistrike
laws. The five-month teachers' strike quickly spread beyond narrow sectoral demands: Students, workers and slumdwellers joined
the teachers in mass demonstrations against the increased cost of
living. Meanwhile, peasant rebellions in the form of occupations of
idle land grew more frequent.

The Coca-Cola Workers' Struggle

The struggle to organize workers' and peasants' unions sharpened. Urban activists in the unionization campaign faced firing,
boycotting by the combined employers and the specter of starva-
tion—if not instant death at the hands of the regime's terror
squads—if their activities became known to their bosses or the
police. When the workers at the Coca-Cola plant attempted to
form a union, over 150 of them were fired and replaced by scabs.
The union partisans then occupied the plant. Police forcibly
evicted them, arresting 14. After the workers rallied solidarity
from the rest of the labor movement, the company rehired the
union activists and, in 1978, recognized the union. The Coca-Cola
workers' struggle helped spark the formation of the *Comité
Nacional de Unidad Sindical* (CNUS—National Committee of
Labor Union Unity).

But then the real repression began. In the following years, eight
union organizers, including two general secretaries, were kid-

---

*This presents a contrast to El Salvador, where the urban working class is
older, more consolidated, and thus more subject to conservative and opportunist political influence.

napped and murdered. To protest the repression, an international labor union boycott of Coca-Cola products was launched in 1980, and found active support among workers in western Europe (above all, Sweden). With Coke's international sales sagging, a contract was signed between the company and the International Union of Food and Allied Workers (IUF), which the Guatemalan workers had joined. The Coca-Cola workers thus emerged with one of the best organized unions in the country, and a base wage of $4.50 *per day*—far more than the average Guatemalan worker receives.[27] They also compelled the company to set up a fund to support the widows of the workers killed in the anti-union repression.

In February 1984, the Coca-Cola franchise that held the bottling plant declared bankruptcy and closed the plant. The 460 workers, charging that the franchise owners had deliberately sabotaged the company's finances to break the union, occupied the plant and lived there round the clock, guarding the equipment against removal or destruction. Unable to resume full production and marketing, and surrounded by the military dictatorship while in a dangerously static position, the workers appealed to national and international solidarity once again. "It doesn't matter if I'm killed," declared Rodolfo Robles, the current general secretary of the union, "because there are other workers right behind me, ready to take my place in the struggle. It's not a new generation, it's the same generation of workers, but with even greater conviction." Urban and rural workers from around the country put their lives on the line to bring truckloads of food to the Coca-Cola workers. A new international boycott was launched against Coca-Cola in April. In May, Coca-Cola workers in Norway and Austria went on strike in solidarity with the Guatemalan workers. In late May 1984, the company gave in, reversed the workers' layoff status, and agreed to pay them to stay in the plant and care for the machinery until new franchise owners are found.

The Earthquake and the People's Movement

The earthquake that devastated Guatemala in February 1976 exposed the gaping chasm that separated the military regime from the increasingly aroused masses. As the military and bureaucratic bourgeoisie indulged in corrupt profiteering off the international aid that poured in following the earthquake, the affected masses struggled to rebuild their lives. Radicalized students and catholic priests, nuns and layworkers went out among the urban slum dwellers and rural Indian communities that were the worst damaged. They helped organize the people to build new schools and hospitals, showed them how to plant new crops and taught them to read.

These democratic and revolutionary forces faced competition from U.S. imperialist agencies such as the Peace Corps and Agency for International Development (AID), whose cadres were also active in the same areas, building community organizations to accomplish similar tasks in the hope of "saving" the people from the revolutionary movement. AID, the Peace Corps and local officials carried out their organizing activities in close collaboration with the army, which took the opportunity of the reconstruction campaign to plant its authority more firmly in the rural towns and villages. But even these reformist, pro-imperialist reconstruction activities, by sowing hope among the people that they could better their lot through active self-organization, propelled them in a progressive direction which brought them into an increasingly violent clash with the regime. Many of the local leaders who arose in the course of the reconstruction campaign were murdered by the army and its death squads in the subsequent years of struggle.[28]

Masses of peasants and rural workers ruined by the earthquake poured into Guatemala City in search of a livelihood; the slums ringing the city grew and changed profoundly in their social composition. Whereas traditionally the slumdwellers had been heavily lumpenproletarian and thus difficult to organize, now their ranks were swelled by laboring people driven into destitution. The slum settlements (*colonias*) that sprang up after the earthquake became well organized and highly combative against the regime.[29] The urban slumdwellers of rural proletarian and peasant origin became the highly elastic social cement uniting the mass movement of the city with the countryside, preparing the stormy transition from the struggle for social reform to the struggle for social revolution.

As the broadened intellectual horizons of the laboring masses led to surges of creative combativity, local struggles escalated swiftly into national struggles. In November 1977, owners shut down a tungsten mine in the far northwest, laying off 300 workers and driving to break the union. The Mam Indian miners hit upon a new tactic to break out of their mountainous isolation: a 400-kilometer protest march into Guatemala City. "Immediately, miners at the Oxec mine and construction crews at the huge Chixoy and Aguacapa hydroelectric plants downed tools in sympathy.

"As the workers and their families trekked down the Pan American highway, Quiché Indians ran from their homes offering food, clothing, money and moral support. Further along, Cakchiquel Indians and Ladino peasants did the same.

"By Tecpán, [90 kilometers] short of the capital, the miners learned their demands [for resuming their jobs and a new collective bargaining agreement] had been met. Yet they walked on to their destination in support of striking workers from the Pantaleón sugar mill, who in turn brought out sympathizers from the industrial estates around lake Amatitlán. From both directions, streams of workers poured onto the cloverleaf by Roosevelt hospital, merging with a throng of waiting urban supporters. 100,000 took to the streets. Never before had workers and peasants, Indians and Ladinos, and Indians of different ethnic groups shared such solidarity."[30]

'We Don't Want Elections, We Want Revolution'

As the March 1978 elections approached, repression against the militant workers became more murderous. Yet the people were in no mood to endure another fraudulent election in passivity. Workers still on stike against the Aguacapa hydroelectric plant, along with other striking workers, camped in front of the national palace. Thousands of public employees went on strike, demanding higher wages. On election eve, over 50,000 people marched through the streets of the capital city, chanting, "We don't want elections, we want revolution."

"...There was a sense of exhiliration that the 'streets belonged to the people,' that their strength was indestructible. Yet at that very moment, general Romeo Lucas García was declared president in fraudulent elections, with a clear mandate from the army and the ruling sectors to annihilate the mass movement and all opposition."[31]

Rise of the Committee for Farmworkers' Unity

On May Day, 1978, the *Comité de Unidad Campesina* (CUC— Committee for Farmworkers' Unity*) publicly announced its exist-

*The Spanish word *campesino(-a)*, literally "countryman" (or -woman), traditionally has meant the equivalent of "peasant" (or small farmer). However, with the rise of agricultural capitalism in recent decades in Central America and the wholesale or partial transformation of masses of peasants into agricultural proletarians (wageworkers), the term *campesinos* has shifted in

ence on the streets of Guatemala City. The CUC mobilized the largest Indian turnout for a May Day demonstration ever in Guatemala's history. Entire families of Indians participated, some carrying hoes, machetes and torches. They marched in disciplined formation, having organized their own careful security system. Indian orators stepped to the fore, also a first for May Day in Guatemala City.

The CUC had been five years in the making. It arose from a fusion of agrarian cooperatives, peasant leagues and christian base communities. Its leaders had been tempered in the fires of bloody repression by the big landowners, who viewed even the mildest cooperative movement as a dangerous threat to their ready supply of supercheap farm labor. Vowing to "uproot the tree of exploitation," the CUC's leaders worked in almost complete clandestinity. Yet the CUC was built as a truly mass democratic organization, whose decisions were made by mass and delegated assemblies at the local, regional and national levels—until the intensifying repression made such open assemblies impossible.[33]

While the CUC's founding leaders were mostly Indians, they soon embraced a perspective of Indian/Ladino unity in the mass and revolutionary struggle—inspired by the rising tide of joint Indian/Ladino labor struggles led by the CNUS. Strategically broadminded, tactically elastic and energetic, they shattered the defeatist myth of the traditional Left that it was "impossible" to organize and politically mobilize the migrant laborers, due to their great ethnic and linguistic diversity and their volatile conditions of time and space—650,000 families from widespread towns and villages, often migrating to a different plantation each year.

The CUC has seized on both aspects of the dual social existence of the peasants/farm laborers—organizing them as peasants in the highlands and as proletarians in the coastal lowlands. Publishing and circulating its newspaper, *Voice*, in several Indian languages as well as Spanish, the CUC has joined forces with the revolutionary vanguard organizations—especially the EGP and ORPA—in conducting political agitation and education, mass armed selfdefense work, and guerrilla sabotage and harassment of the army.[34] With a mass membership whose majority are Indians,

---

meaning, to embrace *both* smallholding peasants *and* agricultural (semi)-proletarians. In the case of the CUC, its members define themselves *primarily* as agricultural workers.[32]

who in turn make up the superoppressed majority of Guatemala's population, the CUC is today the most important mass organization in the countryside, indeed in all of Central America.

The Semi-Insurrection of September 1978

The Lucas García regime immediately resorted to the methods of civil war to crush the mass movement. In May 1978, its troops fired machineguns upon a public gathering of peasants who had come to the town square in Panzós to protest the seizure of their land by the big landowners. Over 100 unarmed Ketchí men, women and children were killed. Panzós lies on the eastern edge of the mineral rich Alta Verapaz region. The massacre there provoked outrage all over the country, and a protest demonstration united over 100,000 people from all sectors of the popular movement. "Murderous army, out of Panzós!" was the cry that resounded through the streets of the town—a cry that was to be echoed in hundreds of villages in the coming years.[35]

In the cities, the regime was making peaceful street demonstrations more and more impossible. Its elite, paramilitary police forces, trained by professional U.S. thugs, attacked and broke up mass demonstrations.

In September, the unionized bus drivers in Guatemala City went on strike for a wage increase. Hoping to drive a wedge between the strikers and the consuming public, the regime authorized a doubling of the urban bus fare from 5¢ to 10¢. In a country where over half the people do not have the 68¢ per day estimated as necessary to buy a sheer minimum amount of food,[36] this 5¢ change would be a terrible added hardship: Even employed workers were already having to shell out 15% of their income on daily travel fares.

A CNUS general assembly of workers, slumdwellers and students immediately decided upon a general strike in the public sector. The strike was 60% effective, and economic activity in the capital was paralyzed. Spontaneously, insurgent youths tore up paving stones to build barricades, burned tires to protect themselves against teargas, and scattered thumbtacks through the streets to deflate the repressive forces. Their insurrectionary tactics, and the face masks they wore to prevent their identification by the police, were inspired by the mass revolutionary upheaval in Nicaragua just weeks earlier, which they had witnessed on television before it was crushed by Somoza. Streetfighting broke out in the capital and in the western highlands. The insurgents were pitifully armed, and police attacks killed over 30. The uprising lasted a week before the government made a concession: The fare hike was withdrawn, and the regime decided to subsidize the private bus company owners to accommodate a partial wage increase for the drivers. But besides the 1,300 people arrested in the course of the uprising, hundreds of union activists were fired, and their unions banned. And the corpses of slumdwellers arrested at the barricades were later found along roadsides.

Carter's 'Break' with the Lucas García Regime

Frightened by the smallscale "dress rehearsal" for revolution it had just confronted, the Lucas García clique was still more frightened by the triumph of the Nicaraguan revolution in 1979 and the destruction of the very prototype for a military/bourgeois oligarchy in Central America: the Somoza dynasty and its national guard. In the manner of a neurotic puppet whose illusions in the omnipotence of his master have been shattered, the Lucas clique blamed U.S. president Carter for "betraying" his loyal ally Somoza (presumably by not making a fullscale invasion of Nicaragua the way Kennedy, Johnson and Nixon did against Vietnam). By 1980, Lucas was publicly denouncing Carter as a "communist." He was furious at Carter and his state department's "human rights" diplomacy.

Carter aimed to avert another Nicaraguan revolution by maneuvering "moderate" civilian politicians into power in the embattled Central American "republics," with a mandate (from the U.S. state department, CIA, and Agency for International Development) to carry out partial social reforms to placate the aroused mass movement. Thus the Carter administration actively supported the October 1979 overthrow of the Salvadoran military dictator Romero by "radical" junior officers, who proceeded to adorn their dictatorship with a figleaf of civilian politicians, above all Duarte, announcing "sweeping" financial and agrarian reforms whose implementation was accompanied by still bloodier repression against the masses (see ch. 1).

In Guatemala, the parvenu military bourgeoisie had supplanted the traditional landowning oligarchy as the kingpin of the ruling class. The military dictators' entire fortunes and new found social status were bound up with their political and bureaucratic office holding, and the wholesale corruption that went with it. Thus they saw *any* threat to their monopoly on officeholding as "subversive" and "communist"—whether it came from the revolutionary movement of the workers and peasants, or from the reformist machinations of Jimmy Carter and the bourgeois opposition parties he was trying to line up for a piece of the political pie. To destroy any possibility of a rerun of the "military/civilian" regime in El Salvador, the Lucas clique launched a reign of terror against *all* social and political sectors in the country outside the ruling caste and its most slavish supporters. This included the murder of dozens of politicians and mayors of the petty-bourgeois and bourgeois opposition parties, such as the social democrats and christian democrats.

But if Lucas García could denounce and break with the Carter regime on a *tactical* level, the two were still deeply united in their *strategic* aim: destroying the revolutionary movement and maintaining capitalist/imperialist rule over Guatemala. Indeed, Carter needed Lucas more than Lucas needed Carter. So Carter's celebrated "disengagement" from the Lucas regime in 1977 in a row over the regime's atrocious human rights record was, in reality, no disengagement at all. While *official* U.S. military aid to Guatemala was stopped, the actual flow of U.S. military hardware continued pouring in. In the last two years of Carter's term (1979-80), over $34 million worth of U.S. military equipment arrived in Guatemala, most of it under contracts licensed by the U.S. commerce department.[37] Still more importantly, Carter pulled the same razzle-dazzle tactic in the field of military policy towards Guatemala that he did in the final months of the Somoza regime, to keep the U.S.' diplomatic hands clean while continuing to arm the regime to the teeth against the revolution: He funneled an enormous amount of military aid through Israel, the prime U.S. proxy in the world which, as an "international pariah" in diplomatic matters, can more conveniently keep its military transactions secret.

Massacre at the Spanish Embassy

As the army increasingly occupied rural towns and villages, terrorizing all suspected grassroots activists, groups of peasants—mostly women—trekked into Guatemala City to denounce the army's occupation campaign and demand the release of their kidnapped relatives. As with the "long march" of striking miners into Guatemala City in 1977, the peasant marchers gathered active support among workers, christian base community groups, slum-dwellers, and students as they made their way into the capital, spreading the word against the army's rural repression.

On 31 January 1980, a delegation of peasants from Quiché and their urban supporters, unable to gain a hearing in the mass media, peacefully occupied the Spanish embassy to press their grievances. The Spanish ambassador agreed to mediate between the peasants and the regime, but the regime was in no bargaining mood. It ordered the police to storm the embassy and evict the peasants. When they refused to surrender, the police sprayed them with incendiary material. In the resulting fire, 39 people were burned alive. Only the ambassador and one peasant sur-vived. The next day the peasant, hospitalized with serious burns, was kidnapped from his hospital bed and murdered.

Like the mass demonstration on the streets of San Salvador nine days earlier, which was shot up by the national guard and suffered dozens dead (see ch. 1), the massacre at the Spanish embassy was a turning point in Guatemala's modern history. Both Indians and Ladinos perished in the flames. And the mili-tary terror over the countryside was driven home to the masses of Guatemala City as never before. "People were stunned for days; they said little, or exchanged tense whispers."[38]

Farmworkers' Mass Strike

In the countryside, the politicized masses were long used to exchanging tense whispers to prepare the next eruption of their struggle. And within a month of the Spanish embassy massacre, the CUC led sugarcane cutters out on a mass strike, demanding wage hikes from $1.12 to $5.00 per *day*. Laborers on cotton and coffee plantations joined in the strike, swelling its numbers to 75,000. The CUC's seven years of patient organizing to unite the entire rural labor force against their exploiters bore fruit. "United action by Indians and Ladinos, resident workers and temporary day laborers was unprecedented in Latin America."[39] The strik-ers were armed only with their machetes, but they made the most of them. Surging onto the Pan-American highway, they blocked all the mill entrances, sabotaged machinery and burned crops stockpiled for export.

After two weeks of mass strike against the stonewalling land-owners, the government declared a new rural minimum wage of $3.20 per day. While the CUC agreed to this partial concession at the urging of other CNUS unions,* the government quietly informed the landowners that it had no intention of enforcing the new minimum wage. And over 10,000 laborers were fired when the strike ended. But the psychological impact of the struggle eclipsed the fact that the strikers made no tangible gain from it. "We are witnessing," wrote a conservative journalist, "a new scene with actors different from the Indian who removes his hat, places it over his chest and humbly asks his boss for a few cents more, by the grace of God."[40]

Indeed, by early 1982, even the U.S. embassy admitted that 80% of the revolutionary guerrilla fighters were Indians. And the Guatemalan army noted warily that "entire families join in as strategic collaborators [with the guerrillas]."[41] The Indian masses were no longer a mere ally of the revolutionary movement; they were now the guiding heart and brains of the revolution. In the Indian regions, the EGP and ORPA, whose origins and leadership are markedly Indian, are known by the people as "our army."

Lucas Garcia's Armored Car Race to Hell...

1 May 1980 saw the last mass May Day demonstration in Guatemala City to date. The people well knew that they were staking their lives by coming out into the streets. Over 100 of them disappeared into the hands of the police and armed forces. And under Lucas García and his successors, there have scarcely been any political prisoners—only political corpses.

As the counterinsurgency war in the countryside began to take on genocidal proportions, there was heightening insecurity among all social classes. In Guatemala City, disappearances into the hands of the military and its unofficial death squads, and the inevitable discovery of the mutilated corpses along some byway, became a daily occurrence. Among the corpses were workers, slumdwellers, students, teachers, priests, liberal professionals and politicians. Unable to solve any of the country's burning economic problems as the world prices for Guatemala's key export crops plummeted, the Lucas clique threw its energies into fattening its own pockets—no matter what the cost in class stability or human life. Military corruption and gangsterism became routine and rabid. The agro-exporting capitalists, having hoisted the military

*With the CNUS threatening to call a general strike of industrial workers in the cities, the regime moved to defuse the situation by formally raising the urban workers' minimum wage from $2.00 to $4.90 per day.

U.S. military attaché, George Maynes, surveys the scene in Nebaj. The revolutionary consciousness and action of the local Ixil people, and of all Guatemala's oppressed peoples, threaten the security of imperialism.

Laura Santos

The civil defense patrols are compulsory for all males from the ages of 18 to 50.

Frank Manuelo

A column of EGP members in the jungles of Ixcán.

Por Esto

(from *Compañero)*

dictatorship to power, now found that the dictator's jackboots were starting to squash their own lust for profit: Lucas brusquely ignored their pleas for tax breaks, in fact *raising* coffee export taxes to insure a stepped up flow of state revenues into his clique's pet financial projects.[42]

Even within the military itself, the base of the regime narrowed dangerously. Lucas was concentrating the graft and plunder in the hands of a smaller and smaller military/bureaucratic clique— freezing out the middle and lower ranking officers. The young officers in the field, despite their mass slaughters of unarmed villagers, were themselves suffering heavy casualties at the hands of the armed revolutionaries: 57 of their kind were killed in 1981.[43] Demoralized by their inability to win the war and their increasing difficulty in rallying young Indian conscripts to murder their own people, the field officers began casting resentful glances at Lucas and his cronies sitting comfortably in Guatemala City and enjoying their monopoly on the spoils of corruption.

...and Rios Montt's 'Born Again' Dictatorship

The elections of March 1982 were yet another exercise in vote fraud in favor of the military's preferred candidate. The bourgeois opposition politicians who had escaped arrest howled foul play. The military officer corps had already decided to get rid of Lucas García in their own preferred way. Two weeks after the election, they ousted him in a bloodless coup. The new dictator was José Efraín Ríos Montt, a seasoned general who had himself been defrauded of the presidential election in 1974.

Ríos Montt, trained at U.S. counterinsurgency facilities and well versed in psychological warfare, promised to end corruption, guarantee human rights and improve Guatemala's image with the U.S. As for corruption, while the flagrance of the Lucas clique's racketeering subsided, Ríos Montt never carried through his promised purge of the clique, nor did he bring a single of its members to trial. As for human rights, some 300 Israeli military advisers who had aided in the coup that brought Ríos Montt to power, proceeded to place their counterinsurgent stamp on his regime; in the summer of 1981, sophisticated Israeli and Argentinian computer hardware and analysis had been key in the detection and murderous military destruction of two dozen "safe" houses operated by EGP and ORPA militants in Guatemala City.[44] And as for improving Guatemala's relations with the U.S., Ronald Reagan was already in the White House.

In his flamboyant attempt to convince the people that his regime marked a serious change in course, Ríos Montt flaunted his "born again christian" credentials, peppering his televised speeches with invocations of god and related absurdities. During his years of political obscurity and depression following his frustrated presidential bid, Ríos Montt had been recruited into an evangelical protestant sect called Gospel Outreach, based in Eureka, California. Founded among drifting leftovers of the hippie counterculture movement of the 1960's and taken over by an aggressive preacher/entrepreneur, Gospel Outreach, upon arrival in Guatemala, concentrated its proselytizing efforts on the upper middle classes of Guatemala City, cashing in on their boredom with traditional catholicism and insecurity over the simmering civil war. Stridently anticommunist and apocalyptic in its world outlook, Gospel Outreach is sharply opposed to the catholic movement of liberation theology, and to those rare protestant sects which support the people's struggle for social liberation.

When their prize proselyte Ríos Montt seized the reins of state, the Gospel Outreach leaders grouped themselves into a clique of "spiritual" advisers to the new dictator. In intimate collaboration with the army and using lavish funds provided by its richer members back in the U.S., the sect played a key role in implementing Ríos Montt's "civic action" programs in the countryside, designed to "win the hearts" of the peasants battered by military occupation and forced relocation. "*Frijoles y fusiles*" was the name Ríos Montt gave his counterinsurgency scheme: "beans and rifles." Gospel Outreach cadres spooned out beans to displaced and destitute peasants in army commissaries, and the army pressganged the local men into "civil defense patrols," outfitting them with a few old rifles to "combat communism."

This arrangement allowed Gospel Outreach not only to greatly expand the scope for its reactionary preaching in Guatemala, but also to lobby in Washington for increased and open U.S. support to Ríos Montt—on the grounds that his regime was adhering to "human rights" standards. Indeed all the conservative, big bourgeois U.S. evangelists, including Billy "Cracker" Graham and Jerry "All in the Family" Falwell, became fanatic supporters of Ríos Montt. This was ironic on the part of the evangelical bigots, who equate woman's right to abortion with "murder." For Ríos Montt's troops soon became notorious for driving their bayonets into the pregnant bellies of Indian women.

A Counterinsurgency Verging on Genocide

As he geared up for an all-out military assault against the rural zones where the revolutionary movement was strongest, Ríos Montt made an "evenhanded" offer of amnesty to the Left and the extreme Right, calling on both to lay down their arms. At the beginning of 1982, the armed Left—including the EGP, ORPA, FAR, and a radical faction of the PGT—had come together to form the *Unidad Revolucionaria Nacional Guatemalteca* (URNG —Guatemalan National Revolutionary Unity), which allowed for closer tactical/military coordination against the government's army. As Ríos Montt well expected, the revolutionary organizations refused to lay down their arms, denouncing the amnesty as a ploy to absolve army rapists, murderers and other criminals against the people, from all legal responsibility. And in a speech before a business convention, Ríos Montt pulled no punches in explaining why he had offered amnesty to the Left: "The amnesty gives us the juridical framework for killing. Anyone who refuses to surrender will be shot."[45]

The army now concentrated its forces against the "Ixil triangle," a zone in El Quiché demarcated by the towns of Nebaj, Chajul and San Juan Cotzal (see map, p. 116). The EGP had grown tremendously among the local Ixil Indians, who were clamoring for arms and organization to resist the repressive forces. The EGP, in fact, had become by far the largest of the revolutionary vanguard organizations, with a membership over half the total membership of the URNG. But it had grown so rapidly that it had not been able to train and arm nearly all its fresh recruits and sympathizers in preparation for the more ferocious battles looming. So when Ríos Montt's forces invaded Nebaj, a municipal capital of between 3,000 and 4,000 people, many EGP members and supporters, and civilians generally, were massacred without offering systematic resistance. The rest of the people of Nebaj fled to the neighboring mountains, where they lived with the EGP guerrillas under desperate conditions.

The army swept savagely through the Indian highlands. Between March and August 1982, the army and airforce destroyed 212 Indian villages, killing from 10 to 300 people in each village. Tens of thousands fled in terror across the border into Mexico, and some one million *internal* refugees were created out of a total population of 7.2 million. Many of them were rounded up into the army's "model village" resettlement projects where, deprived of any chance of making a normal livelihood, they became the beneficiaries of the "beans and guns" program under the iron ring of military occupation. The refugees of Nebaj, after living in the mountains for a year under near-starvation conditions, were compelled to return to the town, now a "model village" under army occupation.

The Army's Model Villages and Civil Defense Patrols

The "model village" program, inspired by U.S. and Israeli counterinsurgency experts, is patterned after the "strategic hamlet" tactic pursued by the U.S. military and its puppet army in south Vietnam. The idea is to drive a lethal wedge between the revolutionary guerrillas and the people by destroying the people's traditional scattered villages and massively relocating them into dense compounds where they are tightly supervised by the army, and materially dependent on the "humanitarian" aid programs it dispenses. In Guatemala, the UN's World Food Program sent basic food supplies, which reached the desperate people through the hands of regional military commanders and their Gospel Outreach agents. The U.S. AID built new housing units, so that some peasants could live more comfortably under the rule of the army which had destroyed their traditional homes and slaughtered their relatives.

All ablebodied men between the ages of 18 and 50 were conscripted into the "civil defense patrols"—a tactic reminiscent of the "civil guard" movement implemented by the Diem regime in south Vietnam in the early 1960's. Pitifully armed civil patrol units have been used as human shields to protect the army's regular troops in their offensives against revolutionary fighters.[46]*

But as in south Vietnam in the early 1960's, the revolutionary movement in Guatemala's countryside is too deeply rooted to be fully isolated from the people and liquidated, even by the most strenuous counterinsurgency measures. The situation today is dramatically different from the struggle of the 1960's, when the rural masses' level of political participation and consciousness was so low (largely thanks to the false policy of the Left) that many could be armed and intimidated by the fascist regime into becoming active agents of the counterrevolution. Today, the arming

*Some of the "civil defense patrols," on the other hand, are the old rightist death squads with a new name.

of the people—no matter how pitifully, and for how reactionary a purpose—can only be a prelude to a nationwide mass insurrection. The "civil defense patrol" movement, which has swelled to some 700,000 men—10% of Guatemala's population— is bound to turn into its revolutionary opposite. In fact, many of the "civil defense patrol" conscripts are themselves revolutionary guerrillas.

To be sure, the counterinsurgency *blitzkrieg* of 1982 ended in a serious defeat for the revolutionary Left—above all, for the EGP, which found itself sharply reduced in numbers and morale in the aftermath. In a November 1983 interview, EGP commander in chief Rolando Morán admitted that he and his organization had made a terrible mistake in the course of their work prior to the assault: "We seriously underestimated the enemy, both internally and internationally." With most of its cadres withdrawn further into the mountains or into exile, the EGP is retrenching, wasting the army's forces through guerrilla harassment tactics and preparing for the next upsurge in the people's struggle. The ORPA, which had a tighter and more compact cadre organization in its zones of influence than did the EGP, was better able to withstand the counterinsurgent assault.

Economic Devastation...

Since the laboring masses are the producers of all social wealth, and thus of the fortunes of the rich, the rulers can never exterminate them with impunity. Ríos Montt's counterinsurgency campaign, while sharply setting back the revolutionary movement, further wrecked the Guatemalan economy. The "model village" and "civil patrol" campaign, by imposing rigid social control and separating the rural producers from the land, has thoroughly disrupted the agricultural cycle. Not only has local subsistence farming been gutted; the seasonal migration of farmworkers to the southern coastal plantations has also been disrupted. Indian men began refusing the annual trek to the southern coast, because they were being branded guerrillas and killed by the army; moreover, they wanted to stay and defend their home villages against army massacres. In the aftermath of the 1982 counterinsurgency drive, the seasonal labor migration ground nearly to a halt.

To be sure, this had little immediate economic impact, since coastal agribusiness was already in a deep slump due to plummeting world market prices for its export crops, and it had been hiring far fewer workers anyway. But the Guatemalan ruling class will be hard pressed to revive labor migratory "business as usual" once the agroexport business revives. It may well have to return to the forced labor conscription of the past. Already the army has forcibly recruited Indian laborers to hack out new roads through the highlands and replant the forest stripped bare by capitalist lumber companies.

...and Another Turn in the Military's Fortune Wheel

Presiding over an insoluble economic quagmire, Ríos Montt ran up against sharpening contradictions with rival sectors of the ruling class. Big private businessmen resented Ríos Montt's aggressive state intervention into the economy; they called for dismantling all import controls, to make Guatemala more attractive to international commerce and investment. They also resented the regime's tight credit policy and high interest rates, as well as its desire to increase taxation of the private sector to fund the counterinsurgency war.[47] The catholic church hierarchy, traditionally profascist and pro-regime, was alarmed by Ríos Montt's aggressive protestant evangelism. His fellow military officers found their caste and national pride wounded by the influence of his clique of California-based "spiritual" advisers. Finally, Ríos Montt, evidently having his hands more than full in Guatemala, was balking at the Pentagon's plans to revive the Central American Defense Council (Condeca, an alliance of U.S. puppet military regimes in Central America, shattered by the overthrow of its linchpin Somoza) for active collaboration with the Salvadoran army and the counterrevolutionary invaders of Nicaragua.

In August 1983, Ríos Montt was ousted in another military "coup by gentlemen's agreement." Only a couple soldiers were killed, and Ríos Montt continued drawing his salary. The U.S. embassy actively assisted in the coup, and the new dictator was general Oscar Humberto Mejía Víctores, who had been deputy defense minister under Lucas García and defense minister under Ríos Montt.[48] As far as the masses were concerned, the only significant change was the revival of ferocious military repression in Guatemala City.

Despite Reagan's fond hopes that Mejía Víctores could help patch Condeca together again, this has yet to materialize. Far from being able to overcome the jealous tensions between the ruling military cliques in El Salvador, Honduras and Guatemala, Mejía was unable to unite the feuding factions within his own military hierarchy. Moreover, in late 1983, three bilingual teachers from U.S. AID were murdered by government forces in Guatemala. When Mejía covered up the murders, the U.S. ambassador became infuriated and left the country, vowing not to return.

The Best Men of the Counterrevolution Step to the Fore

Driving to streamline his army for the campaigns to come, Mejía embarked on a major housecleaning of the "old guard" of the military hierarchy. In December 1983, he forcibly retired 10 generals and 25 colonels, including the last four heads of state: colonel Arana, and generals Laugerud, Lucas García and Ríos Montt. In their place a new generation of colonels has stepped to the fore, military base commanders who won their spurs in the counterinsurgency warfare of recent years. Their leading representative is col. Rodolfo Lobos Zamora, who commanded the military zones of Huehuetenango, El Quiché and Quetzaltenango—three regions where the counterinsurgency war has been most ferocious. Mejía promoted Lobos to chief of staff of the armed forces and deputy chief of state.[49]

The Guatemalan army is not, like the Salvadoran army, a "nine to five, Monday through Friday" army which likes to bomb and sweep through a revolutionary zone, massacring those civilians who could not flee fast enough—only to deploy back to barracks, allowing the guerrillas and their supporters to return and continue the struggle. The Guatemalan army, being a dominant economic and social as well as military force, is intent on hammering spikes into every pore of Guatemalan society, building everywhere a permanent bastion for counterrevolution among the people. With well over a decade of anticivilian warfare under its cartridge belt, it is the most seasoned and systematic army of counterrevolution in Latin America.

The U.S. Stake

It has to be. U.S. corporate investment is higher by far in Guatemala than in any other country of Central America. Five of the *Fortune* top ten corporations—Exxon, Texaco, Gulf Oil, ITT, and IBM—all have operations in Guatemala, and Bank of America has long been a leading investor. Moreover, the resident U.S. businessmen (many of them participants in the 1954 CIA coup) grouped into the American Chamber of Commerce in Guatemala City, are the most rabid partisans of military counterrevolution at all costs. They supported the scandalously corrupt and murderous Lucas García right up to his ouster—even as the Guatemalan big businessmen were breaking with him and huddling with the U.S. embassy to ease him out.[50]

And the local American Chamber of Commerce, for all its lack of political finesse, clearly represents the vanguard moneybags of U.S. domination in Guatemala. Its interests objectively coincide with the "greater good" of U.S. imperialism. For the struggle in Guatemala is taking on a political significance far beyond the economic stakes involved within the country itself.

Latin America's Future

Just as the historical conditions of Guatemala have given rise to the most experienced and powerful counterrevolutionary army in Latin America, so also have they given rise to the most experienced and, in the end, powerful revolutionary movement in the Americas. The Guatemalan revolutionaries have confronted the most complex array of social and ethnic questions, debated conflicting strategies and tactics, tested them out in the fire and blood of revolutionary warfare, and selected and honed the best of them. In their theory and practice, they are spanning the compressed historical epochs separating the village community of the ancient past from the proletarian socialism of the liberating future. More than any other revolutionaries in the hemisphere, they know that proletarian socialism does not mean the destruction of ancient, communal cultures—but rather the *extension* of their communal property relations, freedom and equality through *all* of society, raised upon the advanced technology inherited from decadent capitalism.

If the Guatemalan revolutionaries continue to develop their liberating theory and practice, the "domino theory," so dreaded by the imperialists and their lackeys, will become a reality. The victory of the Guatemalan revolution will impact immediately upon Mexico, long simmering with peasants' and workers' revolt. The giant Brazil, with its own complex mosaic of social and ethnic structures, cannot be long behind in entering the epoch of revolution, and will benefit greatly from the Guatemalan experience. In a real historical sense, the fate of the Americas will be decided in Guatemala in the coming years.

Chapter 5

The Church Torn by Class Struggle

"Is it not true that many youths are awaiting that heralding of a Christ who saves, and liberates, who changes one's heart and foments a peaceful yet decisive revolution, the fruit of christian love?"

—Pope John Paul 2, addressing the catholic priests and religious workers of Central America at San Salvador's metropolitan cathedral, March 1983.[1]

Liberation theology is "the heresy of our time."

—Cardinal Joseph Ratzinger, leading Vatican theologian.

"I tried to save the situation in a christian way, in the peaceful sense, trying to lift the people through their own resources or those of the government. But I realized that all this was a lie, a big deception. I began to get discouraged to see that so much work brought no result...because people went on living the same."

—Gaspar García Laviana, a Spanish missionary in Nicaragua who, after working for years in a peasant community, joined the FSLN in 1977, became a *comandante* on the southern front, and died in battle against Somoza one year later.[2]

Heresy comes from a Greek word meaning "free choice." Christianity originated as a radical, communistic movement among the lower classes of Mediterranean societies in protest against the worldly and moral corruption of the businessmen and orthodox religious castes which oppressed and deceived "their own" people. The early christians actively asserted their free choice by organizing themselves into austere communes of associated consumers on an egalitarian basis, in defiance of the big landowners, slavemasters, businessmen and monarchs of the Roman empire. For their heresy, they were murderously persecuted by the Roman emperors and their local lackeys.

When the emperors got wise to the stubbornly popular christian doctrine, they coopted it, adopting it as the official religion of their decadent empire. Christianity was turned into its opposite. From a religion of the *oppressed*, it was transformed into a religion of the *oppressors*, above all the feudal landowners. Official christianity, embodied in the Roman catholic church, with its vast domain of landholdings and annual wealth extracted from the toil of enserfed peasants, became a mass murderous hunter of heretics on a world scale.

Those who attempted to reassert the communal, antislavery and antiwar values of the original christians—values they often combined with the pagan beliefs of the pre-christian village community—were branded as heretics by the Vatican oligarchy. For their exercise of free choice, they were slaughtered—either by the swift sword of the crusades, or the slow fire of the inquisition. Those peoples who were not christian to begin with and refused to convert to the official feudalist religion—the Jews, the Muslims, and "pagan" communities and civilizations around the world—were branded as "infidels" by the Vatican, and subject to periodic mass extermination and expulsion from their homes.

As capitalist industry, commerce and scientific thought gained a foothold in pockets within feudal Europe, the church lashed out against the new men of property and the scientific freethinkers, branding them first as heretics as later—as the Vatican clique grew more desperate and morally depraved—as "witches." The wealthy men who were strangled, beheaded and burned by the Vatican's henchmen—as well as the hundreds of thousands of poor people, above all women, who suffered the same and worse fates—all had their property confiscated by the sacred church.

The Vatican Moves with the Times

In today's capitalist world, the Vatican has become a modern capitalist/imperialist institution, cleverly blending a kaleidoscope of bourgeois ideology including liberal "humanitarianism" and pacifism, with its old feudal ideology of the corporate serf-owner. The Vatican maintains, and works to expand, its financial/landowning empire, through its transnational bank and its well heeled church holding companies around the world. Small wonder that its leading propagandists, the cardinals and archbishops—robed "chairmen of the board" of the holy capitalist corporation—tend to uphold the established social order and oppose the new heresy, liberation theology.

But the Vatican no longer has its own military arm and judicial network of prisons, torture chambers, inquisition chambers and execution plazas to enforce its reactionary ideas. In this respect it has stepped aside to make room for the secular institutions of modern imperialism, centered in Washington and Wall Street. This has brought a big moral advantage to the Vatican: Its hands are no longer directly covered with the blood of the hundreds of thousands of oppressed people slaughtered by the empire of propertied wealth. The death squads and counterinsurgent armies of El Salvador and Guatemala are not under the command of the Vatican, but of local ruling cliques supervised by the Pentagon, the CIA, Chase Manhattan Bank and the Bank of America. So the Vatican can posture as an "independent" spiritual force "rising above" the fierce struggle between imperialist reaction and the people's revolution. Preaching "universal" love, disarmament, and a purely spiritual "revolution" on the basis of the existing social order, the Vatican serves the aims of imperialism in urging the insurgent masses to lay down their arms and submit once against to the tyranny of their rulers.

The New Christian Movement

On the other side are those catholic priests, nuns and lay-workers who, in Central America, the Philippines and elsewhere, have plunged into the struggle to liberate the laboring masses from the poverty, ignorance and spiritual misery imposed upon them by imperialism. These preachers and practitioners of liberation theology, through their organizing and mobilizing of the rural masses against the structures of exploitation, have headed into a violent clash with the local oligarchies and their death squads. They have also found themselves up against an increasingly strident propaganda assault by the Vatican oligarchy headed by the pope.

Both poles within the catholic church claim to follow the true message of Jesus. But they face each other—whether willingly or not—from opposite sides of the bloody barricade between revolution and counterrevolution. Which side represents the true banner of christ? More importantly, which side represents historical justice and the future of humanity?

Origins of Christianity

Christianity did not emerge out of the blue, any more than Jesus himself emerged from the womb of a virgin. The christian movement was a product of definite economic, social and historical conditions prevailing in Palestine and other parts of the Roman empire ringing the Mediterranean.

Christian thought and practice, in fact, was directly preceded and influenced by a heretical Jewish sect, the Essenes. The essenes lived in isolated agricultural and pastoral communities, holding their land and farm animals in common and sharing their consumption goods equally. They were celibate, vegetarian, and semi-monastic, living austerely and making their own clothing. They rejected the temple sacrifices of animals offered up by the pompous Jewish rabbinical caste. They believed in the transmigration of souls, a belief apparently borrowed from the Persians. They practiced baptism and upheld Mosaic law. They denounced social inequality, slavery, and war.

The Roman empire, sterile and parasitic from the start, became more corrupt and degenerate the more it expanded. The Roman republic was originally based on the produce of free peasants laboring on the Italian peninsula, who sold part of their harvests to the city. As the Roman state became militarized to conquer foreign lands, the Italian peasants were increasingly conscripted into the imperial army. As its once healthy home economic base eroded, the empire enriched itself by looting the economies of its conquered territories, imposing massive tributes on the produce of their peasants and artisans. The republican government in Rome, deprived of any productive base of mass support, became an easy target for overthrow by victorious military thugs like the Caesars. The prisoners of war captured by the Roman army were enslaved and shipped to Italy, where many were worked to death on plantations owned by big landowners, usurers and tax collectors. The luxurious splendor of the imperial clique and the big landowners and usurers formed a more and more scandalous contrast to the desperate poverty of the people. And in the conquered territories of the empire like Palestine, the Roman occupation added another crushing burden to the land taxation and usury practiced by the local propertied classes upon "their own" people. The local businessmen and ruling religious caste established a *modus vivendi* with the Roman military administration, betraying their own people in the bargain.

It was in this social context that the reformist charlatan, Jesus "Turn the Other Cheek" Christ, appeared on the scene. Jesus and his disciples sanctified the poor and the dispossessed, railing against the moral corruption of the rich, especially the money-lenders. "Go...now, you rich men, weep and howl for your miseries that shall come upon you. Your riches are corrupted, and your garments are moth eaten. Your gold and silver is rusted; and their rust shall be a witness against you, and shall eat your flesh as it were fire... Behold, the hire of the laborers who have reaped down your fields, which is of you kept back by fraud, cries: and the cries of those who have reaped are entered into the ears of the Lord of sabaoth." (James, 5.1-4).

Internal Contradiction of Jesus' Teachings

But in Jesus' preachings to the oppressed masses, there was always a sharp *contradiction* between the concept of salvation for the poor *on earth* and salvation for the poor *in the "afterlife"*. In the first book of the new testament, we find the famous watch-word, "Blessed are the meek, for they shall inherit *the earth*." (Matthew, 5.5—emphasis added). This worldly watchword has been embraced by the preachers of liberation theology. But just two verses earlier, we read: "Blessed are the poor *in spirit*, for theirs is the kingdom *of heaven*." (Matthew 5.3—emphasis added). This heavenly hype has been embraced by the pope and his crony theologians.

The contradictory kernel of christian teaching was neatly summed up by the young Marx: "Religious suffering is at the same time an *expression* of real suffering and a *protest* against real suffering. Religion is the sigh of the oppressed creature, the sentiment of a heartless world, the soul of soulless conditions. It is the *opium* of the people."[3]

The oppressed masses of Palestine, both Jewish and non-Jewish, were seething with discontent, searching for some way of deliverance from the double yoke of Roman imperialism and the local propertied classes. Instead of rallying them for a *class* and *national liberation struggle* against their oppressors, Jesus poured cold water on their class hatred, subduing them with paci-fist and "universalist" rhetoric: "...But I say unto those of you who hear, love your enemies, do good to those who hate you. Bless those who curse you, and pray for those who spitefully use you." (St. Luke, 6.27-8). Jesus' only acts of real class struggle were confined to "substitutionist" political stunts like driving the moneylenders out of the temple *by himself, without* a mass mobilization—thus failing to show the way to the *social overthrow* of the moneyed exploiters.

The anti-revolutionary logic of Jesus' politics was exposed when the elitist priests and scribes of the Jerusalem temple publicly confronted him with the question: "Is it lawful for us to give tribute unto Caesar, or no?" This question, which the priests and scribes intended as a baited trap, really posed the burning choice of *capitulation to*, or *struggle against* Roman imperialism. Jesus' evasive response was: "...Render...unto Caesar the things which be Caesar's, and unto God the things which be God's." (St. Luke, 20.22, 20.25). This "marvelous" response took Jesus "off the cross" for the time being; but it had a disarming and demobilizing effect on his followers. Clearly, a bold renunciation of payment of tribute to Caesar would have been a call for popular revolt against the imperial tyranny. But Jesus was dead set against just such a revolt.*

Jesus' radical social preachings frightened the ruling classes, but his lack of a mass struggle orientation left him and his disciples out on a limb—so that his unarmed movement could be crushed without a serious struggle. His execution left the masses woefully unprepared to struggle for their social liberation. If, instead of wasting the people's time and energy with his faith-healing hustles, Jesus had raised the banner of people's war against the Roman imperialists and their local lackey classes, mass insurrection would have become the watchword throughout Palestine. With his social and ethnic broadmindedness, Jesus would have been able to unite diverse groups of people, who had previously faced the Roman legions alone, in common struggle against the empire.

But instead, Jesus chose to preach not only against the oppressive Pharisees and Scribes, but *also* against the revolutionary Zealots, a militant Jewish sect who pursued armed struggle against the Roman occupiers. Thanks to Jesus' opposition, as well as their own religious and ethnic sectarianism, the zealots were defeated and their leaders put to death by the Roman rulers—shortly

---

*In this light, the *sandinista* leaders of Nicaragua today can rightfully claim to be adhering to christian principles when they slavishly uphold the huge money debt to U.S. imperialism they inherited from Somoza, and continue paying it off—thus "rendering unto Rockefeller the dollars which are Rockefeller's."

before Jesus' own execution. Thirty-seven years after Jesus' death (70 AD), the long simmering Jewish mass insurrection broke out in Palestine. The Jewish king Agrippa and other members of the local ruling classes opposed the revolt and defected to the side of the Roman imperialists. The zealots in the lead of the insurrection had to wage a "red terror" against the rich traitors, in the course of their struggle against the armed might of the Roman procurators. The insurrection ended in defeat.

Christianity Spreads to the Dispossessed of Rome

In Italy, meanwhile, the free peasantry was completely ruined by the depredations of the big landowners, who came to rely on an inexhaustible supply of slave labor to work their plantations. The expropriated peasants, driven into the capital city, could find no livelihood there, since Roman industry was pitifully backward and stagnant. They were reduced to a mass of lumpenproletarians, roaming the city begging for food, at times threatening to revolt, at times banding together for mutual defense. The imperial cliques vying for power competed for the political allegiance of the lumpenproletarians by tossing them some of the surplus from the state granaries from time to time. The contrast between the poverty of the many and the wealth of the few was for all to see, as the clique of landowners, tax collectors and imperial officeholders wasted their time and wealth in orgies and debauchery.

In this situation of mass misery and yawning social injustice, the new christian, communal doctrine quickly captured the imagination of the dispossessed. The christian apostles demanded that the rich share out their scandalously acquired wealth equally among the people. And they organized communities in which they put their doctrine into practice on a limited scale. The rich men recruited to the new religion had to sell their land and houses, and lay the proceeds at the feet of the apostles. The apostles then purchased basic goods for the community, which were distributed to each according to his (modest) needs. Plain and simple living was the order of the day for christians travelling between towns and spreading their new gospel. When they arrived in a town or city, they would sojourn with the local christian community, which would supply them with food and clothing. The christians carried out no commerce among themselves, fulfilling each others' material needs through simple barter or outright gifts. They lived and ate communally. All the individuals and families recruited to christianity within a city would combine into "one big christian family," with forms of group marriage practiced in some cases.[4]

Thus the early christian movement evolved forms of *primitive communism*, reviving certain aspects of the original communal, egalitarian mode of human society. Despite ferocious persecution, it gained popularity among the lumpenproletariat, the slaves, and loftyminded members of the propertied classes. But it was only a communism of associated *consumers*, not a communism of associated *producers*. Christianity attempted to abolish social inequality without overthrowing the social class conditions of the Roman empire which daily produced and reproduced gaping inequalities.

And christianity, even during this radical communal phase with its "brotherhood of man" rhetoric, never criticized or struggled against the social oppression of women. Indeed, the apostle Paul exhorted married women to "submit yourselves unto your own husbands as unto the Lord" (Ephesians 5.22), opposed the right to divorce (1 Corinthians 7.10-11), forbade women to teach (1 Timothy 2.11-12), and mandated: "Let your women keep silence in the churches: for it is not permitted unto them to speak... And if they will learn anything, let them ask their husbands at home..." (1 Corinthians 14.34-5). The antisex maniac Paul denounced all nonmarital sex, and railed against homosexuality, both male and female (Romans 1.26-7).

To be sure, *no* social or political doctrine, in that epoch, could have led to the victorious overthrow of the oppressor classes and the reconstitution of society on a revolutionary basis. For the Roman empire did not spawn a *revolutionary class* capable of tackling such a world historic, liberating mission. Roman imperialism involved a monstrously parasitic political/military superstructure that rested on a precariously narrow and shrinking productive base. There was no largescale manufacturing industry of the sort later developed by modern capitalism; industry remained largely of an artisan type. Once the peasants were ruined and expropriated by the landowners, the only laboring class with some degree of social coherence were the slaves on the plantations. But the inexhaustible supply of slave labor from the conquered provinces meant that the owners had no incentive to reproduce new generations of slaves, and could simply work the existing slaves to death. Shackled in the countryside, the slave gangs were isolated from each other, and from the city, where they could find no class ally capable of giving centralized direction and support to their struggle. The slaves did rise up in sporadic and often magnificent revolts, led by men like Spartacus who were far more radical and heroic than Jesus. But they were in every case crushed, their crucified corpses becoming a common sight along the byways of the countryside.

Social Contradictions Emerge
within the Christian Movement

Given christianity's hopeless task of peacefully equalizing the wealth of a society whose motor force was based on the *in*equality of opposing classes, it was inevitable that social inequalities would emerge within the christian movement itself. As the movement spread over a wide expanse of the empire, it became more difficult to maintain the pure convictions and practices of communal self-organization. "The christians no longer lived like one family," observes Rosa Luxemburg. "Each took charge of his own property, and they no longer offered the whole of their goods to the community, but only the superfluity. The gifts of the richer of them to the general body, losing their character of participation in a common life, soon became simple almsgiving, since rich christians no longer made any use of the common property, and put at the service of the others only a part of what they had, while this part might be greater of smaller according to the goodwill of the donor. Thus in the very heart of christian communism appeared the difference between the rich and the poor... Soon it was only the poor christians...who took part in the communal meals; the rich, having offered a part of their plenty, held themselves apart. The poor lived from the alms tossed to them by the rich, and society again became what it had been. The christians had changed nothing."[5]

Priests who held fast to the original, communitarian principles of the faith carried on a passionate agitational struggle against the creeping christian "revisionism." But they could not overcome the objective logic of history. As the social inequalities within christianity widened, so did the separation between priests and laymen. The priests and especially bishops, originally *elected* by the community members and subject to recall by them, grew into fulltime officeholders and came to separate themselves off from the laypeople as a permanent, privileged caste. When the bishops began organizing themselves into councils, those heading the richer and stronger congregations rose swiftly to prominence and power. At the top of the heap was the bishop of Rome, who installed himself as pope. By the fourth century after Jesus' death, christianity had become so "tamed" and corrupted by the dynamics of class society, that it was coopted as the official, state religion of the Roman empire.[6]

The Pontius Pilates of the Vatican against the Christs of the Peoples' Movements

The Roman catholic church became the leading institution of the feudal tyranny that spread over Europe in the wake of the collapse of the secular Roman empire. Where the Roman procurators had once crushed the peasants of the conquered territories with secular taxes on their produce, now the official church crushed the enserfed peasants with "holy" taxes on their produce: The "tithe" tax imposed by the church upon the peasants, in practice, tended to amount to *far more* than one-tenth of their crops. With this fabulous revenue extracted from the sweat and blood of the peasants, the church built magnificent cathedrals and established a parasitic hierarchy of bishops, cardinals and popes living in luxury, fully irresponsible and unaccountable to their parishioners. The Roman catholic oligarchy carried on in the depraved tradition of the Roman imperial oligarchy, adding only a strident note of hypocrisy: The Vatican, to prevent the fragmentation of its corporate landholdings, imposed the discipline of celibacy on the lower clerics—while the bishops (and often popes as well) amused themselves with their kept mistresses, who often bore them children.

The masses, the neediest among whom were tossed the crumbs left over from the bishops' table, were kept ignorant and illiterate. The bible was hoarded by the bishops' oligarchy in its exclusively Latin form; translations into the living languages of Europe were forbidden. This made it easy for the bishops and their servile priests to distort the gospel of Jesus and his disciples, eliminating all references to salvation for the poor on earth and stressing the concept of unconditional subservience to all earthly authorities, for the sake of salvation in the afterlife.

Once a persecuted sect which had sanctified the poor and scorned the rich, christianity now became a *persecuting* church ruthlessly exploiting the poor through its corporate feudal landholdings, and savagely wiping out any opposition to its worldly and spiritual rule. Those groups and social movements—whether neochristian or pagan—which preached and practiced communal, egalitarian principles similar to those of Jesus and the early disciples, now became the heretical sects which the Vatican set out to exterminate.

The Inquisition and 'Witch' Persecutions

On the other side, the sporadic rise of the capitalist mode of production and commerce in different parts of Europe, undermining the foundations of feudal economy, presented an equally dangerous threat to the absolute authority of the church—as well as an irresistible opportunity for the church to enrich its own coffers. The church's desperate struggle against the restive and heretical oppressed people on the one side, and the rising bourgeoisie on the other, culminated in the inquisition beginning around 1200, and accelerated with the hysterical hunts and judicial executions of "witches" beginning in the late 15th century.

Torture was approved as a method of discovering heresy by pope Innocent 4 in 1257, and later popes reaffirmed the holiness of torture—even *mandating* it as a means of forcing deadly confessions and denunciation of "accomplices" by accused witches. The accused were presumed guilty until proven innocent, a carryover from Roman imperial law, the same law that had executed Jesus. The accused had to pay out of their own pockets for the upkeep of their interrogators, torturers, jailguards, judges and executioners. The rest of the victims' property was scooped up by the church. Pope Innocent 4 noted that the threat of property confiscation hung like a sword suspended over the heads of heretics and secular princes.[8] During "witch" trials, it was customary for the judges and their coteries to have a lavish banquet after each session, and after the execution—all paid for by the victim.

From Protestant Revolution...

The emergent bourgeoisie, despite the catholic terror, was gradually subverting feudal economic and social relations, bringing larger areas of Europe under the sway of the manufacturing system and its market economy. The invention of the mechanical printing press shattered the church's monopoly on intellectual life, and new translations of the bible into the living languages of Europe were produced in massive numbers by the second half of the 15th century. Modern scientific thinkers, their ideas increasingly testable by the new devices being produced by capitalist industry, began to raise their heads—although at the risk of having them cut off by the church. The bourgeoisie began groping for a more flexible religion that would serve their class interests and help them combat the religious, as well as worldly supremacy of the Vatican and its bishops. The result was protestantism, which upheld the authority of the biblical scriptures as against the institutional authority of the church, and upheld bourgeois thrift as against aristocratic profligacy.

Emergent protestantism was the "liberation theology" of its day. A deep class division had developed within the catholic clergy, between its upper and lower layers. Many rural and urban preachers, of mostly plebeian origin and subsisting on crumbs tossed to them by the fatcat bishops, came to champion the cause of the peasants and artisans in the face of the feudal/churchy tyranny. The new, vernacular bibles became their prime ideological weapon against the feudal princes and the church hierarchy. The biblical agitation of Jesus and his disciples against the rich exploiters became the raw material for fiery speeches by the radical, heretical priests to their poor congregations.

And within protestantism, there emerged two contending political camps, the moderate and the revolutionary. The moderate (or "opportunist") camp, headed by Martin Luther in Germany, wanted to break the secular power of the catholic church, but was afraid of a mass mobilization of the peasants, which would threaten to get "out of hand" for the bourgeoisie. Lutheranism reflected the selfish aspirations of the rising bourgeoisie to replace feudal exploitation with capitalist exploitation. Lutheran protestantism needed a social movement against the feudal/catholic order, but needed protection at all costs against a genuine people's revolution that would challenge *bourgeois*, as well as feudal property. The contradictions inherent in this bourgeois strategy were expressed in Luther's wild political vacillations. He preached ardently against the church hierarchy and moneylenders, but conciliated with the *secular* princes/landowners, who were eager to profit from the expropriation of church lands. At first Luther preached violent struggle against the catholic oligarchy. But when the peasants rose up in rebellion throughout Germany in 1525, he shifted to a pacifist stance towards the catholic rulers, and then to violent denunciation of the insurgent peasants, calling on the princes and the armed legions of the "holy Roman empire" (the catholic domain over Germany) to drown the peasants' revolt in blood.

The revolutionary camp in protestantism was headed by the radical priest Thomas Münzer in Germany. Münzer used the more radical preachings of Jesus and his disciples as his *starting point* in raising the peasant masses up for revolution. He emphasized communal and egalitarian social values—which the German peasants readily embraced, preferring their village communities of recent memory to their present enserfment. Demanding the immediate establishment of the kingdom of god *on earth* through the people's violent assault against the "antichrist" cliques of bishops and princes, Münzer preached with a passion and practical political commitment that went far beyond Jesus' insipid spiritualism. He built a network of likeminded revolutionary preachers (including the Anabaptists) extending across Germany, preparing the rural and urban masses for insurrection. When preaching among his revolutionary cothinkers, Münzer broke sharply with christian dogma, declaring that Jesus was a mere man, that the bible was not the final authority for human activity and that the real conditions of social life were fundamental.[9]

When the revolt broke out in 1525, Münzer placed himself at its head, as a political and military leader of the people. Tragically, when he came briefly to power, he was unable to overcome the historical limitations imposed by private property, and found himself conciliating with the bourgeoisie. When the feudal armies prevailed over the insurgent peasants and slaughtered them, Münzer was captured and beheaded.

...to Protestant Reaction

Protestantism, thus purged of its revolutionary wing, soon showed that, far from storming the citadel of catholic reaction in revolutionary fashion, it preferred to *take over* some of the most oppressive features of the catholic tyranny. Jean Calvin, the French protestant leader whose movement established a bourgeois republic in Holland, was a notorious witchburner; his most famous victim was Miguel Serveto, a Spanish physician and theologian who was on the verge of discovering the process of blood circulation when Calvin had him roasted alive. Luther, for his part, closed ranks with the catholic hierarchy by denouncing the Polish catholic priest/astronomer Nicholas Copernicus as a "fool" who "wishes to reverse the entire science of astronomy." Coperni-

cus had discovered that the earth rotates around the sun, rather
than *vice versa*, as the blockheaded bible implied. And the lutheran church excommunicated the German astronomical theorist
Johannes Kepler, who had discovered that the planets rotate not
in perfect circles, but in ellipses about the sun.

The People's Revenge

In France as in Germany, a sharp class division developed
within the catholic clergy. The lower clergy, standing close to the
people and sharing in much of their suffering, eagerly joined in
the people's revolutionary uprising of 1789. As the revolution made
deeper and deeper inroads against big landed property, climaxing
in the Jacobin "dictatorship of public safety" of 1792-3, the
aroused masses waged a red terror against the upper clergy and
their pompous institutions of worship.

One probable mass psychological factor which has not been
taken into account by historians of the French revolution is the
aspect of *historic revenge* for the mass murders perpetrated by the
catholic church against the people, first through the inquisition,
and then through the "witch" persecutions and burnings. A similar mass psychological factor was likely at work in the Spanish
revolution of 1936: The victorious proletarians of Barcelona, led by
the anarchists to crush the reactionary armed forces, carried out
a spontaneous red terror against the catholic clergy, including
many priests and nuns whom the workers identified with the parasitic, oppressive hierarchy. The pre-revolutionary upheaval in Madrid, which led to the overthrow of the Spanish monarchy in 1931,
had begun with the spontaneous burning down of several churches
of the dominant jesuit order. The jesuit catholic hierarchy owned,
and still owns today, an enormous amount of land and other capitalist property in Spain. And the jesuits played a crucial role in
the Spanish colonial conquest of Latin America.

The Church Moves into the Capitalist Epoch

The catholic church eagerly participated in and profited from
the Spanish colonial campaign of genocide, enslavement and land
expropriation of the indigenous peoples of "Latin" America. In
1810, in the face of a bourgeois democratic revolutionary movement sweeping the continent, pope Pius 7 condemned Latin America's liberation from Spanish colonial rule. With the rise of politi-

cally independent, bourgeois nation states in Latin America, the church saw much of its institutional power and feudal style land-holdings reduced. In Central America, an attempt was made to bring the tiny and fragmented countries into a single political and territorial union. The Honduran born radical warrior Francisco Morazán, in the course of his decade long struggle to create and maintain the Central American union (1829-39), took a number of radical bourgeois social measures, including expropriating much of the church's land and secularizing many church schools. At the end of the 19th century, liberal bourgeois governments in the Central American countries carried out agrarian reforms which dealt a sharp blow to the remnants of natural economy, ushering in the epoch of big capitalist and imperialist domination over the land. The liberal land reforms expropriated (semi)communal lands still held by the indigenous peoples on the one hand, and feudal style estates still held by the church on the other.* The church, while still a quite wealthy institution in the Central American context, had to fall back more on its purely "spiritual" mission. This it discharged by supporting a succession of oligarchic and military dictators installed at the service of U.S. imperialism.

In Europe, meanwhile, the hoary old church was showing a remarkable ability to adapt itself to the latest word in capitalist exploitation. The convents, token refuges for the homeless and the desperately poor during the feudal epoch, were transformed into capitalist production enterprises. "The convents became literally hells of capitalist exploitation, all the worse because they took in the labor of women and children. The law case against the Convent of the Good Shepherd in France in 1903 gave a resounding example of these abuses. Little girls 12, 10 and 9 years old were compelled to work in abominable conditions, without rest, ruining their eyes and their health, and were badly nourished and subject to prison discipline."[11]

...and Competes against the Marxist Workers' Movements

By this time, the marxist movement (then called the Social Democracy) was making great headway throughout Europe,

---

*In El Salvador, the church tried to take advantage of the liberal land reform to *increase* its landholdings, joining the state in expropriating the peasants' communal lands and attempting to seize full control over the village community organizations (*cofradías*) in the face of sharp resistance by the peasants. This struggle ended in the destruction of the *cofradías*.[10]

organizing millions of workers into labor unions and consumers' cooperatives, educating them through daily socialist newspapers and pamphlets on the burning political issues of the day, and (supposedly) preparing them for the socialist revolution against capitalism. In this situation, the Vatican moved cleverly to deflect the workers' economic and political movement back into channels harmless to the *status quo*. In 1891, pope Leo 13 issued an encyclical criticizing the manifest evils of capitalism, such as ferocious exploitation in the factories and unrestrained economic competition. At the same time, Leo rejected socialism, and maintained a deathly silence about capitalist *imperialism*. After all, the European powers' mad scramble for Africa and China was opening up vast new territories for missionary work by the church. Thus the church gave its blessings to the European colonial invasion of Africa, including Belgian king Leopold's millionsfold genocide against the peoples of the Congo. Within Europe, the church began organizing christian labor unions and cooperatives, equipped with the newly "enlightened" social doctrine, to compete against the socialist mass organizations.

By 1930, the European Social Democratic parties had gone over heavily to the side of "their own" imperialist bourgeoisies, and the mass based Communist movement appeared as the new threat to capitalist rule. That year pope Pius 11 "updated" Leo's social doctrine, giving it more of a left cover appropriate to the deepening radicalization of Europe's impoverished working masses. Pius was more critical of the rights of private property, and cautiously advocated a "mitigated socialism" (i.e., the *bourgeois* socialism aspired to by the social democracies), as against communism.[12]

The threat of proletarian revolution and its international spread continued to prod the church into mass political action to save itself and capitalism. In the wake of the Cuban revolution of 1958-9, the Christian Democratic parties of Latin America, formed in the years following world war 2, scrambled to the left. Using populist and even anti-imperialist rhetoric while engaging the parties of the landowning oligarchies and military cliques in electoral skirmishes, the Christian Democracies quickly became the parties of the rising, modern middle class layers of urban society in Latin America: the liberal professionals, younger industrialists, engineers and technocrats united with middling layers of the clergy. Agitating for moderate land reform and sending cadres out among the rural masses, the Christian Democracies gained a mass base of support among the middle peasants, as well as the more privileged industrial workers, whom they organized into christian labor unions.* Their reformist work, designed to head off a genuine social revolution of the workers and peasants, meshed neatly with the Alliance for Progress counterinsurgency campaign organized by the catholic U.S. president John Kennedy. The liberal pope John 23, who served from 1958 until his death in 1963, pushed the Vatican's social doctrine a notch further to the left, criticizing the gaping inequalities between the rich countries and the third world countries, proclaiming the need for economic aid to the third world, and admonishing the well fed to provide for the malnourished, without "imperialistic aggrandizement."[14]

In Brazil, the franciscan catholic order, a large corporate landowner, began conducting a "revolution from above" in order to head off a people's revolution from below. Under the bourgeois nationalist Goulart regime, the franciscans returned considerable tracts of land to poor peasants, organizing them into cooperatives. From this movement emerged a major theoretician of liberation theology, the franciscan philosopher Leonardo Boff. Living in a monastery outside Rio de Janeiro, Boff has advocated a grassroots people's church, a church that takes the side of the poor in their social struggles. He has been criticized by the reactionary church hierarchy and government officials for combining marxism with catholicism and creating "a parallel, almost heretical church."** When Goulart was overthrown by a CIA sponsored military coup in 1964, not only the peasant masses but also those franciscan priests who had led them in the land reform movement were ruthlessly suppressed. The big landowners and U.S. transnational corporations feared that the ferment unleashed by the franciscans' agrarian reform would threaten to undermine their permanent pool of supercheap labor, and even develop into a challenge to the whole capitalist system in Brazil.

---

*By the early 1960's, the Christian Democratic labor unions included perhaps 15%-20% of the organized workers in Latin America.[13]

**Today there are over 40,000 christian base communities in Brazil. In September 1984, the Vatican, having investigated Boff's writings for several years, summoned him to Rome for a stern hearing. Friar Boff was accompanied by several supportive Brazilian bishops and cardinals when he came before the Vatican trial commission, which acted as his "judge, prosecutor and jury." On the eve of his hearing, the Vatican issued a statement denouncing liberation theology as "a doctrine dangerous to christian faith." The closed door hearing apparently ended in a stalement, for the time being.

The Second Vatican Council

The second Vatican council of 1962-65, strongly influenced by the social encyclicals of the late pope John 23, gave an official stamp of approval to the church's revitalizing efforts to compete with revolutionary and marxist currents for influence in Latin America's mass movements. The bishops assembled at the Vatican council proclaimed that the church is in and of the world, with concerns ranging well beyond the purely spiritual. Without renouncing their own social and material privileges, they defined the church as a community of equals by baptism; all catholics had talents and responsibilities to share.[15] This encouraged a shift in the church's institutional power downwards from the Vatican oligarchy and the archbishops to local bishops organized in national bishops' conferences, and secular catholic leaders.[16] Vatican 2 "evenhandedly" criticized both communism and capitalism, urging governments to guard against "misuse" of private property.

Thomas Melville, a North American Maryknoll* priest who struggled to put the progressive ideas of Vatican 2 into practice in his work among Guatemalan Indians and was kicked out of the country and suspended by the maryknoll order, wrote: "Many of us have been pleased at the attention that Latin America received from John Kennedy and pope John, but not with the results. And what are these results? Simply that the old order of injustice and tyranny has been strengthened and not weakened by this interest."[17]

The Medellin Conference, 1968:
The Bishops Espouse Liberation Theology

Three years after Vatican 2 ended, bishops from all over Latin America gathered in Medellín, Colombia to further elaborate the

*The Maryknoll Missioners, a North American order of the catholic church, were founded in 1911, and began their missionary work in China. Functioning as a humanitarian arm of U.S. imperialism in Asia, the maryknoll order spread to Korea and Japan. It was suppressed in the Japanese empire after the outbreak of war between the U.S. and Japan in 1941, but continued work in China until the triumph of the revolution there. Maryknoll missionaries entered Latin America in 1942, and Africa in the 1950's. A growing rift between the radicalizing maryknoll nuns, priests and layworkers and the conservative hierarchy of the order led to a radicalization of the leadership itself in the 1970's, with women coming to play a prominent leadership role. Maryknoll missionaries have since worked closely with the christian base community movement in El Salvador. In December 1980, four maryknoll sisters were raped and murdered by the national guard outside San Salvador.

church's social doctrine. "Preferential option for the poor" was their keynote theme. "For the first time in Latin America, church prelates recognized that evil may be embodied in social institutions that perpetuate poverty and injustice. The bishops followed this finding with an analysis of the violence inherent in such unjust social structures."[18] They declared that the church must "defend the rights of the oppressed" and "denounce the unjust action of world powers that works against selfdetermination of weaker nations."[19] Urging that liberation theology be put into practice through promoting grassroots organizations of the oppressed people, the bishops stressed the formation of *christian base communities* in Latin America. They even declared that, in situations of severe socioeconomic injustice reinforced by institutional violence, armed resistance was not immoral.[20]

The historical moment was uniquely ripe for the bishops of Latin America to voice such a radical, even revolutionary sounding doctrine and formula for social practice to their priests, nuns and layworkers throughout the continent. The armed revolutionary movements inspired by the Cuban revolution had been smashed, thanks mainly to the strategic ineptitude of their *foco* designs and their resultant lack of an active mass base of support (see ch. 4). Che Guevara had been captured and murdered by the U.S. advised counterinsurgency campaign in Bolivia, and his isolated movement liquidated. Camilo Torres, a rural priest in Colombia who had broken with christian pacifism to join the revolutionary guerrilla movement, had suffered a similar fate. The Guatemalan guerrilla groups were being ruthlessly hunted down and killed, along with thousands of unarmed peasants. The Cuban regime, meanwhile, was beginning to lose its inspirational force for the radical youth of Latin America, as the rising state/party bureaucracy headed by Castro disarmed the Cuban workers, brought the Committees for the Defense of the Revolution under its political thumb, and became more and more a vassal of the conservative Soviet bureaucracy. The "official" Communist parties of Latin America remained as opportunist and anti-revolutionary as ever, ensconced in the bureaucratic apparatuses of the labor unions of the relatively privileged urban workers, holding themselves aloof from the deepening misery of the rural masses, and engaging in endless electoral coalitions with bourgeois opposition parties like the christian democrats and social democrats.

An enormous vacuum of social and political leadership had thus been created in the face of the worsening conditions of land expropriation and desperate poverty of the masses of the countryside and urban shantytowns. Into this vacuum stepped the movement of liberation theology. As priests, nuns and church layworkers studied the documents of Vatican 2 and Medellín with intense interest and motivation, the bishops of Central America took stock of the fact that their priests were bunched up in the cities, leaving vast sections of the rural masses outside the institutional sway of the church. The liberal bishops set the christian base community movement into motion, deploying more priests and nuns to the countryside and allowing for more flexible programs to train catechists (lay teachers) and "delegates of the word" (lay preachers).

Fired by a new sense of mission, priests taught the social gospel to idealistic youths recruited in the cities. Many of these youths became leading cadres in the christian base communities in the countryside. By the mid-1970's, liberation theology had been translated into a mass social and political movement, rallying tens of thousands of peasants and farm laborers to build selfgoverning agrarian cooperatives, which had to struggle to expand under the guns of the reactionary army and the landowners' death squads. This new christian movement, which in fact marked a liberating return to the *old* communitarian values of the *early* christian movement, reached far deeper and more dynamically among the superexploited masses than did the older Christian Democratic organizations. The liberation theology movement, founded upon the crushing defeat of the revolutionary insurgencies of the 1960's, became the mass mobilizing and energizing force that prepared the way for the mass based revolutionary insurgencies of the 1970's and 1980's. And nowhere was this more true than in El Salvador.

El Salvador

With its dense population and rapid communications between city and countryside, El Salvador provided fertile soil for the growth of the christian base community movement. In a sharp break with the church's traditional practice, the priests, nuns, catechists and lay preachers of liberation theology did not attempt to impose the new organizations from above. Instead of treating the people with condescending contempt, as passive objects to be manipulated into the church's financial and spiritual racket, the apostles of liberation theology relied from the start on the people's active initiative and capacity for selfgovernment. The priest or religious leader of the fledgling community *served* the community as a facilitator or resource person. The people themselves decided, through democratic participation and decisionmaking, the tasks and activities of the communities. And these tasks inevitably involved collective practical work to overcome the material misery and social injustices confronting the people. The base communities organized agrarian cooperatives and provided literacy classes and paramedical training for their members.

Maryknoll sister Joan Petrik, who worked among the peasants of the mountains of La Libertad for seven years, related that when she first arrived in Tamanique, "every time a child died, the family would say 'It's the will of God.' But after the people became involved in the christian communities that attitude began to change. And after a year or so I no longer heard people in the communities saying that. After a while they began to say, *'The system caused this.'"* The psychological transformation of the participating peasants was visible in the way they carried themselves daily. Community members, as Petrik recalled, would "walk upright, their heads held high, with selfconfidence."[21]* Peasants not involved in the base community movement, on the other hand, continued to shuffle along with their heads bowed, in the old posture of the submissive slave.

The christian base community movement greatly expanded the breadth and depth of the rural class struggle. While the apostles of liberation theology were by no means preaching the revolutionary overthrow of the big landowners and their armed forces, the landowners viewed the agrarian cooperatives as a dangerous threat to their ready supply of supercheap plantation labor. The ruling oligarchy and its military clique in San Salvador clamped

---

*"We started being less afraid of priests," relates Manlio Argueta through a fictional peasant woman of Chalatenango, where liberationist priests helped organize agrarian cooperatives. "[The traditional priests] used to instill fear in us; we believed they were like magicians who could annihilate us with the simplest gesture. Besides, we didn't trust them. They would speak in hoarse voices, as if from other worlds or from the profundities of God. It seemed as if they walked on air, from here to there, in their long black robes. They'd ask us for a few pounds of corn and some chickens. We couldn't say no because we considered it a sin to deny anything to a priest of the Church."[22] The liberationist priests broke sharply with this parasitic relationship towards the peasants.

down with increasing violence against the christian base community movement and the popular movement in general. As catholic priests, layworkers and community members were cut down by the bullets of the oligarchy, the bishops were compelled to choose sides—either with the people and their own radical priests, or with the oligarchy. Under the radicalizing pressure from their base, some bishops, including archbishop Luis Chávez y González, took the side of the people.

In late 1974, the national guard killed six coffee workers in Tecoluca. When the bishops condemned the massacre, colonel Molina, military dictator at the time, blamed the activities of local priests for the incident. In July 1975, the military attacked a peaceful demonstration of students in San Salvador, who were protesting the invasion of the University of El Salvador's Santa Ana campus. Over 37 students were killed. Archbishop Chávez and other clerics held a mass for the victims. Also protesting the massacre, a group of priests, peasants, workers and students occupied the metropolitan cathedral for a week.[23]

The jesuit Universidad Centroamericana José Simeón Cañas (UCA) declared in a manifesto that "an indiscriminate...repression has been unleashed by private persons, pressure groups and above all...the police and security bodies. We condemn...the violence of a tremendously unequal distribution of land, income and social and political power which favors a small part of the population and oppresses, dispossesses and denies the possibility of a dignified life to the majority of Salvadorans." UCA was bombed six times during 1976.[24]

What made the UCA rectors' denunciation of the oligarchy and its state repression all the more remarkable was that UCA had been founded as a catholic university in 1966 *at the behest of*, and with funding from the oligarchy, who were afraid of sending their children to the autonomous and secular University of El Salvador. In the 1970's the national university indeed became the focal point of revolutionary political and cultural ferment unsurpassed in Central America, inspiring many youths from middle class families to stake their lives on revolutionary ideas and passions. But UCA did not turn out to be the "safe," reactionary haven from radical social and political teachings that the oligarchs had expected. The jesuit educators of UCA, embracing liberation theology, were determined to expand the social and moral horizons of the children of the oligarchy and bourgeoisie who had become their students.

Not afraid to counteract the class interest of their financial bene-
factors, UCA's jesuit rectors issued a manifesto in 1970 calling for
agrarian reform.[25]

The most dramatic expression of the social and political ferment
brewing at UCA was the political trajectory of Salvador Samayoa,
a philosophy student of the jesuits who went on to become a
member of the UCA faculty. Samayoa became minister of education in the first "radical civilian/military junta" following the
ouster of general Romero in October 1979. As the intensifying
military repression shattered the reformist illusions of the liberal
ministers and drove them out of the government, Samayoa resigned his government post at the beginning of 1980. Six days
later, the 29-year-old Samayoa made the surprise announcement
that he was joining the revolutionary FPL. He later stated in an
interview: "...As a university teacher, I've always been concerned
with following the political lines—both theoretical and in practice
—of different trends the popular movement has followed... And it
seems to me that, so far, the organization with the most coherent,
solid and consistent line for combining the different revolutionary
instruments and the armed struggle with the mass movement is
precisely the FPL."[26] Samayoa then took to task the urban liberal
intelligentsia, including his jesuit mentors, for maintaining a
purely moral sympathy with the popular movement and failing to
make an active practical commitment: "...I feel the most liberal
academic and intellectual petty-bourgeois sectors, which is where
I come from, have committed the very serious mistake of, in practice, having our backs to the popular movement. We've committed
the error of failing to learn to share the people's lives and feel in
the heat of struggle the correctness of their principles and
methods."[27]

Today, in the face of repeated bomb attacks and death threats,
UCA continues to produce the only legal oppositional publications
in El Salvador, including the impressively detailed and courageous
journal, *Eca (Estudios Centroamericanos)*. But UCA's publications have a very small circulation, confined basically to urban
intellectuals and politicians, and failing to connect with the working masses.

Archbishop Romero and the People's Movement

When archbishop Chávez retired in 1976, the Vatican appointed
the conservative bishop Oscar Arnulfo Romero to replace him.

Romero's appointment was "greeted with widespread dismay throughout the archdiocese."[28] Chávez and the radical priests and layworkers had hoped the new archbishop would be Arturo Rivera y Damas, auxiliary bishop since 1960 and the boldest exponent of liberation theology within the church hierarchy. In 1970, Rivera and monseñor Ricardo Urioste had sat in at the defense minister's office to secure the release of José Inocencio Alas, a young priest and peasant movement activist who, on the eve of presenting the church's official position in support of land reform, had been kidnapped, tortured and nearly murdered. Neither the Vatican nor the dictatorship wanted Rivera y Damas as archbishop. "We don't want anyone who is going to oppose the government," a cardinal told Rivera in Rome.[29] Romero, by contrast, was considered by the leaders of the people's church to be a "priest of the oligarchy," and the oligarchy seemed content with his appointment. But they were in for a surprise.

One day after he was installed as archbishop, Romero went to meet with president dictator Molina, and requested the release of Rafael Barahona, a radical priest who had been arrested and tortured two days earlier. "President Molina's response was: 'I will release Barahona, but you cannot ask us to treat them any differently until they go back to their basic business, which is religion. These priests of yours,' Molina continued, 'have become politicians, and I hold you responsible for their behavior.' Romero looked Molina straight in the eye. 'With all due respect, Mr. President,' the archbishop said, 'we take our orders from someone higher.'"[30]

Three weeks later, on 12 March 1977, the jesuit priest Rutilio Grande was assassinated along with two parishioners. Grande, a close friend of Romero, had organized the base communities in Aguilares, a town of 10,000 people in a sugarcane region 32 kilometers north of San Salvador. Declaring to the peasants and farmworkers that "God is not in the clouds, lying in a hammock; God acts and wants you to build the kingdom here on earth," Grande and his colleagues had catalyzed a peaceful strike by sugar mill workers for a wage hike—an event which caused moral conflict for Grande, who had not intended his consciousness raising work to result in mass organization and political action.[31]

For Romero, the assassination of Grande was a decisive turning point. He made a dramatic public denunciation of the murder, pointing his finger at the government. Defying Molina's state of siege, he called for public protest demonstrations. In a letter to Molina, Romero declared that the church would boycott all government functions until all the facts about Grande's assassination were brought to light. He went on to demand an end to repression against the people, an explanation of the murders of other priests and catechists, and the return of priests deported by the dictatorship.[32]

The oligarchy and its hired thugs continued to attack. In May 1977, the jesuit priest Alfonso Navarro Oviedo was murdered by a rightist death squad, which went on to issue an ultimatum threatening the entire jesuit order with death unless they left El Salvador within 30 days. Leaflets appearing in rich San Salvador neighborhoods shrieked, "Be a Patriot! Kill a Priest!"[33] In May the military, not content with having murdered the founder of the Aguilares christian base community movement (Rutilio Grande), forcibly evicted some 150 families who had been occupying farmland there for nearly a month. Killing hundreds of people in the operation, the military displayed its intent to wipe out the new christian movement. It destroyed the insides of a local church and established its barracks there.

Archbishop Romero was deeply affected by this massacre and liquidation of the people's church. For the second time since becoming archbishop, he asked priests to open their homes and church doors to the refugees from the military terror. And for the first time, he met with leaders of the popular organizations. The limits of purely peaceful mass protest actions were becoming clear. And, as he strove to defend what was new, healthy and vibrant in his church, the archbishop was propelled by the ruthless logic of the class struggle into a position where he stood considerably closer to the revolutionary movement than to the military/oligarchic dictatorship.

For the first time in world history, the institutional leadership of a national catholic church became an active supporter of a mass movement of the laboring classes that was beginning to pose a revolutionary threat to the oppressor class. Archbishop Romero used the church's radio station, YSAX, to broadcast liberation theology and rigorous denunciations of the military/death-squad terror throughout the country. His Sunday morning mass, beginning at 8:00 and lasting around two hours, soon became the most widely listened to radio program in El Salvador. From the stalls of San Salvador's central market to remote villages where no priest was present, the masses of people listened avidly to the archbishop over YSAX radio. Using a format inspired by liberation theology, Romero would take citations of scripture as points of departure to discuss the reality of social and political life in El Salvador. The end of his Sunday morning broadcast would be devoted to reading every documented case of people who had been attacked, kidnapped, tortured, or killed in the previous week.

In classic christian tradition, Romero condemned violence against *all* individuals, whether the person involved was a poor peasant or a fascist landowner. But the reality of systematic state and fascist repression against the masses and all their social, religious and political organizations assured that Romero's rigorous account of every known case of torture, kidnapping and assassination would amount to a sharp exposure and denunciation of the military regime.[34]

With the sermons broadcast over YSAX reaching an estimated 73% of the rural population and 47% of the urban, archbishop Romero became popularly known as "the voice of those who have no voice." The regime wasted little time in struggling to strangle this voice. Between 1977 and 1979, the YSAX transmitter or antenna was bombed ten times.[35] And in April 1979, the national association for private enterprise—the organization of the big bourgeoisie, including the oligarchy—demanded Romero's arrest and imprisonment.

The Reactionary Church Hierarchy

Archbishop Romero's remarkable radicalization and emergence as a popular spokesman for the politically aroused masses gave many people outside of El Salvador the impression that the Salvadoran church *as a whole* had radicalized and essentially merged with the national liberation movement of the workers and peasants. This was far from being the case. For one thing, Romero himself, while developing a stance of sincere sympathy and practical solidarity with the popular organizations, continued to condemn the tactics of *red terror* against the oligarchy and its agents, tactics used by the revolutionary organizations as a necessary part of their struggle to overthrow the regime; he publicly criticized, in addition to leftist assassinations of ORDEN members, leftist kidnappings of members of the oligarchy in an attempt to free their imprisoned comrades and extract big ransom money from the oligarchy to purchase desperately needed arms. And, while women were pursuing and ever more prominent role at all levels of the people's movement, including the armed struggle, Romero maintained the church's traditional antiwoman doctrine and practice: The priesthood continued to be an all male organization, divorce was still prohibited within the church, and abortion still rejected as "murder."

Moreover, archbishop Romero, in his consistent practical adherence to the liberation theological documents of Vatican 2 and Medellín under the gun of the Salvadoran dictatorship, was clearly an *exceptional* figure within a church hierarchy that was still *generally reactionary*. Besides Romero, the only Salvadoran bishop who was seriously opposing the military dictatorship was Rivera y Damas. All the other bishops have continued actively *supporting* the dictatorship. Perhaps the most notorious is the bishop of San Miguel, José Eduardo Alvarez. Alvarez is himself a colonel in the Salvadoran army, and is reportedly seldom seen out of his army uniform.[36] Freddy Delgado, secretary general of the *Comisión Episcopal de El Salvador* (CEDES), the organization of the church hierarchy, is reputed to be a member of the White Warriors Union, a paramilitary death squad organized in the 1970's by the fascist Roberto d'Aubuissón.[37] Another rightist bishop was Pedro Arnoldo Aparicio of San Vicente. Aparicio, a feudal style racketeer, organized some 15,000 of his peasant parishioners into *"cofradías"* ("confraternities"),* with each member required to pay monthly dues of one *colon.*** Indoctrinating his *cofradías* with Vatican style "slave theology," Aparicio grew rich off the scheme.

Alvarez and Aparicio led the reactionary bishops' attack against the people's church, and against archbishop Romero during his stormy three year term. When in 1975, the FPL put out an open letter to all "progressive priests" praising them for educating the poor and requesting their collaboration in the struggle, Alvarez, Aparicio and bishop Barrera of Santa Ana publicly denounced the popular mass organizations supported by the radical priests as "atheistic" and "materialistic."[38] In 1977, 10 priests and 300 church layworkers from Aparicio's diocese issued a letter

*The term *cofradía* had originally been used to describe the indigenous people's villages based on communal landownership. The Spanish monarchy awarded the church official control over the *cofradías* in the 18th century.

**One Salvadoran *colon* exchanges for about 25¢ (U.S.) on the illegal market. But for those peasants and farmworkers earning the equivalent of one or two dollars a day, these monthly dues could well be a hardship.

criticizing the *papal nuncio* (resident Vatican diplomat in El Salvador) for supporting the government instead of archbishop Romero in the face of bloody state repression. Aparacio suspended all ten priests. Each of them was then visited separately by the national guard and told he was "fair game" because his bishop had rejected him. Although the priests were eventually reinstated by the Vatican, they had been given a clear message that bishop Aparacio was aligned with the military regime against them and their people's movement. [39]

Democratic Bishops vs. Fascist Bishops

In August 1978, Romero and Rivera y Damas issued a pastoral letter on "The Church and the Popular Political Organizations." It upheld the popular organizations as the only vehicles open to the majority of Salvadorans for political participation, and detailed the state repression against them. It concluded by calling for a dialog between the popular organizations and the church—thus giving official support and encouragement to the already existing relationships between the christian base communities and the popular organizations.

Soon afterwards, the other bishops issued a public declaration *prohibiting* priests and layworkers from involvement with the popular organizations. Warning against the threat of marxism, the rightist bishops rejected any relationship between the church and the popular organizations. The bishops' open "slaveowners' rebellion" against archbishop Romero was given massive coverage in El Salvador's reactionary bourgeois press.

In November 1978 Ernesto Barrera, a priest who had joined the revolutionary FPL, was killed in combat. Romero, though "at first shocked and confused" by the event, decided to attend Barrera's funeral. [40] The archbishop's act of solidarity with the fallen revolutionary priest formed a stunning counterpoint with his refusal, in July 1977, to attend the inauguration of general Carlos Humberto Romero as president, as he did not want to give his blessings to a regime that was sure to continue the repression and corruption. Archbishop Romero was now moving into antagonistic conflict with the oligarchy—and with the rightist bishops, the Vatican, and the U.S. embassy, which were all pressuring him to tone down his opposition to the regime.

Oscar Romero becomes archbishop, February 1977. Flanking Romero are his predecessor, Luis Chavez y Gonzalez (left) and his successor, Arturo Rivera y Damas (right). At far right is Rutilio Grande, the radical Jesuit priest and friend of Romero. Grande was assassinated three weeks later.

Eca

Archbishop Romero sided with the people in deeds as well as words. (Eca)

Ernesto Cardenal (center, wearing beret) is a popular poet, trappist catholic priest, and minister of culture in the sandinista government. Along with his brother Fernando, Miguel d'Escoto and Edgar Parrales, he has staved off the pope's repeated demands that he resign from his government post.

From a huge, handpainted billboard erected by Nicaragua's christian base communities on the occasion of the pope's visit in March 1983. The banner reads: "John Paul: Welcome to Free Nicaragua—Thanks to God and the Revolution."

The Puebla Bishops' Conference, 1979

By now, the Vatican oligarchy had drifted heavily back to the right since the heady days of the second Vatican council (1962-65). The Vatican and most of Latin America's bishops had intended their promulgation of liberation theology as a reformist *alternative* to social revolution, not as an energizing *aid* to the revolution. But the radical priests, nuns, and youthful layworkers of Central America had taken liberation theology much farther in practice than the pope and bishops wanted to go. Under the explosive conditions of class conflict in Central America, where even the most peaceful attempts at rural mass organization and mobilization were murderously suppressed by the ruling oligarchies, the activists of the christian base community movement were confronted with a clearcut choice: either collaborate with the armed revolutionary organizations, or face extermination as a social and religious movement at the hands of the oligarchy's forces. The objective logic of incipient civil war in Nicaragua, El Salvador and Guatemala meant that the bishops' lofty exhortation for the church to "take the side of the poor" had to be translated, in grassroots practice, into taking the side of the workers' and peasants' revolution.

The catholic hierarchy's tactic, begun in the early 1960's, of promoting Christian Democratic parties as an "enlightened," liberal reformist buffer between the big bourgeoisie and the revolutionary Left had failed in Central America: Hundreds of christian democratic youths, inspired by liberation theology and the rise of the rural class struggle in which many of them participated, were breaking with the insipid reformism of their upper middleclass parents and joining the revolutionary armed struggle. In El Salvador, they formed the ERP, which launched the first systematic campaign of guerrilla warfare against the regime in the early 1970's.* In Nicaragua, they formed the *tercerista* faction of the FSLN, which played a galvanizing role in the revolution of September 1978 and was to organize the revolutionary combat along the southern front in the June/July 1979 civil war that crushed the Somoza regime.

*The most famous example of the "generation gap" formed by the gathering of revolutionary forces in El Salvador is the family of José Antonio Morales Erlich, secretary general of the Christian Democratic party, who served as agrarian reform minister in the first Duarte government (1980-82). In the 1970's, Morales Erlich's two sons joined the ERP, and thus came to fight the armed forces of their father's regime in the countryside.

None of this sat well with the Vatican and the majority of Latin America's bishops. From the standpoint of the institutional catholic church—still a big capitalist corporate enterprise on a world scale—the genie of liberation theology, uncorked by the hierarchy in the late 1960's, had developed far too worldly ways, merging far too dangerously with the specter of "communism" (workers' and peasants' revolution); the genie had to be shoved back into the holy water bottle.

The February 1979 Latin American bishops' conference in Puebla, Mexico, personally presided over by pope John Paul 2, marked a sharp doctrinal shift back to the right from the Medellín bishops' conference of 1968. Deploring the growing rift within the church, the pope counterposed purely churchy, spiritual work among the masses to the mass self-organizing around the people's material and social needs emphasized by the christian base communities. As the pope recalled in his 29 June 1982 letter to Nicaragua's archbishop Obando (see below): "...When I myself, in my keynote speech at the Puebla assembly, voiced serious reservations about the denomination 'Church which is born of the People,' I had in mind those dangers which I have just noted."[41]

To be sure, the bishops' final statements at Puebla called capitalism "idolatry of riches in individual form," and denounced repression—reflecting the social and moral pressure that the base community movements were exerting on the bishops. But they also categorically denounced class struggle and marxism.

Romero and the 'Radical Civilian/Military Regime'

The 15 October 1979 coup by "progressive" junior officers, which led to a "civilian/military" regime pledged to deep social reforms, sharpened the contradictions of Salvadoran political life. The middleclass democratic sectors, opposed to oligarchic rule but wary of the revolutionary masses, lacked a coherent solution to the social and political crisis; they were thrown into confusion by the complex and deceptive sequence of events begun when "progressive" politicians and administrators entered a government sitting atop a still intact military dictatorship. Several professors and rectors from the jesuit university (UCA) had been involved in the political preparations for the coup, and ten men from UCA joined the new government.[42]

Archbishop Romero, showing that he had yet to burn his bridges to the liberal bourgeoisie, asked the people and their organizations to reserve judgment on the new government, giving the civilian/military junta a grace period to carry out its promised reforms. This brought Romero some direct criticism from radical young priests of the base community movement, who were personally in touch with the sharpening rural repression being unleashed by the junta under the façade of reform.[43]

By the beginning of 1980 Guillermo Ungo and the other liberal junta members, exasperated that the military officers refused to heed their calls for nonviolence towards the people, resigned from the government. They were replaced by Christian Democratic leaders, soon headed by José Napoleón Duarte. The line of demarcation between the Christian Democracy and the people's church now became a line drawn in blood. Archbishop Romero declared: "The events of this week prove that neither the junta nor the Christian Democrats are governing this country... The real power is in the hands of the most repressive sector of the armed forces. If the junta members do not wish to be accomplices in these abuses of power and outright criminal behavior, they should publicly announce the names of those responsible and apply the necessary sanctions, for their hands are red with blood."[44] But Duarte, Morales Erlich and their Christian Democratic cronies did not heed Romero's appeal, and continued fronting for the military/-death-squad dictatorship.

Romero vs. the Pope

Romero's sharpening radicalization into an alliance with the revolutionary mass movement also set him on a collision course with the Vatican. In a private session with archbishop Romero, pope John Paul 2 evidently scolded him for flirting with communism by throwing his support to the people's church and the popular organizations in the incipient civil war. Romero's response to the pope was humble but firm. "Holy Father," he declared to the pope in a 10 February 1980 homily, "in my country it is very dangerous to speak of anticommunism, because anticommunism is the banner brandished by the Right, not out of love of christian sentiments, but out of an impulse to safeguard their selfish interests."[45]

Six weeks later, and one day after publicly urging army soldiers to disobey their officers' orders to slaughter the people, Romero was gunned down by a rightist death squad member (see ch. 1).

As Rivera y Damas Moves to the Right...

Arturo Rivera y Damas was the only one of El Salvador's four bishops to attend archbishop Romero's funeral; the other three bishops (Alvarez, Aparicio and Barrera) were all on the side of Romero's murderers. Rivera y Damas, whose record of courageous opposition to the military regime predated Romero's radicalization by several years, became acting archbishop—with a loaded gun pressing against his head from the start. Rivera continued espousing liberation theology and working with the church's legal aid office (*Socorro Jurídico*) to expose and denounce military/-death-squad repression. But he markedly shifted his emphasis away from Romero's passionate partisanship for the people's movement, to a more "evenhanded" approach to the developing civil war—which did not fundamentally challenge the oligarchic regime.

Whereas Romero directed the great bulk of his denunciations against the reactionary violence of the military and the Right, Rivera has more heavily "counterbalanced" his denunciations of military/rightist terror with denunciations of leftist violence and economic sabotage actions. Whereas Romero, in his foreign policy, directed his criticisms against the U.S. government for its massive military support to the Salvadoran dictatorship, Rivera has "evenhandedly" called for a halt to U.S. military support to the regime while warning of the danger of "Soviet domination" over El Salvador in the event of an FMLN victory in the civil war. And he suspended a group of liberationist priests from Belgium whom he considered too close to the FMLN in their rural work.

...The People's Church Struggles for its Life

As the Duarte/military regime launched murderous assaults against the liberation theology activists, against the church radio station, and against catholic schools and colleges, the people's church movement was practically exterminated in those areas of El Salvador under the government's control. The people's church was now free to work and flourish only in those zones liberated by the FMLN.

Under these conditions, Rivera's treacherous balancing act between the regime and the people's movement could in no way allow him to remain in active contact with the base communities. As the bloc of reactionary bishops and the pope breathed pungent incense down Rivera's neck, his church drifted away from the liberation struggle of the people, and back towards its old institutional mold. "The power derived from truth, credibility and solidarity with the people is being replaced by power derived from being in authority," wrote the jesuit commentator Iván D. Paredes in his 1982 article, "Evolution of the Salvadoran Church."[46] "Although the Church continues looking out for the poor, it seems more and more to be looking out for itself."[47] With the institutional church less inclined to risk its safety to defend the beleaguered masses, "the word of the Church no longer enters into the collective consciousness as it used to, nor is it considered a compelling point of reference for the knowledge or interpretation of what's happening in the country."[48]

Just after Romero's assassination, the christian base communities of the countryside and urban shantytowns joined together to form the *Coordinador Nacional de la Iglesia Popular* (CONIP—National Coordinator of the People's Church). CONIP continued the people's church's struggle against repression and for social justice, now without the active support of the archbishop. In December 1980, priests and nuns from CONIP occupied San Salvador's metropolitan cathedral to denounce the continuing wave of murders of church activists, including the four maryknoll women missionaries from North America. Bishop Aparicio, in his 28 December 1980 homily, demanded excommunication for all CONIP members and justified the death of religious activists—including archbishop Romero—who "incited rebellion."[49]

The People's Church vs. the Oligarchy's Church

The struggle between CONIP (the people's church leadership) and CEDES (the church hierarchy's organization, dominated by the rightist bishops) became a direct reflection of the civil war raging between the laboring masses and the bourgeois oligarchy. With most of its base communities now located in the FMLN liberated zones, CONIP publicly declared the FDR/FMLN as the "authentic representatives" of the Salvadoran people.[50] In January 1982 CEDES, led by bishop/colonel Alvarez, accused CONIP of "promoting a schism within the catholic church" and exhorted the faithful to "recognize the authority of the bishops as representatives of the holy father." CONIP's public response held that the bishops had "a biased position which reduces their moral authority." CONIP went on to denounce bishops Alvarez and Aparicio for collaborating with the military in its bloody attacks against CONIP activists occupying cathedrals.[51]

In October 1982 several bishops, already notorious for blessing helicopters arriving fresh from the U.S., met with the high command of the Salvadoran armed forces. After the meeting, bishop Aparicio denounced 30 priests for working with the FMLN. Archbishop Rivera, in his sermon the following Sunday, defended the clergy in the FMLN liberated zones, stating that church activists should continue conducting their work wherever the people are.[52] On the other hand, Rivera chided the people's church by remarking: "...In those areas where it has grown and developed, it has become a little too ideological, and this has created some problems of division."[53]

Rivera's Balancing Act

If the struggle between CONIP and CEDES reflects the civil war between the laboring masses and the oligarchy, then the political behavior of Rivera y Damas since becoming archbishop reflects the political vacillations of the liberal bourgeoisie between the two warring camps. Like the bourgeois liberal FDR leadership in exile (headed by the social democrat Guillermo Ungo and the christian democrat Rubén Zamora), Rivera has stressed "*reconciliation*" between the two sides of the civil war. Calling for a dialog towards a "political solution" to the war, he supports the antirevolutionary diplomatic efforts of the Contadora group (see ch. 1), and offers his services as a mediator in negotiations between the FMLN and the dictatorship—as in the token "peace talks" held at La Palma on 15 October 1984.

Prior to the March 1982 elections to the constituent assembly, Rivera expressed doubts about the fairness of the process, from which the FDR/FMLN was violently excluded. However, he evidently came under pressure from the Vatican and U.S. embassy to toe the official line that the elections represented a great "victory for democracy." The elections were characterized by systematic vote rigging; their final results, as was soon revealed, were determined by secret negotiations between the big bourgeois parties, presided over by the U.S. ambassador. Yet Rivera praised the "massive turnout" at the polls, hailing it as a mandate for a peaceful solution, as the people were "tired of violence." He cynically overlooked the fact that the working people were *coerced* into voting by the mechanism of having their personal ID cards stamped when they arrived at the polls (lack of the proper stamp becoming possible grounds for firing and/or death squad terror); and even then, the real vote count was grossly inflated by the interested bourgeois parties and the U.S. embassy—as UCA (jesuit university) researchers later discovered.[54] When the rightist Magaña government installed through the elections reversed the token and demagogic agrarian reform pursued by the Duarte regime, Rivera reversed his position again, becoming retrospectively critical of the 1982 elections and deploring the violently repressive atmosphere preceding the March 1984 elections.

Is the People's Church Struggling to Win?

The cadres of the people's church, for their part, are at a grave disadvantage in their struggle against the reactionary bishops and the oligarchy. For while the bishops clearly aim to liquidate the people's church, the *people's church does not aim to overthrow the reactionary hierarchy.* CONIP has stated explicitly that it does *not* define itself "as a parallel church. [CONIP] is not a church that grew out of the people in opposition to the church of hierarchy."[55] CONIP declares itself open to the poor, the popular organizations, *and* the church hierarchy. This would be like a "people's church" in the southern U.S. in 1863 declaring itself open to the slaves, the radical abolitionists, *and* the slaveowners. The selfdefeating christian doctrine of "turn the other cheek" to the murderous exploiters and their churchy mouthpieces continues to exert its retarding and demoralizing effect on the revolutionary movement of the masses.

To be sure, CONIP, with its insistence on tying its strongest hand behind its back in the social and political liberation struggle, is not fundamentally at odds with the policy of the "marxist-leninist" leaders of the FMLN. For while the oligarchy and its armed forces clearly aim to liquidate the armed revolution, the *FMLN leaders do not aim to liquidate the government's armed forces,* which form the linchpin of capitalist rule in El Salvador.* Rather, they propose to *"integrate"* the revolutionary FMLN army with the counterrevolutionary government army—just as CONIP proposes to "integrate" the progressive christian base communities with the reactionary church hierarchy. Despite their great

---

*The most explicit denial of any intent by the FMLN to destroy the reactionary armed forces has come from *comandante* Joaquín Villalobos, head of the ERP (see ch. 1).

courage and fortitude in the struggle, the CONIP cadres and FMLN leaders have shown that *they do not take their liberating historic mission seriously.* They are less clearheaded and principled in conducting their revolutionary struggle than are the leaders of the oligarchy and U.S. imperialism in conducting their *counter*revolutionary struggle. And this poses the greatest danger to the Salvadoran revolution.

The Pope's Visit

Pope John Paul 2 set the tempo for his dramatic sweep through Central America in March 1983 in his speech from Panamá to the rural masses of the region: "In your search for a better [?] justice and elevation, you cannot let yourself be dragged along by the temptation of violence, of guerrilla warfare or of the egoistic class struggle," because "it is not the road of Jesus christ, nor of the church, nor of your christian faith."[56] The pope would have the masses believe that the struggle by the exploited, starving majority to wrest control of society from the hands of the exploiting minority is "egoistic"—whereas the transnational Vatican bank is an altruistic institution.

Upon his arrival at San Salvador's airport, the pope cheerily greeted the country's ruling, rightist politicians—including president of the constituent assembly d'Aubuissón, murderer of archbishop Romero. The streets of the capital were thronged with people from a broad array of social classes, waiting patiently in the sweltering sun for the pope's appearance and motorcade through the city. The rightist daily *La Prensa Gráfica* gave vent to the messianic illusions in the pope's visit held by broad sections of the masses: "Family groups...patiently awaited the passage of the Holy Father and in each face...hope and faith were demonstrating, with fortitude and courage, that the days of suffering and bitterness were already being left behind..."[57] Naturally the editors of *La Prensa Gráfica*, without demonstrating much fortitude and courage of their own, were hoping that the pope's "pacifying" visit would help assure an outcome to the civil war favorable to the bourgeoisie.

The pope's motorcade made a startling detour from its planned route through the capital city, taking him to the metropolitan cathedral. There, the pope gave an unexpected homily in memory of archbishop Romero. He praised Romero as a "zealous pastor, whom the love of God and service to his brothers led to give up his own life in a violent manner, while he was celebrating the sacrifice of forgiveness and reconciliation."[58] The pope was careful not to indicate *who* murdered Romero, or *why*. After all, any discussion of Romero's passionate struggle against state repression, his support to the people's church and the popular organizations, his upholding the people's right to armed insurrection, and his call upon soldiers of the reactionary army not to fire upon the people, would have undermined the pope's campaign to *reconcile* the people with their capitalist masters.

"Unity of the church" was the signboard behind which the pope threw his support to the reactionary bishops. Speaking before priests and nuns, he declared: "Remain united. Realize that in unity lies the force of the church. Always maintain communion with your pastors. Know how to discern and choose before [?] other preachings and ideologies which are not the message of Jesus christ and his church."[59] The pope chided the activists of the christian base communities: "You are not social leaders, political leaders or functionaries [!] of a worldly power."[60] He assured the priests and nuns that "awaiting your word are generous youths who no longer believe in the facile promises of a capitalist society or [?] who at times succumb to the illusion of a revolutionary commitment, which wants to change things and structures, resorting even to violence."[61] Playing on the real contradiction between the reformist "universalism" of Jesus and the revolutionary momentum of the people's church movement, the pope declared: "...The choice facing the priest is at times a dramatic one. While being firm against error, he cannot be against anyone, for all men are brothers—or, in the extreme case, enemies whom he must love according to the gospel; he must embrace all men, for all men are sons of god, and must give his life, if it is necessary, for all his brothers. Here often lies the drama of the priest, impelled by diverse tendencies, hounded by party-oriented choices."[62]

The FMLN had done nothing to arm the masses intellectually and psychologically against the pope's visit. The FMLN should have boldly exposed the pope as a counterrevolutionary, a corporate capitalist, a suppressor of liberation theology, an enemy of the people's church and thus an enemy of the people; this would have helped the oppressed masses develop the conceptual tools they needed to see through the pope's "humanitarian" demagogy, and offered the activists of the people's church a clear pole of opposition to the reactionary hierarchy, around which they could rally and grow. Instead, the FMLN contented itself with a routine run-down of the mass murder committed by the dictatorship against the people over the past four years—humbly lobbying the pope to take the people's side in the civil war. But trying to convince the pope to support the revolutionary people through a rational, humanitarian argument would be like trying to convince your local bank president to support a miners' strike by explaining to him the marxist theory of surplus value and reminding him of the suffering of the miners' families. The pope had come to dispense opium, not solidarity to the Salvadoran people.

Priest Rutilio Sánchez summed up the feelings of the people's church activists, remarking that the pope "did not address our problems. We feel the pope spoke as if he were in a different country: He never mentioned our war, our political prisoners, the hunger we are suffering, the repression. He spoke as if El Salvador were at peace. We felt very disappointed."[63]

Guatemala

The pope's next stop was Guatemala, where he also "forgot" about the civil war and the military government's genocide against the indigenous peoples. At the airport in Guatemala City, he was cordially received by the "born again" protestant dictator Ríos Montt and his wife. In his speeches in Guatemala, the pope made no direct reference to the execution, just days before, of six young Guatemalan patriots by Ríos Montt—showing that the Vatican's pleas for clemency had been tokenistic. Carrying his attack against liberation theology to the indigenous people of Guatemala (some of whom he addressed in person), the pope declared: "...Let no one endeavor any more to confuse gospel preaching with subversion, and let the ministers of worship exercise their mission with security and without hindrances."[64]

The pope's mission in Guatemala was truly a delicate one: He had to revamp catholic influence among the masses in the face of the aggressive protestant onslaught, but without lending support to liberation theology and thus to the revolutionary movement. This meant, as in the rest of Central America, sternly uniting with the reactionary catholic hierarchy as against the people's church movement. But the ultrareactionary Guatemalan catholic hierarchy, despite inevitable frictions with the protestant up-starts, was supporting the Ríos Montt dictatorship. So the pope's visit to Guatemala, in objective terms, served not so much the cause of catholicism as the cause of imperialism.

Protestant evangelical sects now claim a membership of over 1.6 million in Guatemala, some 22% of the population—by far their highest figure in Central America.[65] The mass traumas caused by first the earthquake of 1976 and then the wholesale army massacres in the countryside from the late 1970's through the present, have provided fertile psychological soil for the protestant evangelical sects with their hysterical preaching of the apocalypse and the second coming. Serving as psychological shock troops for the military regime, the pentecostals and other reactionary evangelical sects—many of them based in, and funded from the U.S.—have warned the rural masses that the earthquake the military massacres were their due punishment by god for their participation in the catholic base community movement and the popular organizations.

The catholic church played a key role in the rightist overthrow of the Arbenz regime in 1954. Responding to fears of the big landowners that Arbenz' agrarian reform was undermining their supremacy by allowing the peasants a measure of economic independence, the church leaders organized the Catholic Action movement. Catholic Action carried out strident anticommunist, anti-Arbenz agitation among the masses, including the indigenous peasants. When colonel Castillo Armas seized power at the head of a column of CIA sponsored mercenaries, the church gave its full blessings to his regime and the fascist political movement (MLN) he set up.

With the aim of propping up military/oligarchic rule, the bishops continued to mobilize the Catholic Action movement to sink deeper roots for the church among the rural masses. This involved training a number of Indian men to become lay cathechists and priests, to spread the traditional church teachings more deeply among the indigenous masses. But as these men, educated under the wing of the reactionary church, emerged as respected moral and social leaders of their communities, they more and more overcame the selfhatred and blind obedience to authority which the ruling class and its church had inculcated in their people ever since the wholesale destruction of Mayan cultures by the Spanish colonial invaders and missionaries. They began to develop the repressed consciousness and abilities of their people in the spirit of the original christian gospel, voicing the people's rising aspirations for an end to their miserable conditions through social and political struggle.

When the liberation theology of Vatican 2 and Medellín reached Guatemala by way of its written documents and those radical priests who struggled to implement it among the most oppressed people, the Indian cathechists and priests were among the most passionate and energetic to embrace the new doctrine. The Catholic Action movement thus turned into its opposite—from a tool of reaction into an ally of revolution. In the face of sharpening state repression against the people's church movement, many of the Indian catechists went on to become leading cadres of the Guerrilla Army of the Poor (EGP), the largest of Guatemala's revolutionary political/military organizations.

Nicaragua

In 1968, the year of Medellín, Nicaragua's jesuits, with the support of the country's bishops, organized the *Centro Educativo para el Progreso Agrario* (CEPA—Educational Center for Agrarian Advancement). The CEPA organizers combined training of peasant leaders in agricultural techniques with biblical teaching in the spirit of liberation theology. As the peasants and farmworkers awakened to social struggle, CEPA published a pamphlet, *Cristo, Campesino (Christ, the Peasant)*, in picture book format. Its repeated message was, "You have a right to land." Thousands of copies passed from hand to hand in the countryside.[66]

Youthful lay preachers trained by progressive priests sacrificed the comforts of city life to live, work and preach among the rural masses. It was not long before the fledgling christian base community movement chafed against the cozy conciliationism of the church hierarchy. In 1970, Miguel Obando y Bravo, a former math professor who had spent ten years of his priesthood in El Salvador, was appointed archbishop. Somoza presented him with a Mercedes-Benz, and Obando y Bravo was seen being chauffered about in it. "The specter of the church hierarchy allied with the country's ruling class evoked an outcry from the base communities."[67]

The 1972 earthquake widened the chasm between the Somoza regime and the people, exposing the corruption and cynicism of the Somoza clique and its national guard for all to see. The social aftermath of the quake sharpened the radicalization within the church. As the church stepped in to provide emergency relief and social services to the desperate masses of Managua, even the bishops were brought into personal contact with the suffering of the people. Obando had by now returned the Mercedes-Benz to Somoza, and the bishops issued a pastoral letter denouncing the government and calling for "a completely new order."[68] Meanwhile the FSLN, having regrouped from its *foco*-ist defeats of the mid-1960's and embraced a perspective of mass organizing towards people's war, was forging firm links with the christian base community movement in the countryside. Several of the youthful lay preachers were to become revolutionary fighters and leaders.

The church hierarchy was being pulled into opposition to Somoza from two angles: *Near the top* of society, the national/liberal bourgeoisie was becoming disgusted and restive with the Somoza oligarchy, which had seized on the post-earthquake situation to enrich itself and increase its monopolistic position in the economy, shoving aside the rest of the bourgeoisie. As the bourgeois opposition grew and maneuvered for the support of the masses, it found a ready ally in the bishops. *Near the bottom* of society, the christian base communities were becoming more active and combative in their mass based struggle against the regime; they suffered sharpening repression by the national guard as a result. In 1974, archbishop Obando declared at the national university: "A situation of violence is crushing the masses. I make a clear distinction between basic or institutional violence rooted in socio-economic structures, and the violence of the oppressed which it engenders."[69]

After 1975, as Somoza imposed a state of siege, the national guard in some areas of the north and east banned all catholic religious meetings, or required a special permit for any such meeting to be held. While church buildings were becoming the main places of sanctuary for rural people fleeing the guard's murderous repression, the guard took over several chapels as temporary barracks serving its counterinsurgent campaign. The christian base communities were driven underground, and into closer collaboration with the FSLN.

In view of the selfserving aims of the bourgeois opposition to Somoza, the christian base community movement publicly drew a sharp line of demarcation between the liberal bourgeoisie and the laboring masses. In 1975, the Christian Organizations of Nicaragua declared that *La Prensa* and the traditional opposition media were controlled by "bourgeois sectors opposed to the Somoza dictatorship, but not committed to the true liberation of the Nicaraguan people."[70] Several CEPA activists went on to become leading members of the rural workers' association (ATC); founded by the

FSLN in 1977, the ATC gave a strong proletarian character to the rural people's movement.

The church hierarchy, standing far closer to the liberal bourgeoisie than to the struggling masses, tried to restrict CEPA's activities and discourage it from collaborating with the FSLN—eventually compelling CEPA to break openly from the official church and become an independent christian organization allied with the FSLN.[71] Archbishop Obando, while mediating between Somoza and the FSLN at key conjunctures in the struggle, tried to block the FSLN's conquest of power by maneuvering the bourgeois opposition into a government that would preside over a still intact national guard. In July 1979, he made a last ditch effort to save capitalist rule in Nicaragua by fleeing to Venezuela with opposition leaders and attempting to negotiate a bourgeois regime without Somoza. Then, on the eve of the people's insurrectionary victory, Obando and the bishops issued a public statement upholding the people's right to armed struggle, as a last resort, against a regime of institutionalized repression.

Superficially, Obando's statement was similar to that made by archbishop Romero in El Salvador a few months later. But Romero upheld the people's right to armed struggle when the Salvadoran civil war was *just beginning*, so that he was boldly supporting the revolutionary struggle at a time when the military dictatorship still held the power of life and death over most of the people in the country—including Romero himself. Obando, by contrast, did not clearly uphold the armed revolutionary struggle until the *very end* of the civil war between the people and Somoza, as the Somoza regime was crumbling and the victory of the people led by the FSLN was well within sight. Far from giving any real support to the Nicaraguan revolution, Obando, with his Johnny-come-lately "revolutionism," was angling to ingratiate himself with the enormously popular FSLN—hoping to "moderate" the new regime and maximize the influence of the liberal bourgeoisie in it.

Christian Charity Serves the Counterrevolution

Obando's honeytongued approach to the victorious revolution paid off for the bourgeoisie and its reactionary longterm strategy —thanks to the christian scruples and political opportunism of the FSLN leaders. Just as they set up an unprincipled coalition government with the liberal bourgeoisie (see ch. 2), the FSLN leaders, fearing an open struggle against the Vatican and the local hierarchy, tried to maintain an unprincipled "unity" between the reactionary hierarchy and the revolutionary people's church— despite the fact that the most radical elements of the people's church, notably CEPA, had already made an open break with the hierarchy.

The first fruits of the FSLN leaders' attempt to combine christian principles with revolutionary policy appeared in their treatment of captured national guardsmen. As a gesture of christian "good will," they set 3,000 *somocista* guardsmen free, without subjecting them to people's tribunals and people's justice; tens of thousands of *somocista* agents and informants, whose names had fallen into the FSLN's hands upon the revolutionary victory, were likewise never brought to trial. FSLN interior minister Tomás Borge paid a visit to the jail where captured *somocista* torturers were being held—including the man who had tortured him while he was a political prisoner of Somoza. Borge told his torturer: "Remember when I told you I would take revenge when I was free? I now come for my revenge. For your hate and torture I give you love, and for what you did I give you freedom."[72] The torturer was set free, despite the outraged clamor of the revolutionary masses for him and other *somocista* war criminals to be shot. Many of the freed national guardsmen came to form the backbone of the CIA sponsored *contra* mercenary butchers based in Honduras—and some of them were no doubt among the 2,000 ex-national guardsmen incorporated into the Guatemalan army and its genocidal counterinsurgency campaigns.

Ironically, while the FSLN leaders have bowed before U.S. imperialism, slavishly declaring time and again that they are *against* "exporting revolution" (i.e., against providing material and human solidarity to the Salvadoran and Guatemalan revolutions), their christian scruples have led them to export *counter*revolution to the rest of Central America, in the form of the "generously" freed *somocista* war criminals. Turning the other cheek has not disarmed the oppressors in the 1980's any more than it did in the time of Jesus.

The Bishops Go Over to Counterrevolution

In 1980, the contradiction between the liberal bourgeoisie and the young workers' state erupted into open class struggle, as the industrialist Alfonso Robelo resigned from the coalition government and aggressively mobilized a counterrevolutionary movement. Obando and the church hierarchy, maintaining their alliance with the liberal bourgeoisie, went over more and more to the side of counterrevolution. With *La Prensa* now in the hands of the reactionary upstart Pedro Joaquín Chamorro Barrios and serving as an aggressive mouthpiece for Robelo, Obando and the pope, the church hierarchy sharply opposed practically every progressive social and political mobilization carried out by the FSLN—from the literacy crusade to the volunteer youth mobilizations for the harvest, to the people's militia movement and the universal conscription law (see ch. 2). The conflict between the hierarchy and the people's church, which continued to work with the FSLN, could no longer be contained.

The People Defend Their Priests

The hierarchy struck the first blows: It demanded that four radical priests in the government and FSLN resign their secular posts, and started transferring liberationist priests from their parishes. In July 1980, the bishop of León dismissed a popular priest from his parish in El Viejo. In protest, the parishioners occupied their local church and then the cathedral in León. A protracted struggle began between the hierarchy and the *sandinista* masses over the fate of their radical christian leaders.

The three radical priests in the FSLN-led government, supported by the revolutionary masses, have stood firm against the hierarchy's repeated demands that they resign. In June 1981 the bishops, backed by the Vatican, issued a pastoral letter declaring: "If the priests holding public office and exercising partisan functions do not give up these responsibilities, in order to take up their specific priestly ministry, we will consider them in an attitude of open rebellion and formal disobedience liable to the sanction of church laws." Two days later, the priests in question—Ernesto Cardenal, minister of culture; Miguel d'Escoto, foreign minister*;

---

*It must be acknowledged that Miguel d'Escoto, a maryknoll priest, is not terribly progressive in his world outlook. Declaring himself a disciple of Martin Luther King, d'Escoto holds fast to "turn the other cheek" pacifism as a theological principle, and considers human martyrdom an end in itself: "To be very frank with you, I don't think that violence is christian. Some may say that this is a reactionary position. But I think that the very essence of christianity is the cross. It is through the cross that we will change."[73] Perhaps d'Escoto also thinks that the CIA was doing him a magnanimous favor when it tried to murder him by poisoning his whiskey.

and Edgar Parrales, minister of social welfare—issued a joint communiqué rejecting the bishops' order and reaffirming their commitment to the revolution. In the face of massive support for the priests' stance by the people's church movement, Obando y Bravo sighed, "One must sadly admit that the Nicaraguan church is divided."[74] The bishops and the Vatican had to compromise, allowing the priests to remain in the government while divesting them of formal priestly functions such as celebrating mass.

In July 1981, the FSLN attempted to broaden the scope of Sunday television broadcasts of religious services, from exclusive coverage of Obando's sermon to coverage of local priests' sermons as well. This meant breaking the hierarchy's Sunday propaganda monopoly, and allowing the people's church to speak its word over the mass media. Obando denounced the government for "suppressing" his mass, and banned the filming of mass in *any* church.[75]

The Pope's Letter to Obando

In the summer of 1982, the contradiction between the reactionary hierarchy and the revolutionary people exploded in a series of controversial incidents and mass struggles—with the FSLN government vacillating clumsily between the two contending forces. On 29 June 1982, the pope sent a pastoral letter to Obando at the latter's request, dealing with the question of unity within the church. "...How absurd and dangerous it is," declared the pope, "to imagine that alongside of—not to say against—the Church built around the Bishop, another Church can be conceived as 'charismatic' and not institutional, 'new' and not traditional, alternative and, as has recently been proclaimed, a *People's Church*.

"'People's Church,' in its most common meaning, visible in the writings of a certain theological current,...means a Church that exhausts itself [!] in the autonomy of the so-called *bases*, without reference to the legitimate Pastors or Teachers... It means—since the term *people* easily takes on a markedly sociological and political content—a Church incarnated in the popular organizations, marked by ideologies, placed at the service of their demands, of their programs... It is easy to perceive—as the Puebla document explicitly indicates—that the 'People's Church' concept is hard pressed to escape infiltration with strongly ideological connotations, along the lines of a certain political radicalization, of the class struggle, of acceptance of violence in the pursuit of definite ends, etc."[76]

La Prensa wanted to publish the pope's letter. The government censors, fearing an open conflict with the Vatican, forbade its publication. Following a reactionary uproar both in Nicaragua and internationally, the government reversed itself and ordered *all three* daily newspapers, including the FSLN's *Barricada* and the pro-FSLN *El Nuevo Diario*, to print the pope's letter—along with a crude explanation of the previous censorship.*

The Struggle in Santa Rosa Parish

On 20 July 1982, the archbishop's office announced that priest José Arias Caldera was to be transferred from Managua's poor Santa Rosa *barrio*, where he had served the people for eight years. Arias Caldera, who had lived and done his early religious work among peasants in the mountains, became one of the first church-people to collaborate with the FSLN, sheltering FSLN founder Carlos Fonseca Amador in a safe house in the early 1970's. His parishioners deeply respected him as "the monseñor of the poor." Bismarck Carballo, head of the catholic radio station and official spokesman for archbishop Obando, declared Arias' transfer to a minor post (which he had already been fulfilling for years) a "routine" change within the church. The recently ordained priest chosen by the hierarchy to replace Arias in Santa Rosa had just received lavish publicity in *La Prensa*.

The same night, some 200 members of the Santa Rosa christian base community occupied the church, demanding that Obando and the hierarchy reverse their decision to transfer Arias. "It's like a *coup d'état* that they've delivered to the whole *barrio*," said one of the parishioners protesting the move against Arias.[77] The next day, 21 July, the people of Santa Rosa took to the streets in defense of their priest. They sounded bells, drums and cimbals and hoisted placards in their protest demonstration. One of the placards read: "Those who love the people and live together with them are true priests, the rest are pharisees who pay lip service to love, but whose hearts are far from the people."[78] As the people's occu-

*The FSLN leaders, vacillating between the revolutionary masses and the reactionary bourgeoisie, have resorted to the hamhanded device of censorship of *La Prensa* on the one hand, and bureaucratic stifling of the masses' spontaneous mobilizations against *La Prensa*'s counterrevolutionary agitation on the other. Clumsy clampdowns against bourgeois reaction, quickly followed by spineless *concessions* to bourgeois reaction, is the swerving logic of an opportunist workers' state leadership under the pressure of the revolutionary masses.

pation of the church continued, they rang the church bells every half hour as a signal of vigilance.[79]

That night, the auxiliary bishop of Managua, Bosco Vivas Robelo, entered the Santa Rosa church together with four other people—including a *La Prensa* photographer—and attempted to remove the church's ritual chalice (*sagrario*). In catholic belief, there can be no church without the chalice. As soon as Vivas Robelo seized hold of it, he was angrily confronted by 67-year-old Margarita Fuentes, curator of the church. She was supported by over 80 parishioners, who surrounded Vivas, blocking his exit. Within seconds, the chalice was back in the hands of the people. Vivas appeared to faint, and complained he had been hit—a charge hotly denied by the parishioners. Bismarck Carballo, speaking again for archbishop Obando, branded the parishioners "a disobedient group manipulated by other groups that are likewise disobedient."[80] Throughout the night, the people of Santa Rosa lit and tended bonfires in the streets.

In an editorial in the FSLN's *Barricada*, Eduardo Estrada wrote: "The Catholic Church too must learn to be democratic and to listen to the people; its decisions should emanate not solely from the hierarchy, but be influenced by the interests of our people. Yet the latest events, specifically the posture taken by father Bismarck Carballo, spokesman of the Archbishop's office, is antichristian and antipopular."[81] Carballo and Obando demanded that the Santa Rosa parishioners ask forgiveness for their "disobedience." When the people refused to be contrite, Obando declared them all excommunicated. Their church was officially closed, and Arias had to accept his transfer.

Against the Counterrevolutionary Sects

The catholic hierarchy was not the only religious body that was provoking the people's wrath. Several evangelical sects, headed by the Mormons, Jehovah's Witnesses and Seventh Day Adventists, threatened their "flocks" with the wrath of god if they participated in the revolution and its social programs. They exhorted their members and followers to refuse health vaccinations, and scheduled prayer meetings on the same evenings as literacy classes. In August 1982, *sandinista* youths took over some 30 buildings owned by these counterrevolutionary sects, and set about converting them into libraries, childcare centers and health clinics. The sects, evidently anticipating the mass action against them, had been busy "decapitalizing" their buildings—removing the furniture, sound equipment, papers and other valuable materials.[82]

The government at first did not interfere with the *sandinista* youths' revolutionary initiative. But after a strident protest by the evangelical sects, the FSLN leaders reversed themselves, admitted that a "mistake" had been made, and let the counterrevolutionary churches reopen.[83]

On 11 August 1982, the pope's 29 June letter to Obando (see above) finally appeared in *Barricada* and Nicaragua's other two daily papers. Part of the letter read: "A 'People's Church' opposed to the Church presided over by the legitimate Pastors is...a grave deviation from the will and plan of salvation of Jesus christ. It is, moreover, the beginning of a cracking and rupture of that unity which He bequeathed as a characteristic sign of the Church itself."[84]

Naked Came the Priest...

On the same day, Bismarck Carballo was seen running naked through the streets of Managua—much like Adam, both before and after his fall from innocence—followed by a naked woman, and pursued by a furious man with a pistol. The woman was a parishioner of Carballo's; apparently her estranged lover had stumbled upon the two while they were engaged in an overly intimate confessional session, and chased them out of the house at gunpoint. When the pursuer caught Carballo on the street, he began pistol whipping the priest—until the police arrived and arrested all three.

With juicy rumors sweeping Managua, the FSLN's *Barricada* made plans to feature the story on its front page the next day. But Tomás Borge, fearing a backlash, ordered the ministry of education to buy out the entire press run, to prevent any copies from reaching the street. And the television footage taken of the incident was never shown publicly.[85] The pro-FSLN *El Nuevo Diario* ran a small front page story, without photos. *La Prensa* took to the offensive, publishing a searing attack against the government and supporting Carballo's claim that the whole incident had been an elaborate frameup by the FSLN to "discredit the church."

Having lost the initiative through his squeamish self-censorship, Borge then reversed himself, and both *Barricada* and *Nuevo Diario* published a series of photos of the incident. *Nuevo Diario* later ran another photo, allegedly taken months before the incident, showing Carballo and the woman lounging together on a local beach.*

But this only had the effect of pouring gasoline over the flames of resentment over the FSLN's crude handling of the whole affair. Politically intermediate sections of the masses and of the church— including many who were generally supportive of the revolution— felt that, whatever the truth of the affair was, the FSLN had played "dirty." The "naked priest" incident, instead of broadly exposing the moral degeneracy of the church hierarchy and further undermining its authority among the masses, ironically turned into a potent rallying cry for the hierarchy and the bourgeois counterrevolution.

...and Up in Arms Went the Reactionaries

Five days after the incident—on Monday, 16 August 1982—a group of young counterrevolutionaries went on a rampage through the streets of Monimbó, the Indian *barrio* of Masaya which had been a stronghold of the revolution. The antisandinistas seized arms by overrunning a police station and disarming some *sandinista* soldiers and militia units. Rallying backward and confused people behind the banner of christianity against the "atheism" and "communism" of the FSLN, the antisandinistas barricaded themselves into a private church school.

The local *sandinista* defense committee (CDS) and unions swiftly mobilized a demonstration of several thousand people to confront the reactionary rebels. A police vehicle ran over and killed a demonstrator in front of the church school. The antisandinistas inside the school claimed it was deliberate murder, and prepared their assault against the mass *sandinista* demonstration approaching the school.[86]

At 5:00 pm, as the *sandinista* demonstration closed in on the school, it was hit by a homemade bomb and a shower of stones. A burst of gunfire was heard from the police station now occupied by the reactionaries. As the demonstrators hurled themselves to

---

*Carballo has maintained that the woman parishioner was a hired prostitute and her "estranged lover" an FSLN agent, who forced Carballo and the woman (whom he claims he scarcely knew and was merely "counseling" in her house) to strip naked at gunpoint. The *Nuevo Diario* photo showing Carballo and the woman together at the beach was, according to Carballo, a laboratory fake. Carballo's claim that the whole incident was an FSLN conspiracy to "morally assassinate" him was generally echoed in U.S. bourgeois press accounts of the incident.

the ground, they came under fire from the occupied church school and from neighboring houses. Eddy Guzmán, a 19-year-old student and militant in the *sandinista* youth, was hit and killed by the reactionaries' bullets. So was Edmundo Castellón.[87]

The demonstrators, immobilized by the reactionaries' relentless gunfire, started shouting, "We want arms! We want arms!" "The shotguns and revolvers of the insurrection," relates *Barricada*, "appeared once again, clutched by militia members in civilian dress, who rushed from their houses to repel the aggression. Without abandoning their positions along the ground and in the thresholds of doors, the people lent courage and spirit to the popular fighters who were advancing towards the Salesian [church school], doing battle with the *contras*."

Manuel González, one of the *sandinista* demonstrators, said: "Look *compañero*, these are the bands of the MDN [Alfonso Robelo's counterrevolutionary movement], they have heavy arms and M-16's, and they're in the houses of the bourgeoisie..."[88] The struggle lasted for over an hour. Groups of *sandinista* demonstrators, freed for action by the initiative of the militia fighters, captured some of the reactionaries. During the night, special troops of the interior ministry took command of the situation and arrested the reactionary *provocateurs*. Only 9 of the 81 people arrested turned out to be from Masaya. Two catholic priests—one Costa Rican, the other Spanish—who apparently had played a leading role in the rightist provocation, were delivered to their respective embassies. And the struggle in Monimbó was by no means an isolated incident: During the same period, 14 other highschools were taken over by antisandinistas—indicating an organized conspiracy by the bourgeois/churchy counterrevolution.[89]

The Pope Meets the Revolution

On Friday, 4 March 1983, as the regrouped *somocista* forces were poised to invade Nicaragua from their Honduran base camps, pope John Paul 2 made his anxiously awaited visit to Nicaragua. The pope set the tempo for his Nicaraguan campaign in León, where he attacked the FSLN government's efforts to regulate the curriculum at all schools, including those run by religious orders. He asserted the "strict right of christian parents not to see their children subjected in schools to programs inspired by atheism." According to the pope, *children* have no right to learn about the reality of the world, humanity and the universe—as long as their parents are "strictly" befuddled by medievalist superstition.* He went on to insist that, when education becomes simple instruction, students are "defenseless against possible political or ideological manipulation."[90]

In contrast to his campaign in El Salvador two days later (see above), where he urged the people, in effect, to peacefully "reconcile" themselves to their fascist oppressors, the pope was in no mood to reconcile himself with the Nicaraguan revolution in power. Upon the pope's arrival at the airport, Ernesto Cardenal, a Trappist friar** and minister of culture, attempted to greet the pope in the traditional slavish manner, kneeling down to kiss his ring. Cardenal and the other priests in the government, enjoying strong popular support, had faced down the pope's and bishops' ultimatums for them to resign from their secular positions—forcing a tense compromise. Now the pope brusquely swept his hand away from Cardenal, a brilliant poet and a man of passionate commitment to the revolution, and addressed him as an errant child. "You must straighten out your position with the church," he chided, wagging his index finger at Cardenal. Friar Cardenal later remarked, with a touch of bitterness: "The situation is that Nicaragua has a revolution, and the pope is not revolutionary, so he doesn't understand Nicaragua."

But if the pope did not understand Nicaragua, far less did the FSLN leadership seem to understand the pope. In crass violation of the *democratic* principle of separation of church and state, the FSLN regime declared the day of the pope's visit a national holiday, and subsidized all the expenses of the hundreds of thousands of people who trekked into Managua—in busses, trucks, tractors and on foot—to hear his sermon. The government spent at least $2 million, using a month's worth of precious gasoline for the people's transportation, and lost three days of production to accommodate

*Moreover, the pope grossly exaggerated the degree of "atheism" of the FSLN leaders and the educational system they have established. Several FSLN leaders—most notably Daniel Ortega, trained as a lay preacher in his youth—are quite open, practicing christians; not a single FSLN leader is an acknowledged atheist. And christian themes were widely used in the curriculum developed for the literacy crusade.

**It has become a widespread misconception outside of Nicaragua that Ernesto Cardenal is a jesuit priest—when in fact he is a friar of the tiny *trappist* order of catholicism, which emphasizes asceticism and contemplative community. The confusion is due largely to the fact that Cardenal's brother Fernando, who headed up the literacy crusade and went on to become education minister, *is* a jesuit priest. But on 4 December 1984, Fernando Cardenal was expelled from the jesuit order, at the pope's instigation.

the pope's extravaganza.* The FSLN rallied the masses to attend the pope's sermons under the muddleheaded and historically false slogan, "Between christianity and revolution there is no contradiction." The christian base communities erected a huge billboard adorned with doves carrying olive branches and reading: "John Paul: Welcome to Free Nicaragua. Thanks to God and the Revolution."

The FSLN's *Barricada*, while lavishly covering its pages with photos of the pope and a sympathetic summary of his churchy career, urged the masses to request that the pope use his influence with "world public opinion" to check the murderous attacks upon Nicaragua by the *somocista contras* operating from Honduras. Reports surfaced in the international press, meanwhile, that the pope had met privately with *contra* leaders just prior to his visit to Nicaragua, and had asked them to delay their imminent invasion until *after* his visit. Clearly, it would have been awkward for the pope to visit Nicaragua riding in a *contra* armored car. But far from stopping the *somocista* invasion—which was not within his power, anyway—the pope was exerting himself to *soften the masses up psychologically for the counterrevolutionary assault.*

Upon his arrival in the airport in Managua, the pope had the gall to greet "not only those who have been able to come to meet me or who are listening to me at this moment by various means; not only those whom I shall meet in León or in Managua during my hours' long stay among you which I would like to prolong; but especially the thousands and thousands of Nicaraguans who have not found it possible to come—as they would have liked—to the meeting places..."[91] Over half a million people**—many of whom, coming from distant regions, trekked to Managua for the first time—thronged into Managua's "19 July Plaza" and waited for

*The FSLN leaders' unprincipled squandering of millions of precious dollars and labor hours on the pope's visit exposed the hypocrisy of their excuse that they "could not afford" the expense of holding nationwide elections immediately following their revolutionary victory in 1979. Ironically, all the political indications were that nationwide free elections held at that time would have yielded an *overwhelming victory for the FSLN*—which would have made it that much harder for the FSLN to justify forming a coalition government with the liberal bourgeoisie. The FSLN's opportunist refusal to allow the revolutionary people to directly elect their government, handed U.S. imperialism a free propaganda bone to the effect that the FSLN regime was "undemocratic" and "totalitarian."

**Barricada* estimated that, in León and Managua combined, over 700,000 people—one-quarter of Nicaragua's population—came to hear the pope.

hours under a scorching sun to hear the pope's late afternoon sermon. The red and black flag of the FSLN mingled with the blue and white flag of Nicaragua and the yellow and white colors of the Vatican in the enormous crowd. The bourgeoisie and upper middle classes had mobilized too, confidently expecting the pope to throw his weight behind Obando and the hierarchy. The broad working masses were eagerly expecting the pope to comfort them for the sacrifices they had suffered in the course of their revolutionary struggle, and to throw his moral weight behind the cause of peace and against the armed *contra* assaults.

Four days before, 17 *sandinista* youth activists had been killed by a *somocista* incursion in the north; they were buried in a mass funeral in Managua the day before. The Mothers of Heroes and Martyrs of the revolution, carrying large photos of their dead sons and daughters, were in the forefront of the people's demonstration of hope and expectations in the pope. Several mothers of the youths just killed by the *contras*, expecting the pope to deliver a mass for their martyred children, were seated on the stage. According to *Barricada*, before the speeches began a struggle took place between Bismarck Carballo and Fernando Cardenal over the placement of microphones: While Cardenal tried to get microphones placed among the crowd, Carballo insisted that all the microphones be confined to the stage.

In his speech of welcome to the pope, FSLN and junta leader Daniel Ortega humbly pleaded that the pope address himself to the Nicaraguan people's revolutionary accomplishments and sacrifices, and in particular the threat of U.S. military invasion. He cited at length a letter written by the bishop of León to a U.S. catholic leader during Sandino's struggle in the 1920's, exposing the savagery of the U.S. marine attacks and urging the U.S. catholic leadership to oppose their government's imperialist aggression against Nicaragua. When Ortega concluded his speech and introduced the pope, the masses chanted "We want peace!" *("Queremos la paz!")* over and over again for some five minutes. During this whole time the pope stood stonefaced—as he had during Ortega's speech—his eyes fixed downwards at his feet.

The pope boomingly proceeded with his prepared sermon, which utterly disregarded Ortega's pleas. His sermon was entitled "unity of the church"—once again displaying the pope's limited repertoire of ideas relating to Central America. It was largely a retread of his 29 June 1982 pastoral letter to Obando and the bishops (see above); in the course of his sermon, the pope directly cited passages from that letter which denounced the people's church. "Jesus christ...came," he declared, "to reestablish the lost unity [of mankind], so that there might be 'only one flock,' and 'only one pastor'...a pastor whose voice the sheep 'know,' whereas they do not know the voice of the alien pastors..."[92]

But the Nicaraguan masses, having made the most profound revolution in the western hemisphere, were not about to act like a flock of sheep harkening to the pope's mind-dulling call. As the pope droned on with his bombastic, scarcely comprehensible sermon, the people grew restive. He ignored the imploring gestures of the mothers displaying pictures of their martyred children. While speaking in pompous religious jargon of the natural disasters (floods and droughts) recently suffered by Nicaragua, the pope made no mention of the 50,000 Nicaraguans killed during the civil war against Somoza—or of the imminent *contra*/CIA invasion. A North American churchwoman was moved "...to see the faces of the people change from love, to questioning, to confusion, to waiting for the pope to say something, to *anger*..."

Finally the repressed energy of the revolutionary people burst through the holy fabric of the pope's sermon. The mothers of heroes and martyrs seated on the stage began shouting, "We want a mass for the dead! We want a mass for the martyrs of the revolution!" Their cries were picked up by the stage microphones and broadcast throughout the plaza. Political pandemonium broke loose. The conservative clerics huddled around the altar desperately prompted their wealthy supporters to chant *"El papa! El papa!* (The pope!)" and "Obando! Obando!" *Sandinista* youths countered with chants like, "We want a church on the side of the poor!" and "People's power!" Soon the intermediate forces prevailed, and the inoffensive chant, "We want peace!" drowned out all the other chants. "...The three members of the government junta [Daniel Ortega, Sergio Ramírez, and Rafael Córdova], who were standing to the right of the pope, and the other eight members of the FSLN national directorate, who were placed to the left, remained impassive, observing the uncontrollable reaction of the people and the surprise of the pope."[93]

The pope droned *"Silencio!"* again and again at the people. But the combative spirit of the "flock" was now soaring, and there was no stopping it. For the next half hour of his truncated sermon, the pope was interrupted in a big way by the people several more times, with the chant, "We want peace!" carrying the day. At one point the pope became so exasperated with the chanting that he departed from his prepared text, exclaiming, "The church is the first to desire peace!" But he could not pacify the people. Returning to his "unity of the church" text, the pope proclaimed: "Beloved brothers: Be well aware that there are cases in which unity can only be saved when each one is able to renounce his own ideas, plans and commitments, including good ones—how much more so when they lack the necessary ecclesiastical reference!—for the superior benefit of communion with the bishop, with the pope, with the entire church."[94] This provoked the people to raise an outcry of "We want a church on the side of the poor!" and "People's power!" One woman later remarked, "The pope only spoke to his friends, the rich and the bishops. He didn't speak to the poor, to the people."*

When he finally brought his hapless sermon to an end, the pope still had to deal with the mothers of heroes and martyrs, many of whom came up to demand that he hold communion with them. In every other Central American country he visited, the pope gave a mass for the dead—but not in Nicaragua. The mothers were shocked, frustrated and outraged. When they came up to the altar for communion, most of them were blocked by the pope's Italian bodyguards, who demanded that they show their identification. Lidia Saavedra, mother of Daniel and Humberto Ortega and their martyred brother, intervened in the dispute, declaring that "the revolutionary mothers have the right to communion. Acts like this are what keeps the church disunited." Only four or five of the mothers ended up receiving communion from the pope.[97]

Alba Bonilla, who works in a sewing enterprise, remarked of the pope's visit to Nicaragua: "It wasn't worth the trouble to stop production for three days to welcome him, because he did not hear what the people were asking for, which was peace in Central America."[98]

---

*Towards the end of his "rump sermon," the pope gave a brief message in the Miskitu language, without translation into Spanish. Not wishing to take any chances, partisans of the revolution started up the chant of "People's power!"[95] According to the *New York Times*, the pope's message was: "I love the Miskitu people because they are human beings. Miskitu power!" Nicaragua's bishops, without having made a selfcriticism of the church's active role in the Spanish colonial genocide against the Pacific coast indigenous peoples, denounced the FSLN's forced relocation of the Miskitu (see ch. 3); at the same time, they refused the FSLN's invitation to visit the Tasba Pri Miskitu resettlement camp.[96]

The Dispute over Military Policy

Since the pope's visit, the contradiction between the church hier-archy and the christian base communities supporting the *sandinista* regime, has continued to sharpen. In the national debate over universal (male) military conscription in the summer of 1983, Obando and the bishops, raising the banner of conscientious objection, denounced the FSLN's campaign to strengthen the nation's defense against the counterrevolution. "This law," declared the bishops, "follows the general lines of totalitarian legislation." But the christian base communities, whose representatives gathered in Managua from all over the country, rejected the bishops' demagogy. Speaking on behalf of those gathered, Luis Rarinas from Managua's San Judas *barrio* declared: "We are incensed at the bishops' conference statement, because it obviously wants to deny us the right to defend ourselves."[99] *Sandinista* youths were outraged by the hierarchy's strident opposition to military conscription. Archbishop Obando has complained of having his car attacked by "mobs" of *sandinista* youths.[100]

Rightist Clerics Join the Contras

In December 1983 the catholic bishop of the Atlantic coast, U.S. born Salvador Schlaefer, joined over 1,000 Miskitu who crossed the border into Honduras.* Conservative priests have also joined up with *contras* operating in southwest Nicaragua out of Costa Rica. In the summer of 1984, the interior ministry exposed a budding conspiracy between a rightist priest and a *contra* leader operating within Nicaragua, to form well armed "christian commando groups" to combat the FSLN regime. Archbishop Obando, providing tacit support to these counterrevolutionary activities, has received $493,000 from the U.S. Agency for International Development (AID) to train religious workers.

---

*The facts surrounding this incident were embroiled in controversy. Several Miskitu witnesses who managed to avoid the trek to Honduras reportedly declared that the entire community of 1,000 Miskitu in Francia Sirpe was kidnapped by a band of Miskitu counterrevolutionaries from the Honduran based Misura organization, and forced at gunpoint to march into Honduras. Archbishop Obando, on the other hand, hailed Schlaefer as a modern day Moses leading the oppressed into the "promised land."

Christians to the Left of Christ,
Marxist-Leninists to the Right of Marx and Lenin

Several sympathetic commentators have puzzled over the "new dialog" and "new relationship" between christians and marxist-leninists brought on by the convergence of liberation theology with the armed revolutionary movements of Central America. The main problem with their commentaries is that they tend to make the *apriori* assumption that the christian activists involved adhere consistently to the principles of Jesus, and that the marxist-leninists adhere consistently to the principles of Marx and Lenin. In reality, the situation is far more contradictory and fluid than that.

The boldest and most radical men and women of the liberation theology movement, by taking up arms in the revolutionary insurrection of the laboring classes, have sharply *broken with* the *anti-*revolutionary pacifism and reformism inherent in the teachings of Jesus—however much theological squeamishness they may continue to carry with them on burning questions such as women's liberation and the punishment of counterrevolutionary criminals. On the other hand, *none* of the marxist-leninist organizations in Central America have seriously propagated dialectical materialist philosophy and revolutionary internationalist politics—the twin hallmarks of marxism-leninism—among the masses. As with the "marxist-leninist" movements practically everywhere else in the world, their world outlook consists of bits and scraps of marxist theory melded with various currents of radical bourgeois ideology —above all, pragmatism and liberation theology.

This contradictory situation has led to the curious irony that, on some important social questions, honest revolutionary christians upholding liberation theology have taken *more radical, more progressive positions* than the "marxist-leninist" leaders. In Nicaragua, many activists of the christian base communities are more sensitive to the abuses of the rising state bureaucracy than are the FSLN leaders, who are more and more cozily sitting atop that bureaucracy. And the trappist catholic friar Ernesto Cardenal, while a strong partisan of the Cuban revolution and generally an effusive admirer of the Castro regime, has publicly criticized the Castro regime for its ferocious persecution of homosexuals.

The "marxist-leninist" Fidel Castro, in a statement to Jamaican priests in 1977, declared that "there are no contradictions between the tenets of religion and the tenets of socialism."[101]* Around the same time, Castro fulsomely praised incoming U.S. president Jimmy "Ethnic Purity" Carter—whose church was notorious for its exclusion of blacks—as "a man of deep religious principles." Such statements by Castro confirmed what serious marxists have long suspected: *Castro has never been an atheist.* As a young revolutionary leader, Castro was an honest christian.** Today, as an old, *anti*-revolutionary bureaucrat, he is a highly *dis*honest marxist-leninist. But he is far more of a christian today than he was back then—as evidenced by his reformist, pacifist diplomacy to "end the conflict" in El Salvador for the sake of the existing class order.

Which Class Does the Bible Really Serve?

In theological terms, liberation theology is seriously flawed. In their treatment of the bible—especially the old testament—the liberation theologians tend to snatch out those rare passages which seem to lend support to their progressive vision of social emancipation—while "forgetting" about the *rest* of the bible, in which a sadistic, capricious and narcissistic god places his stamp of approval on practically every imaginable act of inhumanity. They uphold, for example, the liberation of the Jews from their enslavement in Egypt (as related in the book of Exodus) as a paradigm for the contemporary liberation struggles. But they neglect to mention that the liberated Jews, egged on by their hooligan god every step of the way, proceeded to wage genocidal warfare and plunder against the indigenous peoples of Palestine—as related throughout the book of Joshua. And Joshua condemned the

---

*Compare this to Lenin: "Religion is one of the forms of spiritual oppression which everywhere weigh upon the masses of the people crushed by continuous toil for others, by poverty and loneliness. The weakness of the exploited classes in their struggle against their oppressors inevitably produces a belief in a better life after death...[102]

**Castro's theological outlook during his revolutionary struggle against the Batista regime was not purely christian, to be sure. It was combined with Afro-Cuban "pagan" theology—as evidenced by the fact that Castro, while leading the guerrilla struggle, wore an amulet about his neck bearing the image of Santa Barbara, goddess of warfare.[103]

Gibeonites to perpetual slavery, which was fully approved of by god (Joshua 9.20-7).

King David, who has gained a reputation for great sensitivity and compassion for the poor thanks to his authorship of the stultifying psalms, was a moral degenerate—who, having seized and raped a beautiful woman in the course of one of his military campaigns, set her husband (who was one of his subjects) up for certain death in the next battle (2 Samuel 11.2-17). When the cities he was besieging fell, David had all their inhabitants tortured to death and seized the spoils (2 Samuel 12.30-1). When David's kingdom was threatened by military rivals, he had his ten concubines locked up in life imprisonment, for "safekeeping" (2 Samuel 20.3). Wise old king Solomon, while apparently treating *his* 700 wives and 300 concubines fairly humanely (1 Kings 11.3-8), flew into a rage when an ambitious young competitor threatened to edge him out of his kingdom, and tried to have the upstart killed (1 Kings 11.26-40).

The Jewish high priest Ezra was a racist who, invoking god's wrath, commanded that all men who had taken "strange" (i.e., foreign) wives immediately expel them from Israel, along with all children they had borne; those men who refused to obey the racist order would be excommunicated (Ezra 10.2-8). The high priest Nehemiah, pursuing the same program of "ethnic purity," went to murderous extremes to prevent "his" Jewish people from intermarriage and mutual assimilation with the neighboring peoples (Nehemiah 13.23-5).

In sum, the old testament is a testament to racism, genocide, plunder, slavery, and misogyny—all approved of and fomented by a patriarchal god who was the idealized reflection of the most ruthless and successful priest/kings of the "chosen people" in question. Small wonder, then, that the old testament has been the theological stock in trade for the Boer settlers and conquerors of South Africa, and the zionist settlers and conquerors of Palestine. Liberation theology is standing on treacherous ground when it attempts to invoke the old testament. And the new testament, while reflecting a radical communitarian, universalist break from orthodox judaism, is not exactly a revolutionary document either (see beginning of this chapter).

Unlike the halfbaked "liberation theology" of protestantism, which quickly became the new religion of the rising bourgeoisie of northern Europe in its struggle against the feudal aristocracy centered around the catholic church, the liberation theology of today has yet to make a definitive break with the Vatican and institutional catholicism. Is this because the rising, revolutionary proletariat of Central America, to which the new theology is directed, is still too weak—politically and intellectually—to completely cast off the chains of oppressive catholic tradition? Is it because the revolutionary proletariat has *no objective need* for *any* religion, old or new, since it aspires not to exploit *any* other class or people, but rather to *liberate all* the oppressed people worldwide and bring an end to the reign of classes?

One thing is clear: The revolutionary leaders in Central America, with their unprincipled vacillations between catholicism and marxism, and between imperialism and the world proletariat, are making it that much harder for the Central American proletariat to emerge from its swaddling clothes of liberation theology. They are also making it practically impossible for the most honest and dynamic priests, nuns and layworkers of the christian base community movement to complete the transition from catholicism to atheism and revolutionary marxism.

In the last analysis, *liberation theology* is an absurd contradiction in terms. As laboring humanity liberates itself from all exploiters and masters on earth, it will have no need to recognize any master in the heavens. Once human beings achieve conscious control of their destiny—both collective and individual—they will scorn any idea of a god standing above society and manipulating its destiny. The liberation of humanity from all social oppression means the evaporation of all theology from the minds of men and women.

Chapter 6

Women's Liberation

Human nature is not eternal; it is elastic. Human nature is biologically rooted, but the essence of human biology is humanity's struggle with nature through the labor process, which gives rise to a definite social structure. Upon the foundations of that social structure arise cultural, political and religious institutions which in turn condition and mold human nature. The more society develops, the less human nature is determined biologically, and the more it is determined by the social class structure and the leading cultural institutions that reinforce the structure. When the social class structure changes, human nature changes along with it. That is why every profound social revolution creates, and is created by a profound change in human nature.

Machismo was an historical product of the Spanish conquest and enslavement of the indigenous peoples of the Americas, the *gyno*cidal defeat of the Amazons, the destruction of women's social autonomy, the repression of female sexuality, and the degrading cult of motherhood institutionalized by the catholic church. Alongside the smug *machismo* of the Spanish colonial landlord, who took Indian concubines according to his whim while maintaining his legal Spanish wife in a lofty state of sugary purity, arose the explosive "counter*machismo*" of the indigenous and *mestizo* peasant, deeply stung by the humiliation and degradation of his manhood, by the widespread rape and seizure of his women by the colonial rulers and their lackeys.

As Spanish colonial rule was eliminated and Latin America came under the iron heel of U.S. imperialism, *machismo* was *reinforced* by the intense frustration felt by Latin America's economically active classes—overwhelmingly men—at having their opportunities for development, prosperity and prestige squelched by the domination of the U.S. monopolies. Just as the worker who daily swallows indignities and humiliation at the hands of his foreman "makes up for it" by brutalizing his wife and children at home, the men of Latin America (whether bourgeois or proletarian), in the face of the humiliation, oppression and/or superexploitation meted out to them by the U.S. corporations, banks and political leaders, have tended to "make up for it" by puffing up their chests and aggravating their domination over "their" women.

But when the worker stops slavishly submitting to the capitalist tyranny in the factory and consciously rebels against it, asserting his suppressed dignity through struggle, he no longer has a psychological need to tyrannize his family at home. His rebellion may well have been catalyzed by the rebellion of his wife, by the fact that she has gained a measure of economic independence and no longer needs submit to his oppressive behavior. Likewise, when the laboring masses of Latin America take up arms in conscious revolutionary struggle against U.S. imperialism and its local lackeys, the mass psychology of *machismo* is undermined. The revolutionary struggles in Central America today form a doubleheaded hammer, delivering sharp blows to U.S. imperialism *and* to the demoralizing influence of *machismo*. And the hands that wield the hammer are increasingly the hands of women.

The Trans-Atlantic Inquisition

The Spanish *conquistadores* were well prepared for their mission of suppressing the women of the "new" world. Their invasion of the lower Americas was preceded by three centuries of mass torture and murder of women in Europe under the banner of the catholic inquisition. In a rare selfcriticism issued by the inquisition around 1623, it was admitted that "the gravest errors in trials for witchcraft are daily committed by inquisitors, so that the Inquisition has scarcely found one trial conducted legally, with women convicted on the most slender evidence, with confessions extorted by illegal means, and has had to punish its judges for inflicting excessive [!] tortures. In future, all inquisitors must keep strictly to the rules."[1] Burning at the stake was a common punishment for women thus convicted, and even the "rules" permitted torture to extract confessions to "crimes" often dictated by the perverse imaginations of the inquisitors.

Who were those hundreds of thousands of European women burned, garroted and hung by the inquisition and the subsequent anti"witch" hysteria fomented by the church? No doubt a great number, if not the majority of them were older women living on their own, easy targets for institutional terror since they were not (or were no longer) the property of men—and no one with any power in feudal society had any interest in defending them. How many, among the masses of murdered women, were midwives who, by spreading the practice and knowledge of herbal methods of birth control and abortion, helped give women some control over their reproductive powers and were thus viewed as a mortal threat by feudal patriarchy? How many were lesbians who refused to submit to the patriarchal tyranny?*

One thing is certain: Whatever remnants of *matriarchal* societies that had survived within the cracks of feudal reign over Europe, were exterminated by the inquisition and the anti"witch" terror. And, just as the conquering Spanish cavalrymen used the experience and selfconfidence they had gained through "liberating" Spain from Moorish occupation to conquer and massacre the indigenous peoples of America, so the *conquistadores* used the mass murderous momentum of the antiwoman inquisition to crush the rebellious women of the Americas. In the 16th century, the Spanish inquisition was extended to the new world.

Conquest of America, Conquest of Women

The subjugation of America required the subjugation of the Amazons. These were societies of all or mostly women that existed in many parts of the Americas from Brazil up through California, and did not take lightly to having their lands, labor and bodies robbed. Christopher "Genocide" Columbus first excited interest in the conquest of the Amazons by asserting that some of them lived in caves on Caribbean islands which strong winds preventing him from reaching. The legal contracts between the *conquistadores* and their mercantile capitalist backers often included clauses *requiring* a search for the Amazons.[3]

Why did these hardnosed men of commerce, hardly given to "romantic" flights of fancy, pay such avid attention to the routing out of the Amazon societies? Was it because the Amazons, democratically self-organized and thus able to mobilize their entire communities for armed struggle, offered the most protracted and tenacious resistance to the Spanish conquest? After all, the great

---

*The 1532 criminal code of the "holy Roman empire" mandated: "If a man has lascivious relations with a beast, or a man with a man, or a woman with a woman, they shall lose their life, and following general custom, they should be sentenced to death by burning."[2]

bronze age civilizations—of the Aztecs, Mayas and Incas—collapsed like houses of cards at the first blast of the Spaniards' blunderbusses and thrust of the Spaniards' swords; these hierarchical civilizations, their ruling cliques riddled with corruption and demoralization, proved impotent to mobilize the peasant masses they oppressed, to resist the *conquistadores*. But the Amazons were of a sharply different moral and military fiber. They passionately resisted the overthrow of matriarchy by patriarchy, which had occurred many centuries earlier, but may still have been in the process of occurring when the Spaniards first arrived on the scene. Did they practice lesbian sexuality, reproductive freedom, and such "male" survival activities as hunting? Were they the first to resist oppression by the indigenous patriarchal empires (Incas, Mayas, Aztecs), and the last to resist the onslaught of the *conquistadores*?

Certainly, most of the evidence of the lives, struggles, and deaths of the Amazons has been destroyed by the genocide they suffered (it can be assumed that the *conquistadores* followed the tradition of the inquisitors by burning their women victims to ashes) and the zeal of church censors to prevent any coherent account of the battles against the Amazons from reaching the public. What little objective evidence as remains has been largely overlooked or distorted by male chauvinist anthropologists, archeologists and literary analysts.

The first general strike in Nicaragua was by Indian women, refusing to bear children into conditions of slavery to the Spanish.[4] But once colonial slavery was imposed, the conquest of the indigenous women was nearly complete. Wherever the catholic church extended its authority, abortion, birth control, and divorce were banned. The inquisition terrorized indigenous women who continued to resist the patriarchal colonial regime, as well as European settler women who may have hoped to escape the witchhunting terror in Europe by coming to America.* The widespread rape

---

*According to the *New Catholic Encyclopedia*, the Latin American inquisition was initiated by catholic clergy who came to Mexico in the early 1520's and Perú in the 1530's. The Indian populations of both countries—where numerous Amazon societies were reported—were subject to the inquisition throughout the rest of the 16th century. "The major crimes committed by the Indians were, of course [!], idolatry and sacrifice, superstitious practices, and violations of the church's teachings on carnal relationships."[5] How many Indian lesbians were burned or boiled alive by the inquisition? The *New Catholic Encyclopedia* discreetly avoids raising this question. Nor does it raise the question of whether the catholic church is guilty of "superstitious practices."

of Indian women by Spanish men gave way to widespread domestic enslavement of indigenous and *mestizo* women in the patriarchal nuclear family—intensifying whatever patriarchal features as had existed among indigenous societies prior to the conquest. The dynamic goddesses of the Amazons and the women's communities were suppressed, distorted and transformed into the insipid, domesticated cult of the virgin Mary. Women who did not serve as highly fertile, submissive wives and uncomplaining, industrious mothers were viewed and treated with scorn. In Central America, it took the economic upheavals and deep social changes of the 1960's, and the mass political upheavals of the 1970's to open new and liberating vistas for women.

Capitalist Greed Undermines the Patriarchal Family

As modern agroexport capital, under the impact of U.S. imperialism, flooded Central America in the 1950's and 1960's, the traditional rural social structure was thrown into turmoil. Hundreds of thousands of peasants were expropriated from their meager landholdings, and seasonal wage labor on the big capitalist estates skyrocketed. Just as the peasant producer was separated from his means of production, so were peasant families separated from their once stable homesteads. Families became mobile, as women and children were drawn into the whirlwind of seasonal plantation labor. Rural women emerged from centuries of exclusively domestic slavery, to play an increasingly active role in social production. In Nicaragua, women came to make up 40% of the coffee pickers. In El Salvador, while women make up only 10% of the total rural labor force today, they make up some 50% of the rural *industrial* labor force.

Both men and women thus became directly superexploited by monopoly capital, and women's domestic burdens were not eased in the least. But women's relative economic independence, combined with men's enforced mobility through seasonal migrant labor, meant that the traditional bonds of legalized and sanctified prostitution had to break: The patriarchal family went crumbling. By 1978, 40% of the families in El Salvador were headed by women, and upon the triumph of the Nicaraguan revolution perhaps an even higher percentage of Nicaraguan families were headed by single women abandoned by the men who had fathered their children.[6] This phenomenon has surely been accelerated by widescale repression by the military dictatorships, which has violently torn many families apart; but political repression did not *create* this deepgoing social change. Nor can it be glibly explained by the "irresponsibility" of the men involved, or by the familiar practice of a husband dumping his wife after she has worn herself out bearing him several children, and taking up with a younger, more attractive woman. For in the profoundly changed social and psychological conditions of a Central America in the midst of revolutionary struggle, it is doubtful whether women need men as much as men need women.

El Salvador

The mass recruitment of Salvadoran women into the industrial workforce, especially in the countryside, propelled women into a prominent role in the labor union movement. As urban women gained more access to higher education, women students came to take a more and more active part in the intellectual, cultural and political ferment in the universities. But their career options were still restricted by the male monopolies over the liberal professions, and many turned to teaching as the most effective way to place their educations at the service of the people.

In 1965, teachers took to the streets to protest government repression. Out of this struggle formed the national teachers' union, ANDES *(Asociación Nacional de Educadores Salvadoreños)*. When the government ignored their demands, the teachers launched a strike which gradually shut down almost all of the nation's schools. Women by now made up between 80%-90% of the nation's teachers, and were casting off the traditional mentality of passive submission to their paternalistic employer, the government. The government formally agreed to the striking teachers' demands; but it did not implement the agreement and instead tried to dissolve the new teachers' union. So in February 1968, ANDES launched another big strike, with teachers occupying the ministry of education for 58 days. They received widespread support from the working class. The government cracked down hard, killing several teachers.

Since then, the tension between the teachers and the state has simmered and broken out repeatedly in open conflicts, including long strikes around basic economic demands in 1971 and 1984. As the christian base community movement and the popular organizations roused the rural masses to a new life of dignity, consciousness and struggle, many teachers plunged energetically into the work of the popular organizations. The most combative joined the revolutionary vanguard organizations. For several years, ANDES' secretary general was Dr. Mélida Anaya Montes, who later became a top leader of the FPL. Teachers became a prime target of the "security" forces and allied death squads, which sometimes even burst into classrooms and murdered teachers in front of their students. By January 1983, 309 teachers had been killed, with hundreds more kidnapped and tortured.[7] In the context of the civil war, the Salvadoran government and armed forces consider it a crime of subversion to teach the people how to read and write.

Today, at least 40% of the revolutionary members of the FMLN are women. Women are active at all levels of the popular and revolutionary organizations, including military combat and leadership. And the most combative section of the Salvadoran women's movement is the least known: the Committee of Women Political Prisoners, who daily confront and resist the torture, sexual sadism, and allround violation of their rights by the prison guards and military officers. When visited by the Red Cross, these revolutionary women declared that they do not expect to live to see the people's victory in the civil war: They expect to suffer the same fate as those political prisoners who remained in Somoza's dungeons on the eve of that dictator's overthrow. Somoza's last political prisoners were jammed into a basement, where they all died of asphyxiation.[8]

In El Salvador, it is not only the proletarian women, the peasant women, the oppressed and progressive petty-bourgeois women who have become sharply politicized through the eruption of the civil war. Salvadoran women *across the entire social and political spectrum* have been politicized and drawn actively into the struggle. From the standpoint of the bourgeois counterrevolution, this is most clearly seen in the energetic activities of the women's commission of the fascist ARENA party. On 10 December 1979, some 10,000 rightist and "moderate" women marched through San Salvador, demanding an "end to terrorism, violence and anarchy." Expressing their opposition to the liberal reforms declared by the "civilian"/military government, they were, in effect, calling on the military dictatorship to drown the insurgent masses in blood. But before they could reach the national palace, they were confronted by an outraged group of leftist women from the BPR and other popular organizations. In the ensuing struggle, seven people were killed and the reactionary women's demonstration was dissolved.[9]

The sweeping politicization and mobilization of women in El Salvador, surpassing that of any other country in the world, is the surest sign that a profound social transformation is in the making. Even if the revolution were betrayed, disarmed and suppressed beneath a bourgeois nationalist government—as happened in Zimbabwe, thanks to the class and national treason of Robert Mugabe —the revolutionary experience, initiative and consciousness of the masses of Salvadoran women would not permit a government of traitors to consolidate a neocolonial regime. In the course of the Zimbabwean revolution (1972-79), women were far less widely mobilized and less deeply politicized than Salvadoran women have been over the past several years. If a government of national treason is imposed upon El Salvador through a political settlement between U.S. imperialism, the Contadora group, the bourgeois liberal leaders of the FDR and the opportunist leaders of the FMLN, the revolutionary and progressive women will be the first to resist and prepare a nationwide renewal of the revolutionary struggle. And the very logic of the mass political mobilization of women in the current, revolutionary civil war is likely to prevent such a betrayal from "settling" the contest in the first place.

Guatemala

In Guatemala, women make up only 13.7% of the workforce.[10] Yet as many as 25% of the members of some revolutionary political/military organizations are now women.[11] "...Women now dare to speak in public," notes Silvia, a 25-year-old Ladina revolutionary who has learned the Quiché language in the course of the struggle. "And furthermore, it's almost always women who can speak to Indian communities in their languages. Everyone understands that women work as hard as men and are exploited at least as much as men. Indigenous women have advanced more rapidly than the women of the middle class; peasant women have come a lot farther than women from the capital. They have emerged from centuries of oppression to become the most advanced."[12]

Cristina, an Indian woman from Quiché, taught herself to read and eagerly grasped liberation theology through the radicalizing Catholic Action movement. When the Committee of Farmworkers' Unity (CUC) was formed in 1978, she became a local leader, narrowly escaped an army massacre of her village, and had to flee to Guatemala City to avoid being hunted down and murdered by the army. "Now," she related in 1982, "I am working with poor

Ladino peasants in the east; here I have learned many things. Before I believed that Ladinos were all wealthy and that they despised us for being natives. In the east I have come to know the poor Ladinos, some poorer and in worse conditions than us, because the little land which they possess is very bad and scarcely supports their crops... They have never discriminated against me or despised me. We have learned many things together, because my tasks with them always involve political training. They ask me many questions about the customs of my people, and ask me to teach them the Quiché language. I feel a great brotherhood, because they are also humble and simple like us, and it is with them that we are building a blood alliance for all time."[13]

The revolutionary organizers of the countryside, most notably the cadres of the EGP, have struggled persistently against backward social customs that kept women enslaved in the patriarchal family. With revolutionary men criticizing backward husbands and revolutionary women rousing the wives, the EGP cadres have struggled to end the common practice of wife beating, and the jealous refusal of husbands to let their wives leave home at night to participate in political work.[14] Indian women were traditionally even more oppressed in marriage relations than were Ladina women, and at first tended to be timid upon the approach of revolutionary organizers to their villages and homes. Some Indian groups, even after beginning to collaborate with the revolutionary movement, clung to their custom of purchase of a young woman into involuntary marriage by the family of a young man. As the revolutionary movement brought the Indian and Ladino populations into closer social contact and cooperation, occasional attempts by Indian families to extend their practice of bride purchase to young Ladina women (who, while marrying young, choose their husbands freely), led to painful frictions between the two ethnic groups—within the context of political collaboration against the dictatorship.[15]

As their political commitment freed them from domestic slavery, women became messengers and suppliers, teachers, organizers, public speakers, revolutionary soldiers and field commanders. The richly varied needs of the movement and the shifting hazards of the struggle against military genocide shattered the narrow horizons of the small town and isolated village. Women activists moved from mountains to city and into far flung rural organizing campaigns. The traditional sexual division of labor began breaking down, as women participated in farm labor and men helped out in the kitchen. Especially for the most revolutionary women, the nuclear family dissolved, as they often had to leave their children in the care of other women to go to the mountains for military training and refuge from the army's "woman hunts."

The children themselves, increasingly orphaned by the army's massacres and their own lives endangered by malnutrition and relentless repression, were drawn actively into the revolutionary struggle. They acted as messengers and intelligence gatherers on the army and its agents, carefully keeping the secrets of the revolutionary organization while under the murderous eyes of the army. The older children attend political meetings, work in the fields, and take up arms in community selfdefense. Upon reaching the age of 12 they can go to the mountains to receive more intensive political and combat training, as well as general education. [16] In the austere mountain camps of the revolutionary organization, a new form of family is emerging: a family of women, men and children collectively working and sharing the fruits of the land, sharing in the dangers and preparations for struggle. It provides a glimpse of the socialist relations of the future.

Rigoberta Menchú Tum, a young Indian woman from Quiché, came to the revolutionary movement through the struggle of her parents, both leaders of the people's movement and both murdered by the regime. "Because of the desperate conditions which exist in Guatemala," she relates, "women are developing a political consciousness. We are joining the people's struggle in great numbers... It is said that women have great patience for waging war and are very intelligent. If things don't work one way, women find another. They remain in the trenches until the last bullet of the enemy, whereas many men withdraw sooner. Women are said to be calm, and to have good aim with a gun.

"There are women in the mountains who are commanders, not because they speak well, but because they emerged from the people. They have learned through experience to withstand pain, to be patient and understand clearly which steps to take, and to fight without rest..."[17]

Nicaragua

In Nicaragua, women made up 30% of the revolutionary fighters who destroyed the Somoza regime. Yet the percentage of women in the nine *man* sandinista directorate and in the national government

Women militia fighters in the Guerrilla Army of the Poor (EGP) in Guatemala.

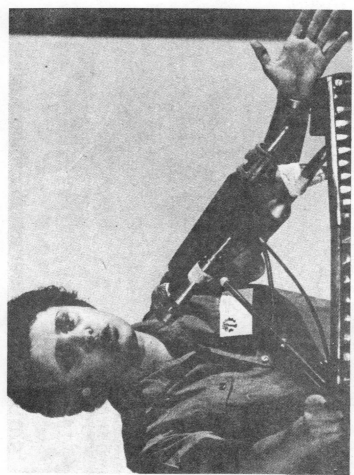

Comandante Dora Maria Tellez, of the Sandinista National Liberation Front (FSLN). In 1979, she led the victorious people's insurrection in Leon, Nicaragua's second largest city. But she, along with the hundreds of other revolutionary women in the FSLN, has been frozen out of government leadership by the male chauvinist FSLN leaders.

Margaret Randall

Nicaraguan mothers of martyrs of the revolution rally against the murderous assaults of the somocista contras, 1982. It was the mothers of heroes and martyrs who daringly interrupted the pope's reactionary sermon in Managua on 4 March 1983, demanding that he address himself to the revolutionary sacrifice their children had made. (Barricada, 27 July 1982).

Militia women in Nicaragua, 1981   NACLA

junta is zero. Ironically, the only woman who has ever served in the national junta has been a bourgeois liberal lady, Violeta Barrios de Chamorro—who resigned from the junta in April 1980, around the same time that the counterrevolutionary liberal Alfonso Robelo resigned. *Revolutionary* women, like *comandante* Dora María Tellez, who led the victorious armed insurrection in León, have been frozen out of the government and the *sandinista* directorate. The FSLN leaders' insistence upon maintaining their directorate and the government as an all male caste, clashes with their rhetoric about pursuing the "logic of the majority."

The conquest of power by the proletariat allied with the peasantry has not eliminated women's oppression in the home or in society at large; but it has opened a wide and fertile field for the women's liberation struggle to advance and develop, both in its practice and theory. The masses of Nicaraguan women, despite their revolutionary gains and heightened selfconfidence, continue to suffer oppression at the hands of the counterrevolutionary church hierarchy and bourgeoisie; they also confront the conservative inertia of the state bureaucracy, the male chauvinism of the FSLN leaders, and the spontaneous tendency of *machismo* to reentrench itself in every aspect of society. Their struggle against these retrograde forces will play a crucial role in determining whether the Nicaraguan revolution becomes truly permanent, or whether it "consolidates" into a bureaucratized miscarriage of itself, squashing the revolutionary aspirations of women beneath a privileged and conservative male caste—as has happened with the other workers' and peasants' revolutions of this century.

The Demilitarization of Women

In the first year after the victory of the revolution, the regime consciously drove women out of the prominent military role they had achieved in the heat of the civil war. Women fighters, proudly shouldering arms on the streets of Managua upon the revolution's victory, were reassigned to secretarial, guard, and political education posts. Many women left the *sandinista* army, and when the first officer ranks were announced in February 1980, there were only 15 women officers out of a total of 230.[18] When the people's militia movement was revived, women flooded passionately into its ranks, over the initial opposition of the FSLN leadership. But the subordinate position of women in the military life of the country, due to the creeping male domination over the regular army, led to a revival of the selfserving mentality among male soldiers that women are basically inferior to men in combat. Women's mass resentment against their programmed degradation in this crucial field was expressed in their political struggle (summer 1983) against the FSLN's sexist double standard in its military conscription bill—which resulted in a rotten compromise, whereby military service became compulsory for young men, but voluntary for women (see ch. 2).

A sign of the pronounced tendency to degrade the masses of women to the level of a "women's auxiliary" to the male army, can be seen in a 1983 publication by the women's organization (AMNLAE). Referring to its mass women's campaign to achieve economic savings through recycling durable consumer goods like bottles, AMNLAE wrote: "This year the savings campaign is aimed at obtaining funds for the nation's defense... Thousands of women are now actively working to raise a million *córdobas* in three months, which will be donated to our Armed Forces as the woman's contribution to the maintenance of the heroic batallions that fight the invaders."[19]

Progressive and Reactionary Women's Legislation

Following the revolution's victory, the government, in consultation with AMNLAE, issued a series of laws and decrees aimed to combat the institutionalized oppression of women. Women were granted full equality before the law. Whereas, under Somoza, male heads of families had held exclusive rights to land property titles, now land titles were granted to couples jointly. All farmworkers were granted equal rights without distinction of sex, ending the old practice of male harvest workers being paid both their own wages and the wages of their wives working alongside them. Equal pay for equal work was enshrined in law. But male workers, in both the industrial and agricultural sectors, have often continued expecting higher pay than women workers performing the same tasks— sometimes even threatening job action to prevent the law from being enforced.[20] Moreover, women still tend to be tracked into the less skilled, lower paying jobs.

The use of women as sex symbols in advertising was banned. All legal distinctions between "legitimate" and "illegitimate" children have been banned—an important advance in a society where over half of the couples are unmarried. Breastfeeding has been actively promoted by the government, AMNLAE and the people's health movement; advertising of milk substitutes for breastfeeding has been banned. Women, as well as men, can now legally adopt children, and the adoption-for-profit racket has been outlawed. Under Somoza, divorce resulted routinely in child custody for the father; now divorce tends to result in child custody for the mother. Prostitution, legal and flourishing under Somoza, has been outlawed,* and a rehabilitation program created to provide former prostitutes with job training, and social and political education.

The laws regulating family relations were passed after widespread debate among both women and men in hundreds of mass assemblies around the country, in the media and in the council of state. One of these laws, the "law of maintenance," requires both parents to contribute to the personal and material support of the children, whether the parents are married or not—or living together or not. This law was declared necessary to protect women and the family, providing a legal mechanism for women to seek economic support from absent fathers. It is accompanied with exhortations to fathers to contribute equally in household chores, alongside mothers.

This law has been praised by muddleheaded radicals as highly progressive. In reality, it is *reactionary*, because it *perpetuates* women's economic dependence on men; it seeks, in effect, to *reinstitutionalize the bourgeois, monogamous nuclear family*, under the utopian signboard of "equality" between men and women within the same old family structure. The requirement that fathers economically support the upkeep of their families (whether intact or not) is backward and patronizing to women, since it presupposes that women will continue to play a subordinate role in the economic life of society, continuing to squander an enormous portion of their life's time and energy on the rearing of their own children.

From a revolutionary standpoint, the *progressive disintegration* of the nuclear family under the impact of capitalist agriculture under Somoza and the people's war against Somoza, should be

---

*While the regime's treatment of prostitutes has generally been progressive and humane, its *outlawing* of prostitution is a clear example of the "legalistic blockheadedness" of the FSLN leaders. As long as commodity production exists, as long as there is unemployment, impoverishment of women and sexual repression, some women will be economically compelled and propelled into selling their bodies for hire to men with the means to pay. Outlawing prostitution—instead of realistically recognizing it as a stubborn social disease inherited from capitalism which can only be eliminated through allsided and protracted socialist development—is bound to criminalize the victims.

carried through to its logical conclusion: the fullscale *socialization of childrearing and housework,* thus liberating women from domestic slavery. Childrearing and housework, instead of being the private responsibility of parents—in reality, mothers—should become the collective responsibility of society as a whole, performed by dedicated public employees, both men and women, receiving decent pay for their socially vital work. This would clear the way for genuine social equality for women, tossing patriarchy and father right* onto the scrap heap of history. It would also allow human beings of all ages to pursue interpersonal and sexual relations freely and to create new forms of "family" groupings, free from the brutalizing and stultifying confines of the bourgeois nuclear family.

Such a communist program, to be sure, could never be achieved within the confines of a single country, least of all a tiny and impoverished country like Nicaragua, under the gun of professional counterrevolutionaries backed by U.S. imperialism. While AMNLAE has pioneered the development of childcare centers and women's economic cooperatives, several of the childcare and cooperative facilities have been destroyed by the *somocista* thugs. And the successful socialization of housework requires substantial technological inputs (washing machines, housecleaning appliances, etc.), eventually including robots, which are currently under the stranglehold of imperialism.

But the fact that the FSLN leaders have failed to cast a beacon light in the direction of this liberating future, insisting on trying to breathe fresh, "revolutionary" life into the stinking corpse of the nuclear family, shows that they still have one foot heavily planted in the old bourgeois, patriarchal society. Their reformist attempt to legislate equality of the sexes within the confines of a social institution (the nuclear family) historically based on the patriarchal enslavement of women and children, has failed miserably.

*"*Father right*" means the reckoning of descent and the inheritance of family wealth through the father. Interestingly, the Hispanic system of family names is less sexist than that derived from other European countries. In the Hispanic system, a woman does not change her name when she marries, and she passes on her father's family name to her children in the form of their "last" name (her *husband's* family name becomes the "middle," and more essential name of the children). This is still, however, *patrilineage,* rooted in the several millennia of enslavement of women and children to men through the patriarchal family. The overthrow of patriarchy also means the overthrow of the oppressive idiocy of father right (patrilineage), and its replacement with the more natural, logical and simple *mother right*: reckoning of descent through the mother.

The renewed official emphasis on the family has reinforced the backward, *macho* attitude among a great many men that, since the revolution has been won, it's time for women to get back to their "natural" place in the kitchen and bedroom. Whereas, during the course of the guerrilla struggle against Somoza, many men washed dishes, few do so today.[21] And many absent fathers have attempted to skirt the "law of maintenance" by denying paternity when women press for child support.

AMNLAE now plans to introduce a law geared to establish guidelines for proof of paternity.[22] Such a law could only lead to a hopeless bureaucratic tangle, and continue to misdirect the social and political energies of women into chasing the tail of the patriarchal tiger. The workers' state, not individual fathers or mothers, should be responsible for child support. That the AMNLAE leaders continue to uphold the law of maintenance as a "liberating" measure shows that, hemmed in by the male chauvinist FSLN leaders, they have yet to solve the theoretical problems of the overthrow of patriarchy.

How Did Henry Hyde Get to Stand on Both Sides of the Barricade in Nicaragua?

The 23 March 1980 issue of the FSLN's *Barricada* newspaper presented a list of areas where women's rights still needed to be improved—including the right to abortion. Today, over five years after the victory of the revolution, the Somoza era law banning abortion remains in force. The only possibility for a woman to have a legal abortion comes when her life is in danger—and even then, she must receive consent from the man. So Nicaraguan women continue to be mutilated and killed by amateur, illegal abortion attempts.

Ironically, this is the same situation facing poor women in the imperialist USA—thanks to the 1977 Hyde amendment, which banned federal Medicaid funding for abortions. And the initiator of that murderous amendment, congressman Henry Hyde (Republican from Illinois), is highly interested in Nicaragua. In the congressional debates over U.S. policy towards Nicaragua, Hyde has distinguished himself with his tirades against the revolution and mouthfoaming advocacy of generous funding for CIA covert operations in support of the *somocistas* fighting against "communist tyranny" in Nicaragua. Hyde argues that, if U.S. covert military operations against the nazis in world war 2 were justifiable, then

U.S. covert operations against the "communists" in Central America must likewise be justified.[23] He overlooks the fact that the *somocista contras*, along with the Salvadoran and Guatemalan armed forces, are playing a role comparable to the nazis' in launching anticivilian massacres and genocide against the oppressed peoples, on behalf of imperialism—not German imperialism, to be sure, but U.S. imperialism. Yet the nazis were fanatically antiabortion—banning abortion among "their" women, under the signboard of "kids, kitchen and church" as women's patriarchal destiny; and in this respect as well, Henry Hyde is in full agreement with nazism. So, thanks to the FSLN leaders' reactionary, antiwoman abortion policy, Hyde has managed to get his way on *both* sides of the barricades in Nicaragua.

In the first years following the revolution's victory, not only did abortion remain illegal, but birth control information and devices were scarcely available. Through AMNLAE's initiative, this latter situation was changed, and now birth control devices are freely available in health clinics and methods of birth control frequently discussed in AMNLAE's popular magazine. The persistent antiabortion policy has been criticized and struggled against by the most politically advanced members and leaders of AMNLAE.

Milú Vargas, chief legal adviser to the council of state, has publicly criticized the existing antiabortion law in a magazine interview, declaring that the law needs to be overturned as soon as possible.[24] Her opinion appears to be shared by several AMNLAE leaders. She adds, however, that "We cannot pass a law on abortion without preparing the people... For many Nicaraguan women, the revolution has come to signify the right to be a mother."[25] It is clear that such preparation, which has yet to begin, can only mean a bold and sharp political struggle to break the murderous power of the catholic church hierarchy, the bourgeoisie, and *macho* men over women's bodies.

Margaret Randall, a North American radical journalist, historian, poet and photographer now living in Nicaragua and politically supporting the FSLN regime, has decided to capitulate to these reactionary social forces before the mass struggle over the abortion question has even begun. Randall has warned that "abortion [rights] legislation...in the context of the present Nicaraguan society, would be a perfect issue for the right wing to exploit."[26] This is similar to the argument put forward by the *right wing* of the North American women's movement that, "in the context of the present U.S. society," it would be a dangerous mistake to "provoke" the "moral majority" and assorted rightwing thugs by struggling for abortion rights and lesbian rights—but that the women's movement should confine its mass activities to "safe" issues like the equal rights amendment and lobbying the imperialist Democratic Party to run a woman for vice president. Opportunists never fail to find an appropriate "context" for their capitulation to the bourgeoisie.

Perhaps Randall would also have solemnly warned the mothers of heroes and martyrs, on the occasion of the pope's extravaganza in Managua, that they must under no conditions interrupt the pope's arrogant and reactionary sermon—for that would become a "perfect issue for the right wing to exploit." But the revolutionary Nicaraguan women are not afraid to struggle against anyone or any institution—no matter how holy—that is trampling on their aspirations. The Right and the Vatican did, to be sure, "exploit" the mass "incident" at the pope's sermon to whip up some more agitation against the Nicaraguan revolution; but there can be no denying that the Right suffered a sharp political setback in Nicaragua that day, thanks to the bold rebellion of the people against the pope.

Randall attempts to bolster her antiabortion position by asserting that "most Nicaraguans are catholic, and that pervades every facet of their life and thought."[27] But this ignores the fact that there are *two opposing camps* of catholics in Nicaragua. Archbishop Obando and his churchy cronies, with their tight links to the Vatican, have a vested interest in maintaining the patriarchal tyranny over women's bodies and thus opposing abortion. But the masses of Nicaraguan women, who tend to adhere to the *people's* church movement, have an *objective interest in breaking the patriarchal tyranny over their bodies and sexual expression.* And the preachers of liberation theology, who uphold the struggle of the oppressed people to gain control of their own destiny, can hardly offer a principled objection to women gaining control of their own bodies.

A bold and principled mass struggle around the abortion issue would surely win masses of women, and several liberationist priests, nuns and church layworkers as well, away from catholicism and into the camp of revolutionary marxism. It would also transform the backward, *macho* consiousness of many working men—who are bound to oppose abortion as long as no mass struggle is waged in favor of abortion rights, and can be expected to vacillate between the two opposing camps when the struggle first breaks out.

The FSLN leaders and their apologists argue that, since the majority of Nicaraguans oppose abortion, it would be "premature" and politically dangerous to grant women abortion rights. But this is narrowminded and shortsighted, glibly accepting the sexist "consensus" imposed upon society by centuries of patriarchal violence against women. It is the method of opportunism to unite with the *more backward* sections of the masses, thus *drowning the most advanced sentiments and ideas* in a reactionary "consensus" which reinforces bourgeois policy and bourgeois ideology over the masses. Since they refuse to conduct an allround mass campaign to win abortion rights for women, the FSLN leaders' forecast that the masses are "not ready" for abortion rights becomes a self-fulfilling prophesy. The marxist-leninist method, by contrast, is to unite with the *most advanced* sections of the masses to educate and rally the broader, less enlightened masses to revolutionary consciousness and action.

Some North American radical feminists, drifting to the right, have chosen to unite with the anti-revolutionary FSLN regime rather than with the revolutionary interests of Nicaraguan women. Adrienne Rich, a prominent lesbian feminist poet and theoretician, has made sharp insights into how patriarchy brutalizes women physically and psychologically by denying them freedom to control their reproductive functions. Upon visiting Nicaragua, Rich decided that her insights do not apply south of the Rio Grande. Echoing the narrow pragmatism of the FSLN leaders, who *counterpose* the struggle against the CIA backed *contras* to women's reproductive rights, Rich accepted their rationale for maintaining Somoza's antiabortion law. She insisted that, when rebuilding a society ravaged by civil war, "you begin by stopping the torture and killing of the unprotected, by feeding the hungry so that they have energy to think about what they want beyond food."[28] But, as Sarah Schulman retorted, "A Nicaraguan woman dead from illegal abortion is just as dead as a woman killed by U.S. backed *contras*."[29]

María Lilian Torres, director of a children's hospital in Valez País, has cited amateur abortion attempts as one of the three major causes of maternal death in Nicaragua (along with toxemia and hemorrhage). One hospital in Managua admits ten women a day due to illegal abortions.[30]

Few North American radical feminists, in the face of *"gringa"* baiting and guilt tripping by "third worldist" opportunists, have had the moral and intellectual courage to publicly uphold the revolutionary interests of Nicaraguan women against the church hierarchy, the bourgeoisie and the male chauvinist FSLN leaders who continue to deny women control over their own bodies. This has left the field wide open for *bourgeois* feminists like Gloria Steinem and Betty Friedan, who basically *oppose* the Nicaraguan revolution, to *counterpose* reproductive rights to support for national liberation struggles against U.S. imperialism.

Some third world male radicals have attempted to justify their backwardness on the abortion question by pointing to the fact that U.S. imperialism over the past quarter century has set up many "family planning" health clinics in Latin America—including Somoza's Nicaragua—which served as cover for a racist policy of population control by coercing or tricking women into sterilization. Indeed, some 40% of all Puerto Rican women have now been sterilized in U.S. colonial hospitals, in a campaign of "slow motion genocide" designed to liquidate the Puerto Rican nation. But only a male chauvinist muddlehead could equate forced (or economically induced) sterilization with a woman's right to a free and safe abortion. The sterilization campaign involves the racist, patriarchal *destruction* of women's reproductive power; legalized abortion involves women's *control* over their reproductive power. Indeed, it is precisely the lack of access to free and safe abortion that has driven many poor women of color to the desperate measure of "voluntary" sterilization.*

The Gay Question

The FSLN regime's attempt to rebuild the nuclear family as the basic cell of society clashes with the liberation of human sexuality, including homosexuality, from bourgeois and churchy constraints. Both Daniel Ortega and Tomás Borge have publicly denounced homosexual activity as a "perversion." These narrowminded moralists are treading on eggshells, because some leading FSLN members themselves happen to be "closet" gays.[31] To date there

---

*In this light, it is no accident that the Reagan administration announced, on 25 June 1984, that U.S. aid dollars would be cut off from any programs of the UN's Fund for Population Activities that involve abortion. "Population activities" is the UN's euphemism for population *control*. Reagan thus insisted on "linking" population control to patriarchy's intensified control over women's bodies.

are no antihomosexual laws in Nicaragua, nor has there been overt state repression against gay men or lesbians. But if the women's liberation movement gets throttled in its current stage of development, if the moral authority of the Vatican and the church hierarchy is not decisively overthrown, and if the state bureaucracy fully consolidates its parasitic rule over the masses, then deep state repression against homosexuals will inevitably set in—as has occurred in most other bureaucratically deformed workers' states (USSR, China, Cuba, etc.).

Women in Catholicism, Women against Catholicism

The FSLN leaders, while lavishly accommodating the pope's visit to Nicaragua with state funds (see ch. 5), have left catholic women in the lurch by failing to raise the democratic demand for the right of women to be ordained as priests in the catholic church. But in areas of the country where no priests are available, women in the people's church movement have taken matters into their own hands, performing religious duties officially reserved for priests— much to the chagrin of the hierarchy. Meanwhile, the struggle for ordination of women as priests has remained the lonely task of liberal catholic women in North America and western Europe. The Vatican, for its part, has been quite right in refusing to budge on this question. Equality between the sexes means the destruction of the catholic church. And the liberation of women means the destruction of all organized religion.

It is a tensile irony of history that the people who have been the most oppressed and brutalized by the catholic church in Latin America—the masses of women—are precisely those who have "traditionally" been the most ardent in their catholic faith. This explosive contradiction can only be resolved through a profound and continuous revolution, which transforms not only the social class structure, but also cultural institutions, human psychology and sexual relations—in a word, human nature. The stunning interruption of the pope's holy sermon by a group of revolutionary mothers—an event without precedent in world history—was the opening salvo of the revolutionary struggle to come.

Once millions of working women have awakened to revolutionary consciousness and plunged into the struggle, the collective release of their pent up psychic, political and intellectual energies will be enough to destroy every economic, political and religious institution of patriarchy—and will sweep the now backward masses of men along with it as well. This struggle will not end until women throughout the world have reconquered, on a higher technological level, the freedom, respect and selfgovernment which they originally enjoyed until their societies were overturned by the patriarchal onslaught several thousand years ago.

The Hemisphere Stood on Its Head

The revolutionary Nicaraguan women, despite being stifled by the opportunist "woman policy" of the FSLN leaders, have succeeded in cutting the incidents of rape down to a very small number, and have made sharp inroads against wifebeating as well. They have done this through their energetic participation in the "vigilance" night patrols organized by the *sandinista* defense committees.[32] In this important respect, Nicaraguan women are already freer than women in the U.S., where rape and womanbeating have long been epidemic. But U.S. imperialism, whose mass media propagandize bestial violence against women as "natural" in order to fuel the mentality of military aggression and invasion, is gearing up to drown the freedom struggles of all the Central American peoples in blood.

But, if the U.S. imperialist tyranny over Latin America intensified the psychology of *machismo* within Latin America, then the revolutionary struggle to overturn *machismo* spells the death knell for U.S. imperialism. The time cannot be far off when the Latin American masses, women and men, mercilessly ridicule and assail the *North American macho* as a relic of the savagery of bourgeois civilization.

Reference Notes

Chapter 1: El Salvador

1. Cited in George Black, *Triumph of the People: The Sandinista Revolution in Nicaragua*, London: Zed Press, 1981, p. 130.
2. As in the U.S., the estimates of the number of participants in mass demonstrations in El Salvador vary widely, from source to source. For this crucial demonstration, I have seen estimates as low as 100,000 and as high as 300,000. The figure of 150,000 comes from the jesuit university journal *Eca (Estudios Centroamericanos)*, February 1984—probably as reliable a source as any. This is also the source I have used for the number of dead and wounded—the figures on which also vary from source to source.
3. Robert Armstrong, "El Salvador: Brink of Civil War?" *Guardian*, New York, 6 Feb 1980. Also *Guardian*, 30 Jan 1980.
4. Laurence Simon and James Stephens, Jr., "El Salvador Land Reform 1980-1: Impact Audit," 2nd edition, Oxfam America, 1982, p. 2.
5. *Ibid.*
6. Penny Lernoux, *Cry of the People*, New York: Doubleday & Co., 1980, pp. 211-13.
7. *Guardian*, New York, 10 June 1981.
8. Leonel Gómez, "El Salvador's Land Reform: A Real Promise But a Final Failure," *El Salvador: Central America in the New Cold War*, Gettleman, Lacefield, Menashe, Mermelstein and Radosh, editors, New York: Grove Press, 1981, pp. 178-81.
9. Martin Diskin, 1982 supplement to Simon and Stephens, *op. cit.*, p. 37.
10. Simon and Stephens, Jr., *op. cit.*, pp. 11-12.
11. *Eca*, Feb 1984. English translation published in *NACLA Report on the Americas*, New York, Mar/Apr 1984, p. 40.
12. Simon and Stephens, Jr., *op. cit.*, p. 9.
13. "Special Law for the Issuance of the Agrarian Reform Bonds," (decree 220), clause "h". Published in English translation in Simon and Stephens, Jr., *op. cit.*, p. 55.
14. *El Salvador News-Gazette.*
15. "Decree 222: Amendments to the Basic Law of Agrarian Reform," art. 2. English translation in Simon and Stephens, Jr., *op. cit.*, p. 56.
16. Philip Wheaton, "Agrarian Reform in El Salvador: A Program of Rural Pacification," Washington DC: EPICA Task Force, p. 15.
17. Diskin, *op. cit.*, p. 30.
18. Simon and Stephens, Jr., *op. cit.*, p. 9.
19. *Eca* no. 403-4, San Salvador, May/June 1982, p. 521.
20. *Ibid.*

21. Diskin, *op. cit.*, p. 31 (calculation from line 7 of his statistical table).

22. *La Prensa Gráfica*, San Salvador, 7 Mar 1983.

23. Interview with a Salvadoran revolutionary, June 1984.

24. *Eca*, no. 403-4, p. 391.

25. Simon and Stephens, Jr., *op. cit.*, p. 17.

26. Wheaton, *op. cit.*, p. 12.

27. *El Salvador's Link*, June 1984, p. 5.

28. Diskin, *op. cit.*, p. 43.

29. Simon and Stephens, Jr., *op. cit.*, p. 1.

30. *Ibid.*, p. 20.

31. Diskin, *op. cit.*, p. 43.

32. *Eca*, no. 403-4, p. 517.

33. Arnon Hadar, "El Salvador: The Struggle for Democracy and U.S. Involvement," San Francisco: Casa El Salvador Farabundo Martí, p. 8.

34. "The Catholic Church in El Salvador," *El Salvador Bulletin*, Berkeley, Dec 1982, p. 5.

35. *Ibid.*

36. D.P. Noonan, "Catholic Church at a Crossroads," *Guardian*, New York, 9 July 1980, p. 20.

37. "The Catholic Church in El Salvador," *op. cit.*

38. Xavier Reyes, "La masacre estaba preparada!" *Barricada*, Managua, 31 Mar 1980, p. 12. Reyes estimated the total attendance at Romero's funeral as over 300,000.

39. Ignacio Martín Baró, "El liderazgo de Monseñor Romero (un análisis psico-social)."

40. *Ibid.*

41. *Ibid.*, and *Eca*, Feb 1984. Reyes gives a far higher tally of the killed and wounded.

42. Mario Menéndez Rodríguez, *Voices from El Salvador*, San Francisco: Solidarity Publications, 1983, p. 2.

43. *Eca*, no. 403-4, May/June 1982, p. 510.

44. *Eca*, Feb 1984.

45. Simon and Stephens, Jr., *op. cit.*, p. 12.

46. *Ibid.*, p. 19.

47. *Guardian* supplement on El Salvador, New York, spring 1981.

48. Menéndez Rodríguez, *op. cit.*, pp. 127-8.

49. *Ibid.*, pp. 131, 130.

50. Ramón Bonachea and Marta San Martín, *The Cuban Insurrection 1952-1959*, New Brunswick, NJ: Transaction Books, 1974, p. 100.

51. "Why is the FMLN Fighting?" Radio Venceremos System, Jan 1984, pp. 25, 26.

52. *Ibid.*, p. 26.

53. Robert Armstrong, "Junta Moves to the Right," *Guardian*, New York, 2 Jan 1980, p. 11.

54. Wheaton, *op. cit.*, p. 11.

55. *Guardian,* New York, 4 June 1980.

56. "What Are the FPL in El Salvador?" International edition of the FPL, 1980, p. 1.

57. *Barricada*, Managua, 10 Apr 1983, p. 3. The original Spanish text read: "La lucha de los pueblos centroamericanos es una sola; cuando Sandino levantó las guerrillas en la montaña, tuvo a su lado a compañeros de todo Centroamérica y toda ella vibró contra el imperialismo en la lucha y las hazañas de los guerrilleros heróicos de Nicaragua; estuvo nuestro principal dirigente revolucionario, el compañero Farabundo Martí, junto a Sandino.

"...Estamos todos los pueblos centroamericanos bajo la agresión del imperialismo norteamericano; estamos luchando contra su invervención en todas las formas dignas que sean posibles, pero también, sabemos que todos los pueblos centroamericanos se convertirán en una hoguera revolucionaria si el imperialismo lleva a cabo sus planes de agresión contra Nicaragua o El Salvador."

58. "Ultima carta de Cayetano Carpio," *El Bolchevique*, no. 25, Los Angeles, June/July 1984, p. 25. The original Spanish text read: "...Pero una cosa es luchar contra el imperialismo y sus intrigas y otra sentir la injusticia, la calumnia y la infamia de parte de los mismo hermanos. Una negra conjura por manchar mi vida revolucionaria y dañar profundamente a las FPL está en marcha y llegando a su culminación...

"No puedo soportar impotente que así se trate a mi querida organización, base de la lucha revolucionaria de mi pueblo y de la unidad consecuente, ni a las exigencias de que ponga sus organismos, redes, miembros y colaboradores en manos de una investigación mal conducida y prejuiciada. Y no puedo soportar el escarnio que se hace de mi persona, la infamia de querer involucrar mi nombre aunque sea indirectamente, la torva insinuación en esa dirección, en el doloroso caso de la terrible pérdida de nuestra compañera Ana María."

59. "FMLN Splits Over Negotiations," *Working Class Opposition*, Los Angeles, June/July 1984, p. 15.

60. "Comunicado de las Fuerzas Populares de Liberación 'Farabundo Martí.'" Mimeographed bulletin, San Salvador, 21 Apr 1983, p. 1.

61. *Guardian*, New York, 18 May 1983, p. 1.

62. "Plataforma Programática para un Gobierno Democrático Revolucionario," FDR, pp. 4-5. The original Spanish text read: "Este Gobierno se apoyará en una amplia base social y política formada en primer lugar, por la clase obrera, el campesinado y las capas medias avanzadas: íntimamente unidas a ellas, estarán todas las capas sociales dispuestas a llevar adelante esta Plataforma; pequeños y medianos empresarios industriales, comerciales, artesanales, agropecuarios (pequeños y medianos cafetaleros y de los otros renglones de la agricultura y ganadería). Comprenderá así mismo, a los profesionales honestos, al clero progresista, a partidos democráticos como el MNR, los sectores avanzados de la Democracia Cristiana, a los oficiales dignos y honestos del Ejército, que estén

dispuestos a servir a los intereses del Pueblo y todo otro sector, grupo, personalidades o segmentos que aboguen por la amplia democracia para las masas populares, por el desarrollo independiente, por la liberación popular."

63. *El Bolchevique, op. cit.*, p. 18.

64. "Comunicado de las Fuerzas Populares de Liberación 'Farabundo Martí,'" 21 Apr 1983, *op. cit.*

65. Communiqué of the central committee of the FPL, El Salvador, 9 Dec 1983.

66. "FMLN Splits Over Negotiations," *op. cit.*

67. Bonachea and San Martín, *op. cit.*, p. 262.

68. *Eca*, Feb 1984. English translation in *NACLA Report on the Americas*, Mar/Apr 1984, p. 16.

69. Ronald Reagan, interview with Malcolm Forbes and Steve Forbes, *Forbes* magazine, 1 Aug 1983.

70. Reagan's speech welcoming Miguel de la Madrid, Washington DC, 15 May 1984 (news dispatches).

71. Murat Williams, "Three Decades of U.S. Aid to El Salvador," *San Francisco Chronicle*, 6 Apr 1983. Originally published in the *Washington Post*.

72. *Counterspy* magazine, May/June 1982. The testimony was given in Cuernavaca, Mexico, where the soldier had escaped to, after himself being imprisoned and tortured by his superiors as a suspected guerrilla. As he is now wanted dead or alive in El Salvador, his name was withheld.

73. D. Fogel, *Africa in Struggle: National Liberation and Proletarian Revolution*, Seattle: Ism Press, 1982, pp. 357-68.

Chapter 2: Nicaragua

1. George Black, *Triumph of the People: The Sandinista Revolution in Nicaragua*, London: Zed Press, 1981. p. 110.

2. *Ibid.*, pp. 109-12.

3. *Ibid.*, pp. 113-15.

4. Cited in *ibid.*, p. 120.

5. *Ibid.*, p. 128.

6. *Ibid.*, pp. 132-5.

7. *Ibid.*, p. 139.

8. "Economic Balance for 1982," *Envio*, Instituto Histórico Centroamericano, Managua, June 1983.

9. *NACLA Report on the Americas*, New York, May/June 1980, p. 19.

10. Black, *op. cit.*, pp. 343-4.

11. Jan Flora, John McFadden, and Ruth Warner, "The Growth of Class Struggle: The Impact of the Nicaraguan Literacy Crusade on the Political Consciousness of Young Literacy Workers," *Latin American Perspectives*, issue 36, winter 1983, p. 49.

12. *Guardian*, New York, 19 Nov 1980.
13. Harry Fried, "Nicaraguan Rightists Plan Return," *Guardian*, New York, 10 Dec 1980.
14. Joseph Collins, *What Difference Could a Revolution Make?: Food and Farming in the New Nicaragua*, San Francisco: Institute for Food and Development Policy, 1982, p. 39.
15. *Ibid.*, p. 33.
16. Black, *op. cit.*, p. 234.
17. Collins, *op. cit.*, pp. 46, 48-9.
18. *Ibid.*, p. 48.
19. *Ibid.*, p. 49.
20. *Ibid.*
21. *Ibid.*
22. *Ibid.*, pp. 90-1, 93-4.
23. *Ibid.*, pp. 89-91.
24. Margaret Randall, "Nicaragua: Women in the People's Militia" (mimeographed).
25. *Womanews*, New York, Dec/Jan 1983-84, p. 7.
26. Kent Norsworthy and Bill Robinson, "Where Draft Resistance is Right Wing," *Guardian*, New York, 5 Oct 1983, p. 14.
27. *Ibid.*
28. *Guardian* supplement on El Salvador, New York, spring 1981, p. 5.
29. *Working Class Opposition*, Los Angeles, Apr 1984, p. 4.
30. "Economic Balance for 1982," *op. cit.*
31. Ramón Bonachea and Marta San Martín, *The Cuban Insurrection 1952-1959*, New Brunswick, NJ: Transaction Books, 1974, p. 330.

Chapter 3: Miskitu Question

1. Interview with Armstrong Wiggins, *Akwesasne Notes*, late autumn 1981.
2. *Navajo Times*, 20 Jan 1984. Reprinted in *Indigenous World/El Mundo Indígena*, San Francisco, vol. 3, no. 2, 1984, p. 16.
3. Population statistics compiled through Nicaraguan government literacy campaign, 1980-1.
4. Interview with Norman Bent, *Sojourners* magazine, Washington DC, March 1983, p. 28.
5. *Ibid.*, p. 25.
6. Interview with Myrna Cunningham, *Nicaraguan Perspectives*, Berkeley, summer 1984, p. 31.
7. Interview with Armstrong Wiggins, *op. cit.*
8. *Indigenous World, op. cit.*, p. 1.
9. Eduard Conzemius, *Ethnographic Survey of the Miskito and Sumu Indians of Honduras and Nicaragua*, Smithsonian Institute Bureau of American Ethnology, Bulletin 106, Washington DC: U.S. Government Printing Office, 1932, p. 84.

10. *Ibid.*, p. 85.

11. *Ibid.*, pp. 86-7, 115. Also Bernard Nietschmann, *Caribbean Edge: The Coming of Modern Times to Isolated People and Wildlife*, New York: Bobbs-Merrill Co., 1979, p. 68.

12. Conzemius, *op. cit.*, p. 87.

13. *Ibid.*

14. *Ibid.*, p. 101.

15. Interview with Armstrong Wiggins, *op. cit.*, p. 6.

16. John Mohawk and Shelton Davis, "Revolutionary Contradictions: Miskitos and Sandinistas in Nicaragua," *Akwesasne Notes*, spring 1982, p. 8.

17. George Black, *Triumph of the People: The Sandinista Revolution in Nicaragua*, London: Zed Press, 1981, pp. 16, 20, 212.

18. *Navajo Times*, *op. cit.*

19. Conzemius, *op. cit.*, p. 39.

20. *Ibid.*, pp. 148-50.

21. Author's interview with a Nicaraguan of African origin from Bluefields, June 1984.

22. *Ibid.*

23. Mohawk and Davis, *op. cit.*

24. Nietschmann, *op. cit.*, p. 176.

25. *Ibid.*, pp. 185-6.

26. Interview with Norman Bent, *op. cit.*

27. *Ibid.*, and Interview with Armstrong Wiggins, *op. cit.*

28. *Ibid.*, pp. 25-6; and Interview with Armstrong Wiggins, *op. cit.*

29. *Ibid.*, p. 26.

30. Black, *op. cit.*, p. 121.

31. Interview with Armstrong Wiggins, *op. cit.*, p. 7.

32. *Ibid.* Also speech by Vernon Bellecourt, San Francisco, 27 Mar 1983.

33. *Ibid.* (Wiggins).

34. *Ibid.*

35. *Ibid.*

36. *Ibid.* Also Interview with Norman Bent, *op. cit.*

37. *Ibid.*

38. Interview with Myrna Cunningham, *op. cit.*, p. 32.

39. Interview with Norman Bent, *op. cit.*

40. Interview with Armstrong Wiggins, *op. cit.*

41. *Ibid.*

42. Interview with Norman Bent, *op. cit.*, p. 27.

43. *Ibid.*, p. 26.

44. Interview with Armstrong Wiggins, *op. cit.*

45. Interview with Norman Bent, *op. cit.*

46. *Ibid.*

47. Interview with Armstrong Wiggins, *op. cit.*

48. Interview with Norman Bent, *op. cit.*

49. *Ibid.*

50. Interview with Armstrong Wiggins, *op. cit.*

51. "Declaración de Principios sobre Comunidades Indígenas," *Barricada Internacional*, Managua, 21 Aug 1981, p. 6. The original Spanish text read: "La Nación Nicaragüense es una sola, territorial y políticamente y no puede ser desmembrada, dividida o lesionada en su soberanía e independencia. Su idioma oficial es el español."

52. *Ibid.*: "Los Recursos Naturales de nuestro territorio son propiedad del pueblo nicaragüense, representado por el Estado Revolucionario quien es el único capaz de establecer su explotación racional y eficiente."

53. "Resolutions of the Summer, 1913 Joint Conference of the Central Committee of the RSDLP and Party Officials," Lenin *Collected Works*, vol. 19, Moscow: Progress Publishers, p. 428. Emphasis added.

54. "Declaración de Principios sobre Comunidades Indígenas," *op. cit.*: "El Gobierno de Reconstrucción Nacional apoya el rescate de las diferentes expresiones culturales, otorgando a las comunidades miskitas, criollas, sumos y ramas de la Costa Atlántica los medios necesarios para el fomento de sus propias tradiciones culturales, incluyendo la conservación de sus lenguas." Note that the terms *rescate* ("rescue," "redemption," or "ransom") and *lenguas* (literally "tongues"—as opposed to the normal word for languages, *idiomas*), have a condescending ring to them.

55. Harriet Rohmer, developer of bilingual educational materials, speech in Berkeley, 19 July 1984.

56. Charles Hale, "Ethnopolitics, Regional War, and a Revolution's Quest for Survival," *Nicaraguan Perspectives*, summer 1984, pp. 37, 33.

57. Interview with Myrna Cunningham, *op. cit.*, p. 33.

58. Hale, *op. cit.*, p. 35.

59. Mohawk and Davis, *op. cit.*, p. 7.

60. *NACLA Report on the Americas*, New York, Jan/Feb 1982, p. 37.

61. *New York Times*, 3 Mar 1982.

62. Interview with Norman Bent, *op. cit.*, p. 28.

63. *Ibid.* Also *Guardian*, New York, 11 Jan 1984, p. 17.

64. *Sojourners* magazine, *op. cit.*, p. 11.

65. Black, *op. cit.*, p. 238.

66. *Akwesasne Notes*, winter 1983, p. 3.

67. According to Norman Bent. Report on the Atlantic coast by Richard Gonzales, KPFA radio, Berkeley, 22 May 1984.

68. Roxanne Dunbar Ortiz, "The Sandinista Revolution in Nicaragua and the Miskito Indians," p. 13.

69. Bernard Nietschmann, "Indian War and Peace in Nicaragua," *Akwesasne Notes*, winter 1983, p. 3.

70. Vernon Bellecourt, speech in San Francisco, 27 Mar 1983.

71. Hale, *op. cit.*, p. 37.

72. Richard Gonzales, "War on the Atlantic Coast: An Eyewitness Report,"

Nicaraguan Perspectives, op. cit., p. 40.

73. Interview with Norman Bent, *Akwesasne Notes*, early spring 1984.

74. Hale, *op. cit.*, p. 34.

75. *Indigenous World, op. cit.*, p. 14.

76. Hale, *op. cit.*, p. 38.

77. *Barricada Internacional*, 25 Oct 1984, p. 1; and 8 Nov 1984, p. 16.

78. Nicaraguan Information Center *Bulletin*, Berkeley, Sep 1984, p. 5.

Chapter 4: Guatemala

1. Eduardo Galeano, *Guatemala: Occupied Country*, translated by Cedric Belfrage, New York: Monthly Review Press, p. 35.

2. "Guatemala's Mayan Heritage," reprint from *Mesoamerica*, vol. 1, no. 9 (Sep 1982); vol. 1, no. 10 (Oct 1982); vol. 1, no. 11 (Nov 1982); vol. 2, no. 1 (Jan 1983); and vol. 2, no. 4 (Apr 1983).

3. *Ibid.*

4. *Ibid.*

5. *Ibid.* Also "Guatemala: Dare to Struggle, Dare to Win," Concerned Guatemala Scholars, revised edition, 1982, p. 61.

6. George Black, "Garrison Guatemala," *NACLA Report on the Americas*, vol. 17, no. 1, Jan/Feb 1983, p. 3.

7. "Guatemala's Mayan Heritage," *op. cit.*

8. *Ibid.*

9. Edelberto Torres Rivas, "Crisis y coyuntura crítica: La caida de Arbenz y los contratiempos de la revolución burguesa," *Política y Sociedad*, no. 4, July/Dec 1977, p. 66.

10. Black, *op. cit.*, p. 4.

11. Ramón Bonachea and Marta San Martín, *The Cuban Insurrection 1952-1959*, New Brunswick, NJ: Transaction Books, 1974. This book gives by far the best historical account of the revolutionary struggle against and overthrow of Batista—of any book I'm aware of.

12. See D. Fogel, *Africa in Struggle: National Liberation and Proletarian Revolution*, Seattle: Ism Press, 1982, pp. 208-16.

13. Galeano, *op. cit.*, p. 18.

14. *Ibid.*, p. 20.

15. *Ibid.*, p. 158. Reprinted from *The National Catholic Reporter*, 31 Jan 1968.

16. *Ibid.*, p. 157.

17. "Guatemala: Dare to Struggle, Dare to Win," *op. cit.*, p. 20.

18. *Ibid.*

19. Black, *op. cit.*, p. 8.

20. Edelberto Torres Rivas, "Guatemala—Crisis and Political Violence," *NACLA Report on the Americas*, Jan/Feb 1980.

21. "Guatemala: Dare to Struggle, Dare to Win," *op. cit.*, p. 22.

22. Black, *op. cit.*, p. 17.

23. *Ibid.*, p. 12.

24. *Ibid.*, p. 32.

25. *Ibid.*, p. 33.

26. "Articles from *Compañero*, The International Magazine of Guatemala's Guerrilla Army of the Poor (EGP)," San Francisco: Solidarity Publications, 1982, p. 10.

27. "International Support Helps Coke Workers Win," *Guatemala!*, Guatemala News and Information Bureau, Oakland, May/June 1984, p. 1.

28. "Guatemala: Dare to Struggle, Dare to Win," *op. cit.*, p. 24.

29. *Ibid.*, pp. 27-8.

30. George Black, "Guatemala—The War Is Not Over," *NACLA Report on the Americas*, vol. 17, no. 2, Mar/Apr 1983, pp. 4-5.

31. "Guatemala: Dare to Struggle, Dare to Win," *op. cit.*, p. 30.

32. *Ibid.*, p. 29.

33. Black, "Guatemala—The War Is Not Over," *op. cit.*, p. 6.

34. *Ibid.*, p. 7.

35. "Guatemala: Dare to Struggle, Dare to Win," *op. cit.*, pp. 30-1.

36. "Articles from *Compañero*," *op. cit.*, p. 10.

37. Black, "Guatemala—The War Is Not Over," *op. cit.*, p. 27.

38. "Guatemala: Dare to Struggle, Dare to Win," *op. cit.*, p. 34.

39. Black, "Guatemala—The War Is Not Over," *op. cit.*, p. 8.

40. *Ibid.*

41. *Ibid.*, p. 9.

42. Black, "Garrison Guatemala," *op. cit.*, p. 25.

43. Black, "Guatemala—The War Is Not Over," *op. cit.*, p. 14.

44. "Guatemala: Dare to Struggle, Dare to Win," *op. cit.*, p. 42. The "high-tech counterinsurgency" involved computer scanning of residential telephone and electricity usage patterns in Guatemala City, searching for unusually high concentrations of such usage. Since the "safe" houses were using lots of electricity to run printing equipment, and making lots of telephone calls for the communication so vital for the revolutionary urban underground, they were vulnerable to the computer scanning, a new tactic in the counter-revolution's arsenal.

45. Black, "Guatemala—The War Is Not Over," *op. cit.*, p. 18.

46. *Ibid.*, pp. 22-3.

47. *Ibid.*, p. 19.

48. *Guardian*, New York, 24 Aug 1983, p. 9.

49. *Central America Bulletin*, Mar 1984, vol. 3, no. 5, Central America Research Institute, Berkeley, p. 2.

50. Black, "Garrison Guatemala," *op. cit.*, p. 24.

Chapter 5: Church Torn by Class Struggle

1. *El Diario de Hoy*, San Salvador, 7 Mar 1983.
2. Cited in George Black, *Triumph of the People: The Sandinista Revolution in Nicaragua*, London: Zed Press, 1981, p. 320.
3. Karl Marx, introduction to "Contribution to the Critique of Hegelian Philosophy of Right," *Karl Marx, Early Writings*, translated and edited by T.B. Bottomore, New York: McGraw-Hill Book Co., 1964, pp. 43-4.
4. Rosa Luxemburg, "Socialism and the Churches," *Rosa Luxemburg Speaks*, New York: Pathfinder Press, 1970, pp. 135-7.
5. *Ibid.*, p. 139.
6. *Ibid.*, pp. 142-3.
7. Rossell H. Robbins, *The Encyclopedia of Witchcraft and Demonology*, New York: Crown Publishers, 1959, p. 269.
8. *Ibid.*
9. See Friedrich Engels, *The Peasant War in Germany*, Moscow: Progress Publishers.
10. "The Catholic Church in El Salvador," *El Salvador Bulletin*, Berkeley, Dec 1982, p. 2.
11. Luxemburg, *op. cit.*, p. 147.
12. Tommie Sue Montgomery, "The Church in the Salvadoran Revolution," *Latin American Perspectives*, issue 36, winter 1983, p. 66.
13. *New Catholic Encyclopedia*, vol. 3, Washington DC: Catholic University of America, 1967, p. 636.
14. Montgomery, *op. cit.*
15. *Ibid.*
16. "The Catholic Church in El Salvador," *op. cit.*, p. 3.
17. *National Catholic Reporter*, 31 Jan 1968. Cited in Eduardo Galeano, *Guatemala: Occupied Country*, New York: Monthly Review Press, 1969, p. 157.
18. Montgomery, *op. cit.*
19. "The Catholic Church in El Salvador," *op. cit.*
20. *Ibid.*
21. Montgomery, *op. cit.*, p. 67.
22. Manlio Argueta, *One Day of Life*, translated by Bill Brow, New York: Vintage Books, 1983, p. 23.
23. "The Catholic Church in El Salvador," *op. cit.*, p. 4.
24. *Ibid.*
25. Montgomery, *op. cit.*, p. 74.
26. Mario Menéndez Rodríguez, *Voices from El Salvador*, San Francisco: Solidarity Publications, 1983, pp. 66-7.
27. *Ibid.*, p. 70.
28. Montgomery, *op. cit.*, p. 76.

29. *Ibid.*
30. *Ibid.*
31. *Ibid.*, pp. 72-4.
32. "The Catholic Church in El Salvador," *op. cit.*
33. *Ibid.*
34. Montgomery, *op. cit.*, p. 78.
35. "The Catholic Church in El Salvador," *op. cit.*
36. *Ibid.*
37. Montgomery, *op. cit.*, p. 68.
38. "The Catholic Church in El Salvador," *op. cit.*, pp. 4-5.
39. *Ibid.*, p. 5.
40. *Ibid.*
41. *Barricada*, Managua, 11 Aug 1982, p. 9. The original Spanish text read: "...Cuando yo mismo en mi discurso de inauguración de la Asamblea de Puebla, hice serias reservas sobre la demoninación 'Iglesia que nace del Pueblo,' tenía en vista los peligros que acabo de recordar."
42. Montgomery, *op. cit.*, p. 75.
43. *Ibid.*, p. 69.
44. "The Catholic Church in El Salvador," *op. cit.*
45. *Barricada*, 1 Mar 1983, p. 2. The original Spanish statement cited read: "Santo Padre, en mi país es muy peligroso hablar de anticomunismo porque el anticomunismo lo proclama la derecha, no por amor a los sentimientos cristianos, sino por el egoísmo de cuidar sus intereses egoístas."
46. Iván D. Paredes, "Evolución de la Iglesia salvadoreña: 24 de marzo 1980/-28 de marzo 1982," *Eca: Estudios Centroamericanos*, UCA, 403-404, May/June 1982, p. 443.
47. *Ibid.*, p. 442.
48. *Ibid.*, p. 440.
49. "The Catholic Church in El Salvador," *op. cit.*, p. 6.
50. Montgomery, *op. cit.*, p. 83.
51. "The Catholic Church in El Salvador," *op. cit.*
52. *Ibid.*
53. *Orientación*, 27 Mar 1983.
54. "The Catholic Church in El Salvador," *op. cit.*, p. 7.
55. CONIP, 14 Nov 1983.
56. *El Diario de Hoy*, San Salvador, 7 Mar 1983.
57. *La Prensa Gráfica*, Edición Especial, San Salvador, 7 Mar 1983, p. 3-A.
58. *Ibid.*, p. 35.
59. *Ibid.*, p. 3. The original Spanish statement cited read: "Permaneced unidos. Pensad que en la unidad está la fuerza de la Iglesia. Mantened siempre la comunión con vuestros pastores. Sepan discernir y elegir ante otras predicaciones e ideologías que no son el mensaje de Jesucristo y de su Iglesia."

60. *Ibid.*, p. 33: "No sois dirigentes sociales, líderes políticos o funcionarios de un poder temporal."

61. *El Diario de Hoy*, 7 Mar 1983. *La Prensa Gráfica* omitted the word "capitalist" from its quote of this speech by the pope—evidently finding the pope's occasional "anticapitalist" demagogy too radical for its rightwing tastes.

62. *La Prensa Gráfica, op. cit.* The original Spanish statement cited read: "...La opción del sacerdote resulta a veces dramática. Aun siendo firme contra el error, no puede estar contra nadie, pues todos somos hermanos o, al límite, enemigos que tiene que amar según el evangelio; tiene que abrazar a todos, pues todos son hijos de Dios, y dar la vida, si es necesario, por todos sus hermanos. Aquí radica con frecuencia el drama del sacerdote, impulsado por diversas tendencias, acosado por opciones partidistas."

63. *Latinamerica Press*, 17 Nov 1983.

64. *Barricada*, 8 Mar 1983, p. 1. The original Spanish statement cited read: "...nadie pretenda confundir más la evangelización con la subversión y que los ministros del culto puedan ejercer su misión con seguridad y sin trabas."

65. George Black, "Guatemala—The War Is Not Over," *NACLA Report on the Americas*, Mar/Apr 1983, p. 20.

66. Joseph Collins, *What Difference Could a Revolution Make?: Food and Farming in the New Nicaragua*, San Francisco: Institute for Food and Development Policy, 1982, p. 24.

67. Kevin McKiernan, "Shrines and Slogans: The Divided Church in Nicaragua," *Mother Jones*, Apr 1984, p. 30.

68. "The Church in Nicaragua: Internal Conflicts and Church/State Tensions," *El Salvador Bulletin*, Berkeley, Oct 1982, p. 5.

69. *Nicaragua—Combate de un Pueblo, Presencia de los Cristianos*, Lima: Centro de Estudios y Publicaciones, 1978, p. 54. Cited in George Black, *Triumph of the People: The Sandinista Revolution in Nicaragua*, London: Zed Press, 1981, pp. 317-18.

70. *Manifiesto a las Fuerzas Cristianas Solidarizadas con la Lucha Revolucionaria del Pueblo Nicaragüense*, June 1975. Cited in Black, *op. cit.*, p. 318.

71. Collins, *op. cit.*, p. 25.

72. *Sojourners* magazine, Washington DC, Mar 1983, p. 16.

73. *Ibid.*

74. "Nicaragua: A Church Divided," *NACLA Report on the Americas*, May/June 1981, p. 48.

75. "The Church in Nicaragua: Internal Conflicts and Church/State Tensions," *op. cit.*

76. *Barricada*, 11 Aug 1982, p. 9. The original Spanish text read: "...De ahí lo absurdo y peligroso que es imaginarse como al lado—por no decir en contra—de la Iglesia construida en torno al Obispo, otra Iglesia concebida como 'carismática' y no institucional, 'nueva' y no tradicional, alternativa

y, como se preconiza últimamente, una *Iglesia Popular.*

"'Iglesia Popular,' en su acepción más común, visible en los escritos de cierta corriente teológica, significa una Iglesia que nace mucho más de supuestos valores de un estrato de población que de la libre y gratuita iniciativa de Dios. Significa una Iglesia que se agota en la autonomía de las llamadas *bases*, sin referencia a los legítimos Pastores o Maestros... Significa—ya que al término pueblo se da fácilmente un contenido marcadamente sociológico y político—Iglesia encarnada en las organizaciones populares, marcada por ideologías, puesta al servicio de sus reivindicaciones, de sus programas y grupos considerados como no pertenecientes al *pueblo.* [I suspect that there was an error or omission in the previous sentence of the text, since the logical flow seems disrupted]. Es fácil percibir—y lo indica explícitamente el documento de Puebla—que el concepto de 'Iglesia Popular' difícilmente escapa a la infiltración de connotaciones fuertemente ideológicas, en la línea de una cierta radicalización política, de la lucha de clases, de la aceptación de la violencia para la consecución de determinados fines, etc."

77. *Barricada*, 21 July 1982, p. 5.
78. *Barricada*, 24 July 1982, p. 1.
79. *Barricada*, 22 July 1982, p. 5.
80. *Ibid.*, p. 1. The *Barricada* report added that "while he was speaking in the entrance of the archbishop's residence, Carballo was escorted by three German shepherd dogs and a lap dog."
81. Eduardo Estrada M., "El anacronismo de la iglesia," *Barricada*, 23 July 1982, p. 3. The original Spanish text read: "La Iglesia Católica también debe aprender a ser democrática, popular, cuyas decisiones no emanen solamente de la jerarquía, sino que estén influidas por los intereses de nuestro pueblo. Pero los últimos acontecimientos, específicamente la postura que ha tomado el padre.Bismarck Carballo, vocero de la Curia Arzobispal, es anticristiana y antipopular."
82. "Es un acto de defensa de la Revolución," *Barricada*, 11 Aug 1982, p. 5. The article described the mass actions as being directed "against three particular sects—mormons, jehovah's witnesses and adventists—which have direct relations with the CIA and carry out counterrevolutionary work inside [Nicaragua]."
83. *Sojourners* magazine, *op. cit.*, p. 12.
84. *Barricada*, *op. cit.*, p. 9. The original Spanish text read: "...Una 'Iglesia Popular' opuesta a la Iglesia presidida por los legítimos Pastores es...una grave desviación de la voluntad y del plan de salvación de Jesucristo. Es además un principio de resquebrajamiento y ruptura de aquella unidad que El dejó como señal característica de la misma Iglesia..."
85. McKiernan, *op. cit.*, p. 48.
86. "Contras tendieron trampa a Masayas," *Barricada*, 18 Aug 1982, p. 5.
87. *Ibid.*
88. "Contras Balean Manifestación," *Barricada*, 17 Aug 1982, p. 5.
89. "The Catholic Church in Nicaragua: Internal Conflicts...", *op. cit.*

90. *New York Times,* 5 Mar 1983.

91. "Primeras palabras de Juan Pablo 2 in Nicaragua Libre," *Barricada,* 5 Mar 1983.

92. "Discurso del papa sobre 'Unidad de la Iglesia,' *Barricada, op. cit.,* p. 9. The original Spanish read: "...Jesucristo, en cambio, vino para restablecer la unidad perdida, para que hubiera 'un solo rebaño' y 'un solo pastor' (Jn 10,16); un pastor cuya voz 'conocen' las ovejas, mientras no conocen la de los extraños (*Ibid* 4-5). El que es la única 'puerta,' por la cual hay que entrar (*Ibid 1*)."

93. *El Nuevo Diario,* 5 Mar 1983, p. 1.

94. *Barricada,* 5 Mar 1983, p. 9. The original Spanish read: "Queridos hermanos: tened bien presente que hay casos en los cuales la unidad solo se salva cuando cada uno es capaz de renunciar a ideas, planes y compromisos propios, inoluso buenos—¡cuántos más cuando carecen de la necesaria referencia eclesial!—por el bien superior de la comunión con el Obispo, con el Papa, con toda la Iglesia."

95. Michael Baumann and Jane Harris, "Visita del Papa agudiza polarización," *Perspectiva Mundial,* 4 Apr 1983, p. 18.

96. *NACLA Report on the Americas,* Jan/Feb 1982, p. 37.

97. "'Nos sentimos frustradas!'" *El Nuevo Diario,* 6 Mar 1983, p. 8. Also *Barricada Internacional,* 28 Mar 1983.

98. *El Nuevo Diario, op. cit.,* p. 7.

99. "Where Draft Resistance is Right Wing," *Guardian,* New York, 5 Oct 1983, p. 14.

100. McKiernan, *op. cit.,* p. 32.

101. Cited in George Black, *op. cit.,* p. 322.

102. Cited in David Shub, *Lenin: A Biography,* Baltimore: Penguin Books, 1966, p. 419.

103. Ramón Bonachea and Marta San Martín, *The Cuban Insurrection 1952-1959,* New Brunswick, NJ: Transaction Books, p. 133.

Chapter 6: Women's Liberation

1. Rossell Hope Robbins, *The Encyclopedia of Witchcraft and Demonology,* New York: Bonanza Books, 1981, p. 269.

2. *Ibid.,* p. 78.

3. Susan Cavin, "Amazon Origins," *Big Apple Dyke News,* New York, Feb 1982, pp. 11-12. Excerpted from her book, *Lesbian Origins,* to be published.

4. According to AMNLAE, Nicaraguan revolutionary women's organization.

5. *New Catholic Encyclopedia,* vol. 8. Washington DC: Catholic University of America, 1967, p. 462.

6. *NACLA Report on the Americas,* New York, Sept/Oct 1980.

7. *El Salvador's Link,* Casa El Salvador Farabundo Martí, June 1984, pp. 3, 7.

8. Ana Guadalupe González, FDR representative, speech in San Francisco, 14 May 1983.

9. *Eca (Estudios Centroamericanos)*, Universidad Centroamericana José Simeón Cañas, no. 403-4, May/June 1982, p. 346.

10. "Guatemalan Women: Their Lives, Their Struggles," from a document of the 31 January Popular Front. Printed in English translation in *We Continue Forever: Sorrow and Strength of Guatemalan Women*, New York: Women's International Resource Exchange, 1983, p. 4.

11. "Two Women in the Struggle of the Guatemalan People," *We Continue Forever...*, *op. cit.*, p. 45.

12. *Ibid.*, p. 41.

13. *News from Guatemala*, Canada, 1982. Reprinted in *Latin American Perspectives*, Riverside, California, winter 1983, issue 36, p. 104.

14. Testimony of María Lupe, one of the first women to join the EGP. *Compañero: Revista Internacional del Ejército Guerrillero de los Pobres*, no. 5, 1982. English translation in "Articles from *Compañero*: The International Magazine of Guatemala's Guerrilla Army of the Poor," San Francisco: Solidarity Publications, 1982, p. 29. This translation read, "...Wife-beating stopped eventually, and now it isn't done any more..." It is an accurate translation of the Spanish original, in which the corresponding sentence read, "...Pero se logró quitar eso, ya no se hace..." A translation of the same testimony by María Lupe, done by the Guatemalan Information Center in Los Angeles and reprinted in *Latin American Perspectives, op. cit.*, p. 106, read: "...But to stop this practice [of wifebeating] is very difficult, and in some cases impossible..." This is clearly a false translation of María Lupe's remarks.

15. *Ibid.* ("Articles from *Compañero*...").

16. *Ibid.*, pp. 30-1.

17. *The Compañeras Speak*, Guatemala News and Information Service, California.

18. George Black, *Triumph of the People: The Sandinista Revolution in Nicaragua*, London: Zed Press, 1981, p. 327.

19. *AMNLAE Update*, AMNLAE, Managua, Aug 1983, p. 4.

20. Black, *op. cit.* Also Joseph Collins, *What Difference Can A Revolution Make? Food and Farming in The New Nicaragua*, San Francisco: Institute for Food and Development Policy, 1982, p. 76.

21. Hermione Harris, cited in *Nicaragua: A Look at the Reality*, Nicaraguan Information Center, Berkeley, 1983, p. 6.

22. Beth Stevens, "Women and Law in Nicaragua," *KPFA Folio*, Berkeley, June 1984, p. 4.

23. "...Now, why deny the president the option of covert aid in Nicaragua? I guess it is how you view the enemy. If it was Hitler, my god, we glorified the French underground, did we not? We did not think they were immoral or indecent, did we? We thought they were great people. We thought they were doing a great job because Hitler was the enemy. Now that it [the enemy] is the *comandantes* of the *sandinistas*, somehow it is not just

gentlemanly to engage in covert activity..." Henry Hyde, speech at the house of representatives, *Congressional Record*, vol. 129, no. 108, 27 July 1983, Washington DC: U.S. Government Printing Office, p. H5733.

24. Susan Sherman, "Nicaragua: Being There," *Off Our Backs*, Washington DC, Oct 1983, p. 9.

25. *Gay Community News*, Boston, 12 Nov 1983, p. 3.

26. *Ibid.*

27. *Ibid.*

28. Adrienne Rich, "A Footnote on 'Being There': Being Here," *Off Our Backs, op. cit.*, p. 11.

29. Sarah Schulman, "Feminist Forum: Provocative, Contradictory," *Gay Community News, op. cit.*

30. *Off Our Backs, op. cit.*, p. 8.

31. Interview with a Salvadoran revolutionary, June 1984.

32. *Womanews*, New York, Dec/Jan 1983-84, p. 6. Also Susan Sherman, *op. cit.*

Index

Acevedo, Angela Rosa: 73.
AFL-CIO (American Federation of Labor-Congress of Industrial Organizations): 4, 8, 66. *see also* AIFLD.
Agrarian question: 221; among the Miskitu, 81, 86, 88, 95; in El Salvador, 3-10, 20, 25, 173-4; in Guatemala, 115, 118-19; in Nicaragua, 58, 67-70, 77.
AID (Agency for International Development): 4, 9, 10, 133, 148, 151, 212.
AIFLD (American Institute for Free Labor Development): *16i*, 4, 9. *see also* AFL-CIO.
Akwesasne Notes: 110-11.
Alas, José Inocencio: 176.
Allende Gossens, Salvador: 120.
Alliance for Progress: 124*n*, 125, 169.
Alpromisu (Alliance for the Progress of Miskitu and Sumu Indians): 90-3 *passim*, 114. *see also* Misurasata.
Alvarez Córdova, Enrique: 6*n*.
Alvarez, José Eduardo: 15, 179, 188, 189-90.
Amazons: 217, 219-20, 221.
AMES (Asociación de Mujeres de El Salvador): *16i*.
AMNLAE (Asociación de Mujeres Nicaragüenses 'Luisa Amanda Espinoza'): *17i*, 60, 70-2 *passim*, 232, 234-6.
Anaya Montes, Mélida: 35, 36, 37-8, 39, 223. *see also* ANDES *and* FPL.
ANDES (Asociación Nacional de Educadores Salvadoreños): *16i*, 222-3.
Aparicio, Pedro Arnoldo: 15, 179-80, 188, 189-90.
Arana Osorio, Carlos: 126, 128, 151.
Arbenz, Jacobo: 118-20, 195.
Arce, Bayardo: 53.
ARDE (Alianza Revolucionaria Democrática): 108, 109. *see also* Pastora Gómez, Edén.
ARENA (Alianza Republicana Nacionalista): *10i*, 7, 18, 26, 47, 223.
Arévalo, Juan José: 117-18.
Argentina: *11i*, 58, 145.

Arias Caldera, José: 202, 203.
ATC (Asociación de Trabajadores del Campo): *17i*, 56, 59, 63, 69, 70.
Austria: 132.
Aztecs: 220.

Barahona, Rafael: 176.
Barrera, Ernesto: 180.
Barrios, Violeta: 60*n*, 231.
Batista, Fulgencio: 29*n*, 40*n*, 121-3 *passim*.
Bazzaglia Recinos, Rogelio: 35, 38.
Bellecourt, Vernon: 111.
Bent, Norman: 80*n*, 92-3, 97, 98, 106, 107.
Boff, Leonardo: 169. *see also* Liberation theology.
Bolivia: 123, 171.
Bolshevik party: 44, 101-2.
Bonilla, Alba: 211.
Borge Martínez, Tomás: 53, 57, 66, 67, 74, 107, 109, 199, 204-5, 239.
BPR (Bloque Popular Revolucionario): *15i*, *16i*, 13, 34, 38, 223. *see also* FPL.
Brazil: 31, 123, 152, 169, 219.
Brest-Litovsk peace treaty: 44.
Brezhnev, Leonid: 99.
British imperialism: 47-8, 82, 83, 84.

Caesars: 156, 158.
Cakchiquel Indians: 134.
California: 146, 219.
Calvin, Jean: 165.
Carballo, Bismarck: 202, 203, 204-5, 209, 255*n*.
Cardenal Martínez, Ernesto: 97, 102, 200, 207, 213.
Cardenal Martínez, Fernando: 105, 207*n*, 209.
Carpio, Salvador Cayetano: *see* Cayetano Carpio, Salvador.
Carrión Cruz, Luis: 53.
Carter, Jimmy: 13, 52, 54, 56, 66, 137, 138, 214.
Castellón, Edmundo: 206.
Castillo Armas, Carlos: 119.

Castro Ruz, Fidel: 40n, 75, 76, 78, 121-2, 171, 213-14.
Castro Ruz, Raúl: 122.
Catholic Action movement: 195-6, 224.
Catholic church: 154-5, 163, 166-7, 168, 171, 185-6, 217, 218, 240; of Brazil, 169; of El Salvador, 11-16, 167n, 172-81, 186-94; of Guatemala, 119, 150, 194, 195-6; of Nicaragua, 65, 71-3 passim, 84, 90-1, 196-8, 200-3, 204-5, 210-12 passim, 237, 240.
Cayetano Carpio, Salvador: 34-6, 38, 39-40.
CDC (Comités de Defensa Civil): 17i, 53, 55, 59.
CDS (Comités de Defensa Sandinista): 13i, 17i, 59, 73, 74, 205.
CEDES (Comisión Episcopal de El Salvador): 179, 189.
Central American Common Market: 26n, 126.
Central American Defense Council (Condeca): 150.
Central American union: 33, 167.
CEPA (Centro Educativo para el Progreso Agrario): 196, 197-8, 199.
Chamorro Barrios, Pedro Joaquín: 60n, 200.
Chamorro Cardenal, Pedro Joaquín: 51, 52, 60n.
Chamorro Cardenal, Xavier: 60n.
Chávez y González, Luis: 174, 175-6.
China: 11i.
Christian base communities: 171, 172-4, 186, 216; in Brazil, 169; in El Salvador, 16, 172, 176-7, 180, 188, 193; in Guatemala, 139, 196; in Nicaragua, 196-8 passim, 208, 212.
Christian Democracy: 168-9, 172, 185; of El Salvador, 16i, 1, 3, 4, 5n, 14, 18, 20, 37, 47, 185, 187; of Guatemala, 138.
Christianity: 153-60, 161-3, 191, 199, 200n. see also Catholic church and Protestantism.
Christian Organizations of Nicaragua: 197.
CIA (Central Intelligence Agency): 9, 36, 99, 103, 109, 111, 120, 151, 169, 199, 200n, 235.
Cienfuegos, Fermán: 15i, 33. see also RN.
Clausewitz, Karl von: 43.

CNUS (Comité Nacional de Unidad Sindical): 17i, 131, 135, 136, 140.
Cockburn, Adolf: 85.
Colombia: 41, 123, 170, 171. see also Contadora group.
Columbus, Christopher: 219.
Committee of Women Political Prisoners (of El Salvador): 223.
Communist Parties: 168; in Latin America, 26, 27, 123, 171; of El Salvador, see PCS; of Guatemala, see PGT.
Congo: 168.
CONIP (Coordinador Nacional de la Iglesia Popular): 189-90, 191-2.
Contadora group: 10i, 37, 41-3, 75n, 76, 190.
Copernicus, Nicholas: 165-6.
Córdova Rivas, Rafael: 93, 210.
COSEP (Consejo Superior de la Empresa Privada): 65, 66.
Creole peoples (of Nicaragua's Atlantic coast): 79-80, 84, 99-100n, 102.
Cuban revolution: 29n, 40n, 77-8, 121-3, 168, 171.
CUC (Comité de Unidad Campesina): 17i, 134-6, 139, 224.
Cunningham, Myrna: 80, 96, 103, 106.

Dalton García, Roque: 31, 32.
D'Aubuissón Arrieta, Roberto: 7n, 18, 179, 192. see also ARENA.
David, king: 215.
De la Madrid, Miguel: 42-3. see also Contadora group.
Delgado, Freddy: 15, 179.
D'Escoto Brockman, Miguel: 200.
Dolores, Ronas: 102.
Duarte, José Napoleón: 16i, 3, 8n, 14, 16, 18, 47, 137, 187, 191. see also Christian Democracy of El Salvador.
Dunbar Ortiz, Roxanne: 96n, 108n, 110, 111.

Eca: 41, 175. see also Jesuits of El Salvador and UCA.
'Economism': 20, 66n.
EGP (Ejército Guerrillero de los Pobres): 16i, 17i, 130, 135, 140, 145, 147, 149, 196, 225.
El Salvador: 10i, 14i, 15i-16i, 1-49, 74-7 passim, 131n, 137, 139, 150, 151, 167n, 170n, 172-80, 185, 186-94, 198, 207, 214, 221, 222-4.

England: 47. *see also* British imperialism.
ERP (Ejército Revolucionario del Pueblo): *15i*, 28-31, 32, 33, 185.
Essenes: 156.
Estrada, Eduardo: 203.
Ethiopia: 6, 76.

Fagoth Mueller, Steadman: 91, 92, 95, 96-7, 98, 99-100, 103, 104, 108-9, 112.
Falwell, Jerry: 146.
FAPU (Frente de Acción Popular Unificada): *15i*, 13, 31. *see also* RN.
FAR (Fuerzas Armadas Rebeldes): *16i*, 124-6, 129, 147.
Farabundo Martí, Agustín: 26, 35.
FCER (Frente Clara Elizabeth Ramírez): *15i*, 38-9, *42n*, 44.
FDN (Fuerzas Democráticas Nicaragüenses): 109.
FDR (Frente Democrático Revolucionario): *10i, 15i-16i, 6n*, 19, 30, 37, 41, 43, 47, 189, 190.
FMLN (Frente 'Farabundo Martí' de Liberación Nacional): *10i, 15i*, 19, 26-41, 47, 48, 188-92 *passim*, 193-4, 223.
Foco theory: 121, 122-3, 124, 130.
Fonseca Amador, Carlos: 202.
FPL (Fuerzas Populares de Liberación/ Farabundo Martí): *15i*, 33, 34-6, 37-40, 175, 179, 180.
France: 43, 166, 167.
Friedan, Betty: 239.
FSLN (Frente Sandinista de Liberación Nacional): *12i-13i, 17i*, 52, 53-4, 55-60 *passim*, 64, *66n*, 67-79 *passim*, 81, 91, 93-101, 102-4 *passim*, 107-8, 110, 111, 112-13, 114, 185, 197-9, 200-13 *passim*, 226, 231-6 *passim*.
FTC (Federación de Trabajadores del Campo): *16i*.
Fuentes, Margarita: 203.

García, Edgardo: 59, 69.
García, José Guillermo: 32.
García Laviana, Gaspar: 153.
Germany: 44, 164-5.
González, Leonel: *15i*.
González, Manuel: 206.
Gospel Outreach: 146, 148.
Graham, Billy: 146.
Grande, Rutilio: 176, 177, 181.
Green Berets: 45-6, 75, 126.

Guatemala: *10i, 14i, 16i-17i*, 18, 41, *42n*, 77, 114-21, 123-52, 170, 194-6, 224-6.
Guerra, Salvador: 36.
Guevara, Ernesto (Che): 31, 121-3, 130, 171.
Guzmán, Eddy: 206.

Handal, Schafik Jorge: *15i*, 27-8. *see also* PCS.
Holland: 165.
Homosexuality: 160, 213, 220, 239-40.
Honduras: *12i, 13i*, 26-7, 33, 66, 82, 88-89, 98, 99, 108, 112, 119, 126, 150, 199, 206.
Huntington, Samuel: 4.
Hyde, Henry: 236-7, *257-8n*.

Ilom, Gaspar: *16i. see also* ORPA.
Incas: 220.
International Development Bank: 128.
International Indian Treaty Council: 110, 111.
International Monetary Fund (IMF): 74.
International Union of Food and Allied Workers (IUF): 132.
Israel: 58, 138, 145, 148.
ISTA (Instituto Salvadoreño para la Transformación Agraria): 4, 5, 7, 8, 10. *see also* Agrarian question in El Salvador.
Italy: 156, 159.
Ixil Indians: 128, 130, 141, 147.

Jamaica: 83.
Jara, Víctor: 15.
Jehovah's Witnesses: 203-4, *255n*.
Jesuits: 166; of El Salvador, 41, 174-5, 176, 177, 186, 189; of Nicaragua, 196, 197-8.
Jesus of Nazareth: 155, 157-8, 163-5 *passim*, 192, 193, 199, 213.
John Paul 2: *see* Pope John Paul 2.
Johnson, Lyndon: 45, 137.
Joshua: 214-15.
Jovel, Ernesto: 33. *see also* RN.

Kampuchea: *13i*.
Kennedy, John: 45, 137, 169, 170.
Kepler, Johannes: 166.
Ketchí Indians: 128, 136.
Kirkpatrick, Jeane: *104n*.

Kissinger, Henry: 46.
Kumi, Baltimore: 112.

Laos: *13i*.
La Prensa: 51, 60, 65-7 *passim*, 197, 200, 202, 203.
Lau, Hazel: 92, 95, 102, 105, 108.
Le Duc Tho: 46.
Lenin, Vladimir Ilyich: 44, 66*n*, 101-2, 213, 214*n*.
Liberation theology: 11-13, 124*n*, 153-5 *passim*, 157, 164, 169, 171-3 *passim*, 177, 178, 185, 194, 213, 215-16, 237.
Lobos Zamora, Rodolfo: 151.
LP-28 (Ligas Populares 28 de Febrero): *15i*, 13, 28. *see also* ERP.
Lucas García, Fernando Romeo: 134, 136-8 *passim*, 144-5, 150-2 *passim*.
Luther, Martin: 164-5.
Luxemburg, Rosa: 161.

Machismo: 217-18, 225, 231, 232, 235, 237, 241.
Majano, Adolfo Arnoldo: 23, 32.
Mam Indians: 128, 133.
Maroons (of Jamaica): 83, 109.
Martínez, Ana Guadalupe: 32. *see also* ERP.
Marx, Karl: 157, 213.
Maryknoll missioners: 124*n*, 170, 173, 189, 200*n*.
Mayas: 115, 220.
MDN (Movimiento Democrático Nicaragüense): 65, 67, 206.
Mejía Víctores, Oscar Humberto: 150-1.
Melville, Thomas: 124*n*, 170.
Menchú Tum, Rigoberta: 226.
Méndez Montenegro, Julio César: 125.
Mexico: 30, 41, 42-3*n*, 82, 85, 147, 152, 220*n*. *see also* Contadora group.
Miskitu Aslatakanka Nicaragua: 113-14.
Miskitu Indians: 79-114, 211*n*, 212.
Misura (Miskitu, Sumu and Rama): 109, 212*n*. *see also* Fagoth Mueller, Steadman.
Misurasata (Sandinista Unity of Miskitu, Sumu and Rama Indians): 93-6 *passim*, 98, 99-100, 108, 114.
Mitterrand, François: 43.
MLN (Movimiento de Liberación Nacional): 119, 126.
MNR (Movimiento Nacional Revolu-

cionario): 28, 37. *see also* Ungo, Guillermo Manuel.
Molina, Arturo Armando: 176, 177.
Mondale, Walter: 13.
Monsanto, Pablo: *16i*. *see also* FAR.
Montenegro, Sofía: *13i-14i*.
MOR (Movimiento Obrero Revolucionario): *15i*, 38, 39.
Morales Erlich, José Antonio: 185*n*, 187.
Morán, Rolando: *16i*, 149. *see also* EGP.
Moravian church: 87-8, 108*n*. *see also* Miskitu Indians.
Morazán, Francisco: 167.
Mormons: 203-4, 255*n*.
Mothers of Heroes and Martyrs: 209, 210, 211, 229.
MRP-Ixim (Movimiento Revolucionario del Pueblo): *17i*.
Mugabe, Robert: 47-8, 224.
Münzer, Thomas: 165.
MUSYGES (Movimiento Unido Sindical y Gremial de El Salvador): *16i*.
Muzorewa, Abel: 47.

Nasser, Gamal Abdel: 6.
Navarro Oviedo, Alfonso: 177.
Ngo Dinh Diem: 148. *see also* Vietnam war and revolution.
Nicaragua: *8i-9i*, *12i-13i*, *14i*, *17i*, 1, 35-36, 41, 49-114, 120-1, 126, 136, 137, 158*n*, 185, 196-212, 213, 220, 221, 223, 226, 231-9, 240, 241.
Nietschmann, Bernard: 110-11.
Nixon, Richard: 137.
Nkomo, Joshua: 47, 48.
Norway: 132.
Núñez Téllez, Carlos: 53.

Obando y Bravo, Miguel: 196-8 *passim*, 200-3 *passim*, 209, 210, 212, 237.
Opportunism: *10i*, 20, 53, 237, 238; defined, 68*n*; of Fidel Castro, 76, 78, 213-14; of the FMLN leaders, 37, 41, 193-4; of the FPL leaders, 38-9; of the FSLN leaders, *12i*, *13i*, 57-9, 67-8, 71-2, 73, 74-6, 93-101, 104, 107-8, 158*n*, 198-9, 202, 204-5, 207-8, 231-2, 233, 234, 238, 239-40; of the Hanoi bureaucrats, 46; of Jesus christ, 157-158; of Latin America's Communist Parties, 123, 171; of Martin Luther,

164-5; of Robert Mugabe, 47-8; of the PCS, 26-7, 28, 34; of the PGT, 123-4, 125; of Josef Stalin, 76; of Joaquín Villalobos, 30-1.
ORDEN (of El Salvador): 5n, 34, 178.
ORPA (Organización del Pueblo en Armas): 16i, 17i, 129-30, 135, 140, 145, 147, 149.
Ortega Saavedra, Daniel: 53, 70, 75-6, 92-3, 97, 109, 207n, 209-11 passim, 239.
Ortega Saavedra, Humberto: 1, 53, 211.

Palestine: 156, 157, 158-9, 214-15.
Panamá: 41, 82. see also Contadora group.
Paredes, Iván D.: 189.
Paris peace treaty (between U.S. and North Vietnam): 13i, 44, 46.
Parrales, Edgar: 201.
Pastora Gómez, Edén: 53, 108, 109, 113.
Paul, apostle: 160.
PCS (Partido Comunista Salvadoreño): 15i, 26-8, 33, 34. see also UDN.
Peace Corps: 124, 133.
Pentecostals: 195.
People's church: see Christian base communities and Catholic Action movement (Guatemala) and CEPA (Nicaragua) and CONIP (El Salvador).
Perón, Isabel: 11i.
Perú: 6, 81, 220n.
Petrik, Joan: 173.
PGT (Partido Guatemalteco del Trabajo): 16i, 118, 123-4, 125, 129. see also Communist Parties.
Pharisees: 158.
Philippines: 155.
Pocomchí Indians: 128.
Pope: 157, 162; Innocent 4—163; John 23—169, 170; John Paul 2—12, 15-16, 153, 186, 187, 192-4, 201-2, 204, 206-11, 237, 240, 253n, 254-5n, 256n; Leo 13—168; Pius 7—166; Pius 11—168. see also Vatican.
Prado, Elmer: 97-8.
Prosterman, Roy: 9. see also AIFLD.
Protestantism: 164-6, 215.
PRTC (Partido Revolucionario de Trabajadores Centroamericanos): 15i, 33.
Puerto Rico: 239.

Quiché Indians: 128, 134, 225.

Radio Venceremos: 28-30. see also ERP.
Rama Indians: 79, 80n, 84, 93, 102, 109.
Ramírez Mercado, Sergio: 95, 98, 210.
Ramírez, William: 95.
Randall, Margaret: 236-7.
Rarinas, Luis: 212.
Ratzinger, Joseph: 153.
Reagan, Ronald: 41-3, 75, 99, 104n, 107n, 145, 150, 239n.
Rich, Adrienne: 238.
Ríos Montt, José Efraín: 145-7, 149-51 passim, 194.
Rivera, Brooklyn: 92, 95, 105, 108, 109, 112-13.
Rivera y Damas, Arturo: 14-16, 33, 176, 179, 180, 188-9, 190-1.
RN (Resistencia Nacional): 15i, 31-3. see also FAPU.
Robelo Callejas, Alfonso: 60, 65, 66, 67, 93, 199-200, 231. see also MDN.
Robles, Rodolfo: 132.
Roca, Roberto: 15i. see also PRTC.
Roman empire: 153, 156, 157, 158-9, 160-1, 162, 163.
Romero, Carlos Humberto: 1, 11, 137, 180.
Romero, Oscar Arnulfo: 11-15, 175-82, 186-8, 192-3, 198, 253n.
Ruiz, Henry: 53.
Russian revolution: 2.

Saavedra, Lidia: 211.
Salazar, Jorge: 66.
Samayoa, Salvador: 36, 175.
Sánchez, Rutilio: 194.
Sandinista National Liberation Front. see FSLN.
Sandino, Augusto César: 35, 85, 209.
Schlaefer, Salvador: 212.
Schulman, Sarah: 238.
Serveto, Miguel: 165.
Seventh Day Adventists: 203-4, 255n.
Smith, Ian: 47.
Social Democracy: 167-8. see also MNR (El Salvador).
Solomon, king: 215.
Somoza Debayle, Anastasio: 51, 52, 54, 55, 57, 58, 66, 67, 72, 80, 88-9, 90, 91, 96, 98, 107n, 123, 136, 137, 196-7, 223, 233, 239.
Somoza García, Anastasio: 51n, 85.

South Africa: 215.
Soviet Union: 34, 76, 240.
Spanish colonialism: 81, 82-3, 84, 115, 166, 195, 217, 218, 219-21.
Spanish revolution: 166.
Spartacus: 161.
Stalin, Josef: 76, 101n.
Steinem, Gloria: 239.
Sumu Indians: 79, 80n, 82, 83, 90, 94, 95, 102, 109. see also Miskitu Indians.
Sweden: 132.

Tellez, Dora María: 56, 228, 231.
Torres, Camilo: 171.
Torres, María Lilian: 238.
Twenty-six (26) July Movement: 121-2. see also Cuban revolution.

Ubico, Jorge: 117.
UCA (Universidad Centroamericana José Simeón Cañas): 174-5, 186, 191.
UCS (Unión Comunal Salvadoreña): 16i, 4, 5n, 8. see also Christian Democracy of El Salvador.
UDN (Unión Democrática Nacional): 15i, 13, 26. see also PCS.
UN (United Nations): 68n, 75, 88, 148.
UNAG (Unión Nacional de Arrendatarios y Ganaderos): 17i, 69, 70.
Ungo, Guillermo Manuel: 23, 27, 28, 37, 43, 75, 187, 190.
United Fruit Company: 117, 119.
United People's Movement (Of Nicaragua): 53, 93.
UPD (Unión Popular Democrática): 16i.
Urioste, Ricardo: 176.
URNG: (Unidad Revolucionaria Nacional Guatemalteca): 16i, 147.
Uruguay: 123.
U.S. imperialism: 9i, 10i, 13i-14i, 74-5, 123, 155, 217-18, 221, 239, 241; in Brazil, 169; in El Salvador, 1, 4, 6, 9, 10, 13, 16, 17, 39, 41-3, 45-6, 137, 180, 190-1, 192; in Guatemala, 117-20 passim, 125, 126, 133, 136, 138, 148, 150-151, 151-2, 195; in Nicaragua, 55, 58, 72, 76, 80, 81, 84-5, 103, 104, 109, 158n, 199, 209, 234; in Vietnam, 4, 9, 44, 46. see also AID, AIFLD, Alliance for Progress, CIA, Green Berets, and Peace Corps.

Vargas, Milú: 236.
Vatican: 11, 12, 153, 154-5, 162-4 passim, 166, 168-70 passim, 175-6, 180, 185-6, 187, 190, 192, 194, 199, 200-2 passim, 209, 216, 237, 240.
Venezuela: 41, 123, 198. see also Contadora group.
Viera, José Rodolfo: 8. see also ISTA.
Vietnam war and revolution: 13i-14i, 4, 9, 38, 44, 46, 123, 148.
Villalobos, Joaquín: 15i, 30-1. see also ERP.
Vivas Robelo, Bosco: 203.

Wheelock Román, Jaime: 53, 62, 68.
White Warriors Union: 179.
Wiggins, Armstrong: 79, 80-1, 84, 94, 95, 110.
Williams, Murat: 45.
Woman question: 217-22; in early christianity, 160; among the Miskitu, 86, 108; in El Salvador, 179, 222-4; in Guatemala, 224-7; in Nicaragua, 56, 60, 70-3, 226, 231-9, 241.

Zacharias, Indira Brigette: 79.
Zamora, Rubén: 27, 190.
Zealots: 158-9.
Zelaya, José Santos: 84.
Zimbabwe: 47-8, 224.
Zimbabwe African National Union (ZANU): 47-8.